NOT ALL SUNSHINE AND SAND

NOT ALL SUNSHINE AND SAND

The Tales of a UK–Middle-East Truck Driver

Paul Rowlands

Illustrations by Brian Wales

Book Guild Publishing
Sussex, England

First published in Great Britain in 2010 by
The Book Guild Ltd
Pavilion View
19 New Road
Brighton, BN1 1UF

Second printing 2010

Typesetting in Garamond by
YHT Ltd, London

Printed in Great Britain by
CPI Antony Rowe

A catalogue record for this book is available from
The British Library.

ISBN 978 1 84624 483 4

I would like to dedicate this book to my darling wife Frances, whose long-suffering patience has been stretched to the limit by my constant complaining about her interference in the writing process, when in fact if it hadn't been for her diligence and total encouragement during the whole process it is unlikely the book would have come to fruition.

Further thanks to my good friend Brian Wales, a fellow 'Middle-East Trucker', for all his unstinting efforts in providing me with the illustrations which so aptly portray the gist of each tale. Wonderful!

Finally, thanks to young Matt Ireland, who unwittingly sowed the seed of the idea in me.

Contents

1	You're Doing WHAT?	1
2	£17 6s 3d	7
3	Thank You Draiver!	19
4	Crunch and Graunch!	27
5	Never Get Any Trouble Round 'Ere	31
6	Got Your Passport Then Son?	41
7	Middle East Here I Come!	49
8	The Day is Nigh	55
9	Big Women!	67
10	Turkey!	73
11	900 Miles to Abadan!	89
12	Any Chance of a Lift Mate?	107
13	Water Melon Man	121
14	Irate Stowaways!	139
15	Ekmek and Egg	145
16	Somewhere East of Plovdiv	155
17	600 Miles East of Ankara!	167

18	Ladas and Lollipops	183
19	Their Eyes are Everywhere!	187
20	Poo Bare!	197
21	Tahir Village	201
22	Charioteer?	209
23	A Bit of a Headache	221
24	Aw Smudger, Don't Do That!	233
25	Human Frailty!	241
26	10,000 Miles of Excitement!	251
27	A Different Tack	269
28	Monte Carlo or Bust!	273
29	Make Do and Mend	281
30	Too Much Potential for Grief?	287

1

You're Doing WHAT?

'You're doing WHAT?' said mother. 'I certainly hope you're not doing any such thing.'

But I was ... I had handed in my notice at the Inland Revenue, and I was going to become a coalman. I could hear the shock and horror in her voice.

'What will the neighbours say?'

'Don't worry mum, I'll creep in and out of the back door,' I said, laughing.

I was to report to the coal yard the following Monday at 8 a.m. to meet the manager Mr Gray, and the foreman, Tel.

Office work wasn't for me . . . I wasn't cut out for it. I was twenty two and wanted to drive for a living.

The final nail in the coffin came when I told Mr Philpot. He was sixty-four, ready for retirement, and sat next to me at our desk in the tax office.

'Jack, I'm thinking of leaving.'

I remember his fateful words.

'Don't be ridiculous Paul, what about your pension when you're sixty-five?'

'What about my pension when I'm sixty-five? I'm twenty-two!'

We all know he was right, but I mean at twenty-two?

The following day I resigned, and a week later answered an advert in the *East Anglian Daily Times* for a coalman at the Co-op coal yard in Stowmarket, Suffolk.

I was introduced to my new work colleagues, who were as big a bunch of hard nuts and punch up merchants as you would ever want to meet, and very well known around Stowmarket for their enthusiasm for anything resembling the noble art of fisticuffs, with or without fists.

Roy Malloy, Cat Mullins, Raspberry Badbold snr and Raspberry Badbold jnr were guys ready for a scrap at the local Chinese any Friday or Saturday night of the year. But you know what? Behind all their bluff and bravado, they were as good as gold to me - eventually.

Here I was, the original nine-stone weakling. A skinny, lanky and pasty faced ex office bod, the Milky Bar Kid, about to become a coalman. I could tell they weren't overly impressed.

'Have you ever humped or loaded bags of coal, squire?' asked Raspberry jnr, with a grin on his face as he admired my 'muscular' arms.

'No,' I replied.

'Should be fun larning you then,' said Roy in his broad Suffolk accent.

The next few weeks were spent with the foreman Tel on his coal lorry learning the trade. I have never been so knackered and bruised at the end of each day as I was in that first month, learning how to fill a sack properly, how to stack a sack properly, how to carry a sack properly, how to tip them into a coal bunker properly, and 1,001 other incidental things such as the different varieties of solid fuel, coal, coke, furnacite, anthracite, coalite, ad-infinitum.

Most of the time Tel would look out for me, but as you can imagine, as soon as his back was turned, I became the butt of all the jokes and tricks from my new workmates.

Roy drove the tractor. I use the verb 'to drive' advisedly, and he was responsible for filling the hopper with whatever type of coal was required. Whoever's lorry was to be loaded next, that driver was responsible for making sure the correct number of sacks, with the correct contents, was loaded for the following day's coal-round.

After the first week, Tel would reverse the lorry up to the hopper and leave me to load while he went off to talk to the manager, Mr Gray.

The first time this happened was on a hot day in late September 1969.

I was standing on the back of the lorry, at the hopper, with just a pair of shorts, boots and specs on, waiting for Roy to put a load of furnacite nuts into the funnel. I had already stacked two rows of coke and was sweating profusely.

My foot was on the control pedal that shut off the chute once there was a hundredweight of coal in the sack.

I wasn't watching Roy, or the rest of the lads. I was concentrating on the chute, and waiting for the furnacite to come roaring down.

But they were watching me.

Up came the tractor, and with a flip of the lever, a ton of coal dust was released into the hopper, and shot straight down the chute like an avalanche, completely engulfing me. *It* went everywhere. The sack was immediately filled to overflowing; it went in my mouth, down my shorts, filled my boots, and my hair was caked in it. I was totally covered in filthy black coal dust.

When it finally settled, so to speak, the lads were doubled up in fits of laughter. All you could see of me was my teeth, and after I wiped my specs, my eyes.

'You look in a bit of a state, old son,' said Tel as he came round the back of the lorry. 'Hoping to audition for the Black and White Minstrels show, then?' Of course that encouraged them into another round of cackling.

'Right you lot, get this mess cleared up before Mr Gray gets here.'

The following day having got back from our round, I was again at the back of our truck, this time loading anthracite nuts. The other lads were waiting to get on to the hopper with their trucks, and were teasing me with their usual unadulterated banter.

I was concentrating on Roy and the tractor; no more episodes like yesterday, thank you. I'd watched him drive into the heap of anthracite, so I wasn't worried that he might have picked up a load of dust again. He drove up to the hopper, released the bucket and once again dropped the load down the chute.

There I was, Mr Naïve, holding open the sack, ready to receive a hundredweight of anthracite nuts, when, with a loud bang, a single lump of anthracite, the size of a whole coal mine, came crashing through the flap and into the sack, banging the scales down with a load clang, and jamming my foot on the shutter control so that I was unable to close off the chute. The rest of the bucket load poured through the open chute, while I stood there helpless, unable to move, with my foot trapped on the control pedal under this huge lump of coal. By the time the whole lot had come through the flap I was knee deep in it. Of course the guys were once again doubled up and cackling like old hens.

They made my life hell for those first few weeks, but as time passed, a sort of mutual admiration grew as I refused to get angry, and was able to accept being the butt of their humour, and to laugh at myself.

Then one morning Tel called me aside to tell me that I was going to be Raspberry snr's mate on one of the lorries, and as Raspberry had lost his driving licence I would be the driver!

This momentous point in time was to become the start of my professional driving career. Little did I know where *this* road would lead in the not too distant future.

I could hardly contain my excitement. I was going to drive a proper truck. Well I thought it was proper at the time, a Bedford TK three-tonner, which could carry *four* tons of coal. This was the big time.

I soon came to know that proper truckers called these little rigid lorries, 'wheelbarrows'.

The following morning I met Rasps in the yard and soon realised this was going to be the Raspberry Badbold show, and that the whole job was tailored around his personal lifestyle and requirements.

This coal lorry was actually just Raspberry's personal limousine, kindly provided by the Co-op to drive him around his fiefdom, and I was his chauffeur!

Each round had its own boundary which we were not supposed to cross under pain of death, but once we'd delivered *our* coal, that dictat seemed to go by the board as off we went on a daily magical mystery tour, with Raspberry directing operations.

'We'll see if we can find some new customers buh[1] 'at'll please old Gray,' said Raspberry. All this was done with a nudge, a wink and a boyish grin.

[1] 'Buh', Suffolk word for boy.

Over the next few months we built up a good friendship. He was the salt of the earth, not an academic; he wouldn't be able to spell it. Yet he knew how many pennies made five.

We'd pull up outside a house somewhere in the depths of Suffolk and Rasps would say: 'Just you wait on here a bit mate, I'll drop a load in this old biddy's bunker. Shan't be too long,' and off he'd go, covered in coal dust, with filthy hands, and a couple of sacks of coal, and I wouldn't see him for half an hour.

Later on, back he'd come, 'cleaning his trousers on his hands', so to speak, and telling me with a grin on his smut-stained face, 'short of cash Paul, she'll pay next week, I'll have to introduce you sometime buh.'

On the odd occasion we'd find ourselves at the other side of the county parked up outside a bungalow in a remote hamlet that I'd never heard of and he'd be off with a couple of bags of slack, while I'd be left twiddling my thumbs and looking round only to see the curtains moving. Funny old place to keep coal, in the bedroom!

And where *did* he put his hands while he was unloading his coal in her bunker? The thought of it brought a smile to my lips.

Over the next few months, the heavy manual labour helped me to fill out and become physically much stronger. By now I was part of the crew and gave as good as I got when the mickey-taking started.

But it was time for me to move on. Driving my little 'wheelbarrow' had given me a taste for bigger and better things.

Mother was right of course, it *wasn't* my type of work. Looking back, it was always only going to be a temporary thing, a means to an end, even though then I had no idea what that end was going to be.

But it was great fun while it lasted!

2

£17 6s 3d

Within a couple of months there was an advert in the *Stowmarket Chronicle* that caught my eye. 'Driver required for local haulage company'. I phoned that same afternoon, and was asked to attend an interview later in the week. The company was George Thorpe Haulage Ltd, Mendlesham, a proper road haulage company.

On Friday afternoon I turned up in my best bib and tucker, and nervously introduced myself to the transport manager, Keith Hammond.

'Very smart young man, but not the sort of clothing we'd advise you to wear if we offer you the position.'

While he was giving me the third degree about my previous driving experience, an older guy walked into the office, and I was introduced to Arthur Tighe, otherwise known as 'Tishy', the foreman.

'Right,' said Mr Hammond, 'when we are done with the formalities, Arthur here is going to take you out on a test drive to make sure you can handle a lorry, and if he's satisfied, we will offer you the job.'

No pressure then!

Inside, the butterflies had got their hobnailed boots on and were giving my stomach a battering, so tightly strung were my nerves.

Tishy took me out into the yard to the Bedford TK that we were going to drive through the country lanes for the next half an hour or so. That was handy; at least I was used to driving TKs, although the coal lorries were smaller than this one. This was a ten-tonner!

Considering the nerves the drive went well and I was offered the job at the princely sum of £17 6s 3d a week, plus overtime. This was *good* money, and I would be able to save up now. Of course this never happened, but hey, when you're young, the maths seems simple.

This was my first proper truck driving job. George Thorpe Haulage Ltd was based at the Old Station Yard in Mendlesham. He had a mixed fleet of about twenty five trucks, loosely based on the agricultural industry's requirements, from cattle floats through to sugar beet lorries.

George was the owner. He was a proper old fashioned boss, and always arrived at the office in a pristine dark green, Jaguar Mk 2. He was short and plump in a suet dumpling sort of way, a bit Toad of Toad Hall, and usually turned up wearing a tweed jacket, shirt and tie. Though kind hearted, and with a benevolent look about him he certainly knew the wood from the trees in transport matters.

I handed in my week's notice at the coal yard the following Monday. I was sorry to be saying goodbye to the gang. We'd become good mates, but I wanted to pursue my career in transport and drive bigger trucks.

A week later I was set to work at Thorpy's. I had two days training in the yard with Tishy and Jim, a sort of deputy foreman, and shown how to rope and sheet. Tying a 'dolly', or a 'gate',[1] in the local vernacular, was a mystery to me, and it took the full two days to get the hang of it, but once I did, nothing I tied on to the truck ever fell off.

Then, on the third day I was off on my own, thrown into the deep end, loading apples from orchards all across East Anglia, and then delivering them to Aldeby Fruit Factory in Norfolk where the hordes of factory girls and their mothers would tease you mercilessly and worse, if they got their hands on you!

This gave me a tremendous grounding in all the basic aspects of haulage: how to stack boxes properly so that the contents didn't get damaged; how to sheet them up to protect them from the rain and not have bits flapping around, and how to rope down a load securely. Within a few weeks I was a seasoned professional and an expert on everything haulage and women!

At the end of the apple season Keith called me into the office and told me I was being moved up to a six-wheeler, an ancient 16 ton Bedford TK with maybe 90 bhp.[2] Strangely enough I remember her registration number to this day, 878 MRT. She must have been the first TK off the production line, and was so old and underpowered it was an embarrassment to drive her fully freighted, tractors would overtake

[1] Dolly or Gate, a mechanism by which you made a special knot in your rope that when it was looped on to your lorry hook allowed you to apply much more tension, and therefore made the rope much tighter and consequently more secure.

[2] Bhp = brake horse power, back in the 1970s the law changed so that the horse power requirement became a minimum of 6 bhp per ton, so even with a thirty-two tonner 196 bhp was sufficient (compare that to today's power houses!). Before the change in legislation anything that could pull the skin off a rice pudding would suffice.

me! I don't think I ever got the old dear into top gear, and she only had five!

I distinctly remember my first 'long job', having to deliver a bulk load of fertilizer from Fisons, Ipswich to Fisons, Immingham. By the time I reached Spilsby on the A16 in Lincolnshire, mid afternoon, the poor old girl was getting tired and in need of a rest and took fright at the infamous long steep hill. A quarter of the way up and in second gear she ran out of puff.

Just before we came to a standstill I tried to slip her into first, but so worn were the gear linkages that it wouldn't drop in. When I finally did find first we were at a standstill and she resolutely refused to move as smoke started to pour out from the clutch housing!

Very circumspectly, I let her roll back down the hill, having to stop every few yards to build up the air. When we eventually reached the bottom I stopped for ten minutes or so to build up the courage for another attempt before putting her in first and with the engine complaining bitterly, very slowly crawled up. It was touch and go for her as well as me, and when I finally reached the top I could have done with a change of clothes.

Within two weeks George retired the old girl from active service and I was given a proper six-wheeler, a 24 ton Bedford KM with a lifting rear axle.

'Now make sure you look after this,' said George, walking me round the newly painted vehicle.

I was overjoyed. No longer was I going to be the 'boy', restricted only to East Anglia. I was going to be let loose on the rest of the country.

There was only one thing: I'd have to take a class two test. The winds of change were starting to blow through the haulage industry's cobwebbed history. New legislation was coming into force and new drivers would have to get specific licences for specific types of trucks.

But within three days I was facing the end of my fledgling driving career!

With a screeching noise, my truck had come to a juddering halt. I'd only left the yard at Mendlesham five minutes earlier and was making my way to the A140.

'Oh no! What was that?' It sounded terminal.

I jumped out and checked the dipstick. It smelled of burnt oil and was as dry as the proverbial bone. I'd got a couple of gallons in the cab, so I quickly poured the lot in until it just showed on the bottom of the stick. Then I walked back to a phone box and called the office, telling Keith that the engine had conked out.

Ten minutes later Alan turned up in the firm's mini-van.

'What's up Paul, you haven't buggered her up already have you?'

'Don't know Alan, she just sort of came to a halt.'

'R-righht! Just sort of came to a halt eh?'

With that he jumped into the cab and turned the key. There was nothing.

'Don't tell me you've seized her up,' he laughed, 'what's the oil like?'

'Fine,' I said, 'up to the mark, I checked it this morning.'

With that Alan pulled out the dipstick.

'I thought you checked it this morning. Looks like you checked it five minutes ago and then topped it up. This is fresh oil,' he said, showing me the dipstick.

'You've bloody well seized her up, you pillock, this'll please the old man.'

So Al had to organise towing it home and I had to see the boss Mr Thorpe.

I was young and naïve and even offered to pay for a new engine: I didn't want to lose my job.

'DO YOU KNOW HOW MUCH A NEW ENGINE COSTS?' he bellowed. 'It's £466, have you got £466, young man?'

I stood there dumbstruck, unable to move my lips.

He gave me a real bollocking, but like a true gentleman gave me one more chance.

'*Don't* let me see you back in here again. Do you hear?'

For the next week I was on jankers and had to skivvy around the yard, painting trailers, washing lorries, anything I was told to do as well as being the continuous butt of the fitters' barbs, until the following Monday when Alan told me my truck was repaired and ready to roll.

Hopefully, I had learned my lesson ...

Most of George's six-wheelers were by now busy working on Fison's Fertiliser, either bulk or bagged, and I joined them, driving all over the country to various Fison's depots, delivering the fertiliser that was being shipped into Ipswich docks. I well remember my first trip to Leith in Scotland. I couldn't have been more excited at the prospect of me, Ivan Brown and Fred Thompson on a night out in Morpeth with proper truckers.

Often we had to deliver fertiliser to local farms and on one occasion, loading out of Ipswich, I was given two deliveries, eight tons in bags to one farm, and the same to a second farm. I made sure that the first delivery was loaded on the front of my truck and that the second was loaded on the back. Satisfied, I roped and sheeted the load and drove off into the countryside to find my first drop.

Now of course, *silly* me, hadn't really thought out the logistics when I was loading, and when I got to the first farm I realised that their bags were at the front when they should have been on the back. One was for ease of unloading, and two, I was soon to find out. Still never mind, learning process and all that ...

I untied the front of the sheet, pulled it back, and started to unload the fertiliser. When I'd finished unloading his eight tons, I was of course left with a large gap at the front of the truck, with the remaining eight tons on the back. This truck had quite an overhang behind the rear wheels but, fingers crossed, it should be fine, as the farmer certainly wasn't about to give me a hand to move eight tons of bagged manure to the front.

After getting a signature, I pulled out of his barn and headed to the second farm about 10 miles away. Initially the steering seemed OK, a bit on the light side maybe, but not a problem. That was until I came to a T-junction on top of a small incline. I was supposed to turn left, and as there was nothing coming, I went to make the manoeuvre. Releasing the handbrake, I pulled away, turning the steering wheel to the left - and went straight across the road! My guardian angel must have been looking down on me because opposite there was an entrance to a field and not the usual ditch; otherwise I'd have been in it!

With all the weight on the back of the truck the front wheels had left the ground and I had no steerage, so I pulled as far into the field as I could, and then moved about half a ton of the bags up to the front of the truck.

Gingerly, I reversed across the junction and down the small incline. Fortunately this was a country road, with little traffic: the weight transference seemed to have done the trick, and very steadily I drove on to the second farm with no harm done.

My life in this job was just a continuous round of learning and even after forty years I've yet to meet the font of all transport knowledge, mind you there are some who think they are!

Three weeks later I'd been booked in for my class two test and arrived at the test station in my Bedford. I was nervous, but confident. I knew my truck, and as it had a synchromesh gearbox, that was one less thing to worry about. In many ways the old Bedford was like an overgrown car.

A couple of hours later I'd passed with flying colours; my words you understand, not necessarily the examiner's.

This result gave me even more impetus to try for my class one.

For the next three months I was back to the grind of agricultural work, delivering load after load of Fison's Fertiliser to farms all across East Anglia. It was here I learned another lesson - cover your load properly.

The pallets of fertiliser sat proud of the buck by six inches on each side. Normally, a fly sheet was sufficient protection against the elements as it covered the length of the load and halfway down the sides just leaving the bottom two bags exposed. It was no problem if it rained as the hundredweight bags were made of thick polythene. But I hadn't allowed for the fact that not all the farms were easily accessible, and well remember after a tortuous drive down a narrow country lane flanked by hedgerows, arriving at one particular farm only to be greeted by the farmer offering me a shovel and asking if I wouldn't mind taking a wheelbarrow back up the lane and shovelling up all the fertiliser! Looking along both sides of my truck I could see that all the exposed bags had been ripped open by the 'vicious hedge', and I had left a quarter mile trail of Fison's 'best' up the lane. This farmer was not Mr Happy and signed for forty damaged bags, two tons of lost 'manure' ...

In between the loads out of Fisons we also carried thousands of tons mostly of grain in and out of Paul's and White's Malt in Ipswich. For this I had a special demountable Tamplin tipper body fitted to my truck, and after weighing in empty we would draw round to the quayside and under the hoppers. The grain poured from the silos out through the hoppers and into our tipper lorries via a flexible hose. I soon became quite adept at judging when I had around sixteen tons on board. Then it was round to the weighbridge, normally grossing near my maximum weight of twenty four tons.

One morning having weighed in, I was told to load maize off the quayside then deliver it to Paul's factory near Bury St

Edmunds. I watched the maize pouring in and climbed on top of the load to guide the flexible pipe, ensuring the maize was evenly spread. When I considered it to be close to my maximum weight I shut the slide across the end of the pipe, clambered back down, climbed in the cab and started up. As I pulled out from under the hopper heading round to the weighbridge the truck seemed to be creaking and groaning more than usual and the old girl didn't seem to want to accelerate very quickly at all. Eventually I pulled on to the weighbridge, jumped out and wandered into the office.

'Feels a little sluggish Chris,' I said to the guy operating the scales.

'Bloody hell, I'm not surprised,' he said, as we watched the needle swing round to 37 tons.

'You're 13 tons overweight; don't tell me you've filled right to the top?'

'I have. Why, what's the problem with *that*? I always fill her nearly to the top.'

'The problem with *that*,' said Chris, 'is that maize weighs more than half as much again as grain.'

'You're joking,' I said.

'Do these scales look as if they're joking and I'm afraid I've got nowhere for you to tip off the excess till later on today,' he said, handing me the weighbridge ticket.

I wasn't going to wait all day and get another rollicking from Keith. So I crept out of the mill and with the old girl groaning and complaining I slowly made my way across Suffolk to the other side of Bury St Edmunds never once able to get above 35 mph. In those days the A45 (A14) was single carriageway, so for the whole trip there was a long tailback cursing the fact that I was on the road. I know, I could hear you!

By now the sugar beet season was in full flow and what a back breaking job *that* was. At first it was all hands to the pump, and any truck that had the facility to carry sugar beet was put in harness.

In the late 1960s, not all the farmers had fully automated loading operations, and it was with a feeling of trepidation that you arrived at a 'new' farm, just in case it had the dreaded 'manual' loading.

Mechanical loading meant no pain; manual loading was all pain!

Mechanical loading was done by a tractor driver, who either tipped the beet straight into your tipper body or on to a riddle. A riddle bounced the sugar beet about, shaking off the excess dirt before dropping it into your tipper. In the early days many farmers liked to use the straight-into-the-truck method, because they could secretly add extra mud to the load when they were shovelling up the beet to give added weight. Extra weight meant extra money.

The factory got wise to this and would sample every load with a special drill. If there was excess mud in the sample the farmer would be paid proportionately less for the load.

Manual loading was something else; every driver carried a sugar beet fork, which if in good condition he guarded with his life!

It's like a large garden fork on steroids, and has special prongs or tines,[3] which have large rounded nodules welded on to the tips, supposedly for ease of shovelling up the beet.

If you were very lucky your beet fork would have a complete set of these nodules in place which would make the job a good deal less traumatic.

To the uninitiated sugar beet have 'arms and legs' and were constantly trying to escape from your fork. If you'd managed to scoop up enough on your prongs, you would then attempt

[3] Tines and nodules – Tines are the prongs on a sugar beet fork, and nodules are rounded bits of metal welded to the ends of the prongs to prevent the sugar beet being stabbed.

to throw them high in the air in the general direction of your truck and hope they would land somewhere inside. Usually, most didn't make it and fell off as soon as you swung your fork back.

Should you be unlucky enough to have a fork with a nodule or two *missing*, then not only would you break your back shovelling the beet, but when it came to throwing them up into the truck, there would be at least a couple stuck on the ends that had been harpooned in action. This required even more wasted energy trying to get them off with your boot.

For me shovelling ten tons of sugar beet into a tipper lorry would make a perfect sentence for the magistrates court to hand down, because once would be enough!

And as to some farmers, they just thought of you as a money saving device, another farm implement, they wanted their sugar beet delivered and didn't want to spend money investing in 'new technology', 'a tractor shovel, wot's wun o they things buh?'

If Steven Spielberg were to make a film about shovelling sugar beet, which is always likely, it would be a disaster movie!

I needed my class one urgently.[4] Then for some proper trucking.

It was 1971, the early days of my driving career. I was twenty four, and I had found what I wanted to do – the freedom to roam and have adventure. The Civil Service hadn't been for me; not much adventure and certainly not much roaming. Mind you, the girls were very pretty. There were not many pretty girls in road haulage in those days:

[4] Class one is a reference to the type of HGV licence. Licences were split into three main groups. Class three was for four-wheeled rigid trucks up to sixteen tons. Class two was for six- and eight-wheeled rigid vehicles up to twenty four and thirty tons respectively. The top licence was the class one which allowed you to drive articulated vehicles and any from the lesser licence groups.

Popeye-style arms were still required, *and* a certain amount of stubble on the chin. They were not my type of woman and they lacked a certain amount of feminine charm.

3

Thank You Draiver!

There were two types of farmer, one with a large farm and one with a small farm. The only things that distinguished one type from the other were the number of holes in their cardigans and the accent.

'Thank you draiver,' said the large farm farmer in his middle-class voice, 'pity abyte the rain, I shall have to sign for whet demmage.'

He reached up and handed back my saturated delivery notes, then, without a backward glance, strode off towards the warm glow coming from the farmhouse kitchen door, rain cascading off his sou'wester.

It was all right for *him*, going back into his nice warm kitchen. How inviting did *that* look? Don't worry about me mate, I'm fine. *Look* at the state of me . . . standing there on my empty flatbed, job done, saturated, with rainwater pouring off me.

I had arrived at this large farm near Bildeston about two hours previously with a ten-ton load of pulp nuts[1] brought from the British Sugar Beet factory in Ipswich.

There had been torrential rain for the last hour, and we'd had to unload in the yard because we couldn't get into the barn; a partly dismembered tractor was blocking the entrance.

The farmer had asked me to roll back the sheet one stack at a time so that the hessian-bagged nuts didn't get too wet.

Never mind me, as long as his nuts were dry. The rain poured down incessantly, it was virtually dark, my clothes were totally saturated, my specs kept slipping off my nose, and rainwater was pouring out of the bottom of my jeans and into my boots. I might as well have been standing under a waterfall.

I heaved the sopping wet canvas sheet, which by now seemed to weigh about half a ton, into an untidy pile against the headboard, and threw a couple of ropes over it to stop it slipping off, then walked round to the other side of the cab and stripped off - totally. I threw all my soaking wet clothes into the passenger footwell, emptied my boots, climbed into the cab, put my 'sodding' wet boots back *on* again, and drove back to the yard stark naked. Good job it was dark!

Bugger this for a game of soldiers I thought, I'll tidy it all up tomorrow. Wouldn't it be nice to be driving somewhere exotic in a warm dry climate?

Back in the yard under the arc lights there was the usual

[1] Pulp nuts are made from the residue of sugar beet after it has been processed to extract the sugar, and then sold on to the farmer as food for cattle, pigs, etc.

good natured banter, especially when my mate Alan Carter, the foreman fitter, saw my state of undress. 'Blimey Paul, you're not expecting to frighten anyone with that are you?' Well, what did he expect? It was *bloody* cold!

The following evening I had one of the worst experiences of my life.

I was on the way back to Mendlesham at the end of the day and driving through Stowupland when a Jack Russell shot out from a driveway right under the front wheels of my truck. I stamped on the anchors. Too late and it was dead in an instant. What shook me up for days after was that a fraction of a second later a tiny young girl trotted out after it and for the longest moment in my life I thought the worst, but with huge good fortune my momentum had taken me past just in time.

The next ten minutes were very distressing as the parents rushed out on hearing the truck screech to a halt and their daughter screaming. I was apologetic, so were they; I was angry, so were they. But after a few tears and lots of hugs for the little girl the situation calmed down, and cautiously I drove back to the yard. To this day the thought of what could have happened still sends shivers down my spine.

Occasionally we were sent down to 72 Park in Felixstowe to load a container. I remember my first time well. These were still early days in the emerging world of container transportation, and, as with many trucks that were used for general haulage, my truck wasn't fitted with twistlocks.[2] The health and safety issue hadn't reared its all-encompassing head as yet and drivers made do and mended as best they could in the way they secured containers on to their vehicles.

[2] Twistlocks became an integral part of flatbed furniture and were designed to sit proud of the buck. The transtainer driver would lower the box on to the locks; the driver would then twist the handle round to secure it in place.

When I think back at some of the things we did, it makes my blood curdle.

The Stalcon[3] driver lowered the 20-ft container squarely on to my flatbed and after he released it I gently pulled off the loading bay to the roadside where I tied the four corners of the box to the hooks along the edge of the buck with *rope*. As it was loaded with ten tons of magazines, the weight kept the container firmly on the truck all the way to Aylesbury. All went well, the container was unloaded and it was time to make my way back to Felixstowe.

How naïve was I thinking that the rope was sufficient to hold an empty container square on the buck! By the time I had got halfway back to Felixstowe the empty box was trying to escape from my truck. The continual bouncing and vibration had loosened the ropes, allowing the container to skew across the bed and it was now sitting at an angle, two corners sticking out on either side by around two feet. I had to do something otherwise by the time I reached Felixstowe the container would be crossways behind me. Fortunately I encountered a few trucks parked up by a burger van in a large lay-by. One of the guys was driving a tipper and he very kindly offered to reverse his wagon against my 20-ft box and try to push it back in place. Finally it was back in some sort of shape and I tied it down hoping it would stay still. Fat chance! By the time I reached the docks it had once again shifted round.

It wasn't until another couple of years later that the authorities banned the loading of containers unless twistlocks were fitted. All this was new and when I think back, what if

[3] Stalcon. This machine was designed to lift and load containers on to lorries, and in the 1970s was the mainstay of container ops. To look at, they reminded you of a prehistoric yellow monster, with the driver sitting about twenty feet up in his cabin controlling this huge behemoth. It was able to lift a container about 18-ft up, enough to stack them three high and usually manoeuvred around the terminal on six elephantine pneumatic tyres.

I'd had to make an emergency stop? There is no way those ropes would have held the container. They would have snapped and likely the box would have slid forward, possibly into the cab. I know it happened to others.

It was a time of great change in road transport. It was out with the old and in with the new.

Haulage was struggling to come to terms with the rapid deregulation of the industry, from the cloth cap and overalls of the old 'A', 'B' and 'C' licences to the jeans, leather jackets and clogs of the 'O' licence era, where virtually anyone who was a person of 'good character' could apply for the new Operators Licence.

British-built trucks had 'reliable' mechanics, and cabs designed to the haulage company owner's specifications.

But what about the poor driver?

Air conditioning was provided by ill-fitting bodywork and holes in the floor through which the foot pedals protruded. In some trucks you could even see the road flashing past under your feet, such was the gap around them. The seat was a vinyl-covered piece of sponge, stapled on to a bit of plywood, which often doubled as a battery cover. The back of the seat was *another* vinyl-covered piece of sponge, screwed to the back of the cab.

A huge engine with practically no sound insulation sat right by your side, and if it wasn't for the fifty blankets your wife or mother gave you to keep the engine quiet, we'd all be deaf . . . pardon, I've got tinnitus! Sometimes, when driving in the bitter cold, you'd spread twenty of them over your lap to stop your legs falling off!

'Heater, driver? You've got your Gardiner engine to keep you warm. This is proper men's work, if you don't like it, there's the door,' was the standard response.

Road haulage was in transition and moving away from the Jurassic era. We were moving on, from British-built AEC's, Atkinsons and ERF's with Leyland or Gardiner engines, to high spec. and civilised European trucks with proper heaters, car-like gear changes, quiet engines and exotic names such as Scania, Volvo, and Mercedes.

My test date had come through: only two weeks to go; I couldn't wait.

For those two weeks, when I wasn't out on class one training with the RTITB,[4] Keith asked if I'd help out in the evenings, loading trailers down at Munton and Fison, the grain factory on the outskirts of Stowmarket.

The idea was that I would have an old shunter[5] down at M&F, then drivers would come and drop off empty trailers, and pick up the ones that I had loaded.

I would use the shunter to manoeuvre trailers under the two loading chutes, and then load them up with sacks of corn.

When the trailer was loaded I would drag it off the loading bay, wind down the landing legs and throw a sheet over it.

I would then couple up to another trailer, reverse *that* under a chute and start the whole process all over again. This was done to give me extra experience in picking up and dropping trailers and manoeuvring articulated vehicles in general.

Of course I became lazy, and instead of leaving the shunter coupled up to the trailer whilst loading, I would back both trailers under the chutes and wait for one of the lads to come into the yard, drop their empty trailer, and then take a loaded one directly off the chute.

All this was all well and good until they sent me a single axle trailer to load rather than the usual twin axle.

My job instructions were that I was to wait under the chute for a sack of corn to come down and fall on to my shoulder,

[4] RTITB. Road Transport Industry Training Board.

[5] Shunter. Usually an old lorry tractor unit that had seen its best days and was used for the general moving of trailers round the yard.

then walk to the front of the trailer and stack it against the headboard. Five sacks were to be stacked against the headboard, then three sacks flat on top of those, then another three, then two and finally one on top, so there were fourteen sacks in a stack. Each sack was one cwt, therefore each stack was fourteen cwt.

By the time I'd got to the fourth row there were now nearly three and a half tons stacked up in front of the landing legs, and I had begun to notice that the back end of the trailer was becoming decidedly bouncy, and with only one axle, there wasn't a lot of weight to hold it down.

Halfway through loading the fifth row and having just taken a sack from the chute on to my shoulder I was walking forward to the stack, when suddenly the trailer toppled gracefully forward, using the landing legs as a fulcrum. Of course I staggered forward with the sack on my shoulder and collapsed on to the remains of the stack, as the top three rows tumbled over the headboard on to the concrete floor.

Needless to say, relieved of the weight of one and a half tons of corn, the trailer then, not quite so gracefully, toppled back on to its wheels with a resounding crash, which brought forth a none-too-happy works manager wondering what the hell was going on. I was ordered back to the yard and given a heavy duty bollocking by the governor with a warning to, 'Grow up, this is a serious business. Munton's a very important customer, and if we're out, you're out. *Understood?*'

Suitably chastened, I returned to complete the job, and for the next two weeks worked my socks off trying to regain some credibility.

On the last afternoon of the last day the export manager came down and invited me up to the second floor where the last of the 9000 tons had been stored for the 'closing out ceremony'. When I got there a group of about a dozen guys were spread out across the deck all armed with various implements, from pitchforks to brooms. At the far end of the concrete floor were the remains of the export order, about forty bags in a stack against the wall. I was handed a shovel and asked him what was doing?

'We're going ratting,' he said, pointing at the pile of sacks. 'Tuck your trousers inside your boots.'

There were tails sticking out from all over the stack and each time another sack was pulled away there was a scurrying sound as the rats tried to squeeze into the slowly reducing space. Eventually there were only a dozen or so sacks left and as the brave guy at the front pulled the next one away all hell was let loose as about thirty rats the size of elephants made a break, scurrying across the floor to make their escape. I won't go into the detail of who won because I was hiding behind the shaft of my shovel, eyes closed while the mayhem took place.

Bring on my class one HGV test!!

4

Crunch and Graunch!

There I was two weeks later, a nervous wreck, waiting at the test station in Ipswich. I could see 'God', the examiner, walking from his car.

'Nothing to worry about Paul, he's not an ogre,' said my tutor, Herbie Green.

'He is, he is,' my mind was telling me.

We were introduced and completed all the formalities.

'OK Mr Rowlands, it's ten o'clock, time to go.'

Other than the gear change test, which will live with me forever, the rest of the morning passed in a haze.

'Pull over when you consider it safe to do so,' said the examiner as we entered Bell Lane in Kesgrave.

I did. This was it: the gear change test.

'Don't panic Mr Mainwaring,' was all I could think about. I couldn't help it, my knees were shaking.

'Right, I'd like you to start in the lowest gear and make your way through the gearbox to the highest gear, and then back down to the lowest gear again, thank you.'

The truck I was driving was a Leyland, with the new 273 bhp engine and a five over five, plus crawler crash gear box.

The requirement was to go from crawler through to ten and back down again; twenty changes, missing a gear meant failure.[1]

The best I can say is that it was less than smooth. Some of the gear changes were horrendous as I crunched and graunched the lever through the box. It was a master class! A baboon could have done better.

Non-synchromesh gearboxes are a joy to drive when there is no pressure, and a certain level of skill is required to do it properly. There *is* a sense of satisfaction and accomplishment as you listen for the right engine tone, then as you dip the clutch, each gear slots seamlessly into place.

'Congratulations Mr Rowlands, it's my pleasure to inform you that you have passed the examination.'

With that he handed me my pass certificate.

I had passed!! I know not how but I had.

As per usual, Herbie drove the wagon back to Mendlesham. He did this because when drivers passed their tests some of

[1] From the late 1960s onwards trucks came with more and more gears eventually ending up with sixteen or occasionally more. In simple terms it was impossible to build a gearbox to hold that number of standard gears due to size limitations, so as in the case of my test vehicle it had five standard gears and after you had changed into fifth there was a small air-powered knob to lift and then you went through the same five gears again using different cogs.

them were a little too excited and not able to concentrate properly.

'You're a good driver Paul, but a bit impetuous, so just take care.'

He was a good bloke, Herbie, one of the 'old school', about fifty and the type of bloke who commands respect. Little did I know I would be meeting him again in about five years to take my Certificate of Professional Competence, more commonly known as the Transport Manager's Licence.

It was back to the yard to give Mr Thorpe the good news and start my career as a proper truck driver. Now I could drive a thirty-two ton lethal weapon on the highways and byways of Britain, legally.

George was pleased. The HGV tests had not long been in operation and all of the other drivers in the company had received their licences by the Grandfather Rights method,[2] so I was the first to pass the official test with Geo Thorpe.

As I stood waiting expectantly for my AEC Mandator George said: 'Well done boy, there you go,' and pointed in the direction of an old AEC Mercury artic, a twenty-four tonner!

'Nooooooo, that can't be right.' I was properly qualified, I wanted a proper lorry.

I wasn't listening to George, who was droning on about: 'Getting the hang of it ... see how it goes ... big responsibility, etc, etc.'

[2] In 1971 when the law implementing the new HGV driver licences came in, the Government agreed that anyone who could prove that they had been driving a heavy goods vehicle for a period of six months during the previous twelve months could obtain a licence without having to take a test, by a term known as Grandfather Rights. Many hauliers took a flexible view on the legislation and signed off drivers who hadn't completed the required minimum time.

5

Never Get Any Trouble Round 'Ere

'But Mr Thorpe, I was hoping for distance work.'

'You will my boy, just give it a few months and see how it goes.'

So it was more farm work, and more farm work.

Then about six months later Keith Hammond, the transport manager, called me into the office and told me that George was moving me up to a thirty-two ton Atkinson Borderer.

'Yessssssss,' at last.

I'd now got a proper truck with a bloody great 12-litre

engine to keep me 'warm'. Being the boy, I was about eighteenth in seniority; it was really all I could expect.

I drove this beast for the next fifteen months, learning all the time, and doing distance work as and when it was offered.

This was the job for me; I loved it, and stopped in digs all over the country, from crofters' cottages near Nairn to B&B's in Plymouth. I also used every opportunity to visit my wider family and as often as possible arrived unannounced at various aunts, uncles, and cousins in South Wales and Gloucestershire, from parking at Cotswold Farm Park, my cousin Jill and Joe's farm, to parking at the bottom of Matexa Street[1] in the Rhondda where I was born. I imposed myself on them all!

The kids in Matexa Street used my flatbed trailer as a visiting playground, playing 'off ground it' or using the trailer as a goal and just generally enjoying themselves.

'Yer in ma pit sonny, get tae f... oot o here.'

The sound of Scotch Corner, proper truck drivers' digs! I only stopped there once, and that was enough. I had paid my 7/6 (33p) for a bed; my room number was nine and I got to bed around 11 p.m. falling straight to sleep.

At some god unearthly hour I was awoken to find myself staring into the face of Shrek's ugly brother: a drunken Glaswegian!

I was trying to focus my eyes on this monster of a man; he must have been 14ft 6ins tall!

'Didja hear wot I seed sonny, coz I'll nae repeat it, this is ma pit.'

Gathering my stuff very rapidly, I mumbled an apology and left the tiny room. As I was closing the door, he was climbing into the bed, overalls, hobnailed boots and all. I checked the number, it read six, the number was loose and had rolled

[1] According to my Uncle Bill, Matexa Street was named after the Greek General Metaxa, but some member of the council mis-spelled the name, which came out as Matexa.

around. I made my way down the corridor and found the proper room six empty, which did for me, so I fell into bed and drifted off to sleep dreaming of hobnailed-booted giants chasing me down the A1.

The following week I was heading out of London on the M4 towards South Wales. It was getting towards dusk, and I was flat out at 51 mph, trying to get to Membury Services before my driving time ran out, when I noticed an Austin 1100 overtaking me very slowly in the middle lane doing about 52 mph. What had caught my eye was the fact that the driver didn't appear to be keeping a straight line and was gently wandering across his lane. As the car very slowly crept alongside me I looked down and instantly saw the reason for his meanderings in the middle lane. He and his semi-clad lady friend were giving an Oscar-winning performance. I was surprised he could even drive let alone keep his car moving in some semblance of a straight line! With my right foot trying to push the accelerator through the floor I urged my old Atki to keep pace, but to no avail, 51 was it and no matter how much I tried to coax an extra half an mph out of her by offering 'sweets and cakes' she was having none of it as I watched the Austin and its romantically-inclined occupants slowly pull ahead of me as they weaved their way up the middle lane into the gathering gloom. I hope they got home in one piece!

I tipped my load of machinery in Carmarthen late the following morning and after reloading in Port Talbot steelworks in the afternoon, phoned my Uncle Glyn to see if it was OK to stay over that night.

My uncle, aunt and cousin Alan were more than pleased, and by six p.m. I was parked outside their house next to a six-foot high chain link fence that ran alongside the road on the edge of the Sandwells estate. My arrival caused a bit of a stir and a few of the local kids started to use the truck as a kind of play area.

'They'll be OK boyo,' said Uncle Glyn. 'Never get any trouble round here.'

I had a pleasant evening and a good night's sleep in a proper bed. Making ready to leave at 6 a.m. I said my good-byes, climbed into the cab and fired 'the old girl' up. Once the air had built up I waved to my aunt and uncle, dropped into gear and pulled away.

Atkis are not the quietest of wagons and it wasn't until I'd got a few yards down the road that I realised I was dragging fifty yards of post and chain link fencing with me.

Oh great, deep joy! Those little buggers hadn't been quite so innocent after all; they'd untied the last two ropes off the trailer and attached them to the fence, which I was now in the process of bringing back to Suffolk!

Fortunately not much damage was done, and once I had untangled the rope from the fence and retied the back end of my load I was ready to roll again. Uncle Glyn said he would sort out any problems, and half an hour later I was on my way.

This time of change was also the start of a transition in the way drivers spent their night-out money. Before the 'O' licence was introduced in 1971, 99% of drivers on a night out, slept in 'digs', some of which, like Scotch Corner, had been around for 'centuries', as had some of the landladies. Until then drivers were paid a night-out allowance to cover the cost. In 1970 that would have been about the equivalent of 75p. At this time there were virtually no sleeper cabs so theoretically there was no option other than to find accommodation for the night. However with the introduction of European trucks into the British haulage industry, this practice rapidly started to change. Many of the European wagons came with sleeper cab options and haulage companies could immediately see a cost-saving. Those drivers with this option could now sleep in the cab thereby allowing the company to cut back on the value of the night-out payment.

The problem with this was that some drivers could *also* see a benefit, in that they could save the night-out money for themselves, All very well if you had a proper sleeper cab, but drivers with non-sleeper cabs felt they were losing out and many started to make temporary beds out of plywood and foam, which at the end of their working day, after shifting all their stuff round their cabs, they would fit across it.

In November 1972 I was driving the old KM for a couple of days as my Atki was in for a service, and parked up for the night at one of the motorway services with a guy called Alan, a driver from Chipping Ongar. Neither of us had sleeper cabs, but I at least, had a shelf behind the seat of the Bedford where I could just about squeeze myself into a sleeping bag and have some semblance of a rest. Remember, we were young and could put up with a lot more discomfort!

Alan was driving an old AEC Mandator and he had cut a length of plywood to fit exactly the width of his cab. The AEC had deep window ledges on the inside of the door and his board was designed in such a way as to sit on them when the doors were closed. We had only met that evening after I followed him off the motorway to the truck parking area, pulling up alongside and as drivers do, had started giving off diesel fumes.[2]

While sitting in our trucks chatting through our open windows a 'lady' with a couple of carrier bags walked around between our cabs and asked if either of us was heading north. This sort of request happened reasonably often and usually from 'travelling ladies'.

It so happened that Alan was heading up to Newcastle, but not until the next day. Betty, for that was her name, stopped and chatted for a while, then as it was cold, asked if she could

[2] Diesel fumes. All drivers ever talk about are trucks, how fast they are, how powerful they are and how much better theirs is than anyone else's. So if a driver walks into a café and says 'it's full of diesel fumes in here,' that's what he means.

sit in the cab. Al being the gentleman said OK, but only till we went for dinner in the café.

About six o'clock we wandered into the transport cafeteria and Betty disappeared off around the lorry park area, presumably to try and get a lift with someone else. It wasn't a night to be outside as a sharp frost had been forecast.

At ten we called it a day in the restaurant (there are only so many diesel fumes you can inhale and cups of tea you can drink) and returned to our trucks. Poor old Al had to reorganise his cab first, then pull his bed from behind his seats and lay it out. At each end of his plywood base he had affixed a vertical piece of wood about a foot high. He said this was to stop his pillow getting damp at one end and his sleeping bag at the other. We said goodnight, pulled our respective curtains round and went to bed.

CRASH! And with it the sound of splintering wood.

'What the hell was that?' I awoke with a start and could hear moaning and a woman's plaintive voice.

'Sorry Alan, you all right Alan?'

I scrambled out of my sleeping bag, pulled on some clothes and jumped out of the cab to be confronted by Alan laying half off his makeshift bed - on the tarmac! A few others had congregated around and someone had run into the service area to get help.

Poor Alan was lying immobile on the deck groaning.

Within fifteen minutes an ambulance had arrived and he was whisked off to hospital. I later heard he had concussion, cracked ribs, a broken arm in two places and damaged vertebrae.

It seems that at around midnight this Betty woman, shivering with cold, unable to get a lift and having no money, had decided to seek out generous old Alan and scrounge a warm seat for the night. She knocked on his door and without waiting for a response had pulled at the door handle. Of course the door flew open and the bed with Alan on it, shot out of the cab like a toboggan on the Cresta Run and crashed head first on to the ground.

When I looked round afterwards she had done a runner and was nowhere to be found.

Poor Al took two years to recover fully from this traumatic experience and he never left the cab unlocked again. Luckily he had the bits of wood attached to the ends of his 'bed' as they had saved him from more serious injury.

As I drove into the yard one chilly morning in February, 1973 I spotted a brand new Guy Big J 4T parked at the top of the yard. I got out of my car and wandered up to look at this magnificent new beast all painted up in George Thorpe's colours of Lincoln Green with red bumpers. As I stood there admiring her there was a call from Keith to see him in the office. 'How do you fancy a change of truck?' he asked.

'That would be great. Is Fred Page's Mandator available then?'

Fred was *the* senior driver. He was about sixty and only had one eye. Those were the days! He epitomised the older type of driver from another era, in that anyone who didn't remember the General Strike of 1926 wasn't old enough to be taken seriously.

'Shouldn't you be wearing nappies sonny?'

'Yes Fred, I've got them on under my jeans.'

Normally only one of the *senior* drivers got these new trucks; seniority was king. But strange to tell, not one of the older guys was interested. They were *all* Mandator men and loved their straight six gear boxes.

'Don't want none of that crap,' was the general consensus.

'I'll have that 'crap' Keith sir, please sir.'

Of course I got that 'crap', only it wasn't 'crap' at all.

'Mr Thorpe reckons you're a grafter, and I couldn't persuade him otherwise, so here are the keys; make sure you look after it and don't seize it up.'

They were never going to let me forget ...

I couldn't believe it, my first brand new truck, ADX 555L, a Guy Big J 4T with a 205 horse Cummins engine,[3] Fuller 9 speed range change gearbox, a black vinyl padded dash, and a heater!

This was heaven. 'Wait till tonight and I tell them down at the Queen's Head in Stowmarket . . .' But by the time I'd got to 'Big J' all I could hear were snores. It was outrageous; these were all my rugby mates. Obviously not everyone was as enthusiastic as me. Couldn't understand that at all.

I even put 'EASY RIDER' plates on the front of my brand new truck. Ah, the innocence of youth.

For the next few months I was like a dog with five bones. I loved the truck and I loved the job. The majority of the time I was working out of Vicon Agricultural Machinery in Ipswich, delivering to agricultural dealerships all over the country. It was proper distance work and I was very often away for the whole week. Much of the time I was in Scotland trying to find small agricultural dealerships in the most obscure places. How I managed to get my beloved Guy along some of those roads I'll never know.

A most unusual experience occurred when I was heading north on the A68 in the Scottish Borders. I had loaded in Ipswich the previous day with numerous pieces of machinery, but most importantly, with eight single axle farm trailers with a spindle rake attachment on the back for flicking straw up into a baler. I had to secure them on my truck with the towing eye down on the deck and the spindle in the air so as not to damage it in transit. All went well on the way up the A1 other than I noticed that the 'old girl' didn't seem to be pulling as well as normal. I knew she was due for a service soon and just got on with the job.

[3] 205 bhp (brake horse power) was par for the course for British wagons back in the 1960s and 1970s. These days a lot of the trucks have upwards of 500bhp. In fact the truck I drive these days pushes out 480bhp.

After a night at Quernhow Café near Ripon I left early the following morning heading into a dull overcast sky. The wind was blowing, and the day ahead didn't look very appetising. Good old EASY RIDER felt even more sluggish today.

Hope it's nothing too serious, I thought as I turned off the A1 on to the A68 heading for Tow Law.

The wind was getting stronger by the hour and when I reached the border at Carter Bar and crossed into Scotland, the rain was lashing down and it was blowing a gale. By now she was really sluggish and then on one particular downhill stretch I had to drop down a couple of gears just to keep going at all. What the hell was going on, changing gear to go downhill?

It was then I had a blinding flash about what was happening. The eight farm trailers which were tilted into the air were acting like parachutes and trapping the wind behind each one. No wonder the poor old thing had felt sluggish on the way up. Next time I'd make sure they were facing the other way!! It was Sod's Law that the weather was crap for the next two days, until I reached the last dealership near Penicuik. I swear that as soon as I had unloaded the last of the trailers the bloody wind dropped and the sun came out. It could only happen to me . . .

There was no reload so I decided to retrace my steps down the A68. At Carter Bar I pulled into the big new lay-by for a cup of tea and a butty at the caravan. As I stood basking in the spring sunshine a flatbed with a humungous lump of rock nearly the length of his trailer drew in and pulled up at the far end of the lay-by. The driver wandered back and ordered some grub.

'That's what you call a headstone mate,' said the burger man chatting away and trying to be nosey.

'Ay, yer right it is,' he said chomping into his butty, 'weighs a bloody fair bit too.'

'Taking it anywhere special?' I asked.

'Stonehenge,' said the driver, 'we're taking a load of them down to fill in all the gaps, then putting a roof on to make a coven for all the witches.'

'You're not, are you?' said Mr Gullible. I was forever the innocent abroad . . .

It transpired that the stone was actually going to be installed in this very lay-by to mark the border between Scotland and England. The driver was waiting for the crane and engineers to arrive and we wandered back to where his truck was parked to view the deep hole in the ground where the monolith was going to be placed.

Many a time in the future I crossed the Bar and listened to the skirl of the bagpipes played by a kilted Scottish soldier standing to attention by the stone.

I loved my job, but something at the back of my mind was still nagging me to stretch my wings and fly away even further. I blame my dad.

Both during and after the Second World War up until 1965 he was in the RAF Motor Transport Division (MT), and during the North African Desert Campaign used to drive Queen Marys,[4] collecting both British and German aircraft that had been shot down.

So being a Forces child, much of my life had been spent with my parents in various parts of the world. I finished my education at Changi Grammar School in Singapore in 1964 so I had obviously inherited the travelling gene from someone!

In the last two and a half years I had travelled the length and breadth of Britain and was looking for new challenges.

[4] Queen Marys were designed to carry plane fuselages and were used in the Second World War to carry plane fuselages. They were an articulated vehicle with a fifty foot trailer and often pulled by a Bedford S type tractor unit. They were used to great effect to recover aircraft that had been shot down in the North African Campaign.

6

Got Your Passport Then Son?

At seventeen and a half I had left home and moved down to Chessington in Surrey to work in the Ordnance Survey. There at Hook Evangelical I met a fantastic group of like minded people. Hook was a thriving church, with a very healthy population of youngsters my own age, and for a few years in the late sixties, like a surrogate family, they provided me with tremendous support and fellowship. At the end of my first year there three of my friends and I decided to go on holiday together in Paul Moulin's 'luxury' Commer Cob van, touring around Europe, moving from one country to another and camping along the way in our nearly waterproof ex scout tent. We had an absolutely brilliant time, as four young lads could back in the mid 1960s.

This continental travel with my mates had whetted my appetite for further European experiences, and now in 1974 I felt I was ready to try doing it for a living.

I often asked George when he was going to start continental work, but his response wasn't always positive.

'Continental, boy, what would I want to be doing that for? I have enough trouble getting money out of the farmer round the corner, without having to do it in French with a French farmer, when I don't even speak French, and *don't* intend to learn.'

Towards the end of June 1974 the Vicon work came to an end, and Keith put me to work out of Felixstowe, doing the odd load for Bob Carter, one of the sons of W Carter of Woodbridge, a long-established Suffolk haulier.

Bob was just starting to make his own way in transport and as yet had no trucks, so sub-contracted his work out. On one occasion I happened to be talking to him while waiting for my delivery notes, and mentioned my interest in continental work.

'I shall be looking for drivers with continental experience when I get established,' said Bob.

That set my mind working overtime.

How do I get the experience? The fact that me and my mates had been driving around Europe on holiday wouldn't do. No, I *had* to get experience driving trucks abroad . . .

I decided to pester Kevin and George. In fact, I pestered anyone who would listen, at every opportunity.

Anyway, a few weeks later Kevin called me into the office and said: 'George wants a word with you.'

What had I done now? Too many alterations on the log sheets or what?

These were the days of written log sheets, before tachographs were even a twinkle in the Ministry's eye. Driving times, on duty times, and breaks were entered manually on daily log sheets.

At the start of each day everything on the sheet would be entered correctly, but as the day moved on and you found that there wouldn't be enough time to complete your day's work legally, then you'd start to make alterations, until sometimes you had made so many alterations the sheet became illegible, so you'd tear it out and tell the boss that. 'It fell in a puddle, guv,' or, 'the dog chewed it up, sir'. They came to be known as the daily lie sheet, rather than log sheet.

In the office George said: 'Right young man, you've been constantly nagging me, and from what I hear just about everyone in the village about the continent. So you've got your wish, and I don't want to hear any more about blooming foreign travel after this, do you hear?'

I couldn't believe my ears. Was this true?

I had to go back into the traffic office to get the details off Keith.

'You've to go solo to Dover Docks and pick up a tilt, whatever that is,' said Keith, 'and you'll get any other instructions when you get there. Oh, and don't forget to pick up the CMR for the delivery, apparently they're continental delivery notes.'

Blimey! A CMR, the real deal.

That night I was at home packing a small suitcase. I was in ecstasy; continental work in my beloved Big J; wait till I tell my mates.

The following morning I was up with the bloke who was going to work the night before. Such was my excitement, I couldn't sleep!

Normally I parked my tractor unit just up the road from our house in the entrance to a field. This morning, no matter how I tried I couldn't get enough traction to get on to the road, my wheels just spun in the mud. Panic, what to do? I'm supposed to be going continental today. It was 4 a.m.

I made a quick sprint home to get my sister Bev out of bed. Maybe she could pull me out with her mini van! Truck = six tons, mini van = half a ton. Prospect: not good. My sister, with a distinct lack of good grace and enthusiasm, said yes.

I tied a length of rope between us and sis tried to haul me out, but my wheels were still spinning. She wasn't giving it enough oomph in her little mini.

'Look Bev, let me have a go, you jump in the truck and I'll pull *you* out.'

I showed her how to get it into gear with the help of the gear clutch, and jumped into the mini. I backed up a foot or two so I'd have a bit of momentum and roared forward. It was just enough, and the truck came out on to the road. The problem was I hadn't told Bev to stamp on the anchors as soon as it shot out of the field, and CRASH, the truck ran into the back of the van. It stopped then all right!

'Look at what you've done to my van,' Bev screamed

'It wasn't me,' I said.

'What do you mean it wasn't you? If it wasn't you, who the hell was it?' She screamed in an even louder voice.

'It was your fault, for not standing on the brakes,' I said.

'WHAT? MY FAULT!' she bellowed, 'you ungrateful bastard, I'm telling mum.'

'OK Bev, look I'm sorry but I've got to go. I'll sort it out later when I get back from the continent.'

It was a glorious morning as I bob tailed with the tractor unit down to Dover. About 8 a.m. I dropped down through the town into the Western Docks Terminal. These were the relatively early days of Ro-Ro (Roll on, Roll off ferries) and there weren't many trailers to choose from.

My instructions were to report to an office in the docks. To this day I can't remember who, though something about Sammy Williams rings a bell, but I could be totally wrong. I was so excited I didn't really care. I went to an office upstairs.

'Come to collect a trailer and CMR for the continent,' I said passing my paperwork over the counter and trying to look nonchalant and experienced.

'Oh yeah, and where do you think you might be going?' said the guy behind the counter.

'Don't know, abroad somewhere, I've got to pick up the details here, mate'

'Your first time here then driver?' he said with a grin on his face. 'Got your passport, son?'

I showed him my pristine new passport.

'Don't worry driver, I don't need to see it, but they might want to see it in Norwich.'

'NORWICH!'

There was some guffawing and chuckling behind me and I went as red as a beetroot. The guy gave me my paperwork, and with a flourish, the CMR, and told me to go to the dock office for the location of my trailer.

This was the start of another very large learning curve. I got my location from the dock office and also a dock pass to enable me to leave the dock with my trailer. I was so disappointed I think I had a tear in my eye.

But worse was to come; it was a catalogue of disasters.

Coupling up to foreign trailers thirty five years ago was a bit of a dark art. Those of you who might have been truck drivers at the time will remember the number of different lenses, bulbs, winding handles, air line couplings, etc you had to carry, because trailers from the different European countries were all of different specification. This was before the days of trailer light boards hanging off the back with bungee straps pinched from someone else's tilt!

I found my trailer, a handsome, newish Dutch trailer with a yellow tilt. I went to reverse under it and almost hit the back of my cab. My fifth wheel had gone right under the pin.

Oh sod it, I thought, I'll have to wind up the trailer landing legs a few inches and try again.

Of course, my British hexagon winding handle didn't fit the

round Dutch spindle. So it was beg, steal or borrow one from somebody else and I scrounged a handle from one of the 'dock shunters', wound the legs up, which lowered the trailer, and successfully coupled up. I then jumped up behind the cab to connect the air lines and Suzie (electrical cable), and would soon be on my way.

The Suzie connection didn't match, and the only air line that fitted was the red one, which released the trailer brakes. The other two, yellow and blue, required a different type of connector, called a palm coupling, which I didn't have. Neither did I have the correct bulbs for the trailer nor the correct lenses for the trailer. I had no correct anything for this type of work. None of the other drivers had any spare equipment, or if they did, they weren't prepared to lend me any. So, I had no trailer brakes and no lights.

I won't bore you with any more details of this mini-drama other than to say the CMR said fourteen tons, and I drove back to Mendlesham on just the unit brakes with no rear trailer lights. It was very hairy, and looking back, very stupid. How I managed to miss the men in blue I'll never know and had I got stopped I would have deserved to have had the book thrown at me. It was a very sheepish driver who arrived back in the yard late that afternoon. Even worse, I'd cooked[1] the unit's brakes and my mate Alan Carter, the foreman fitter was a little scathing to say the least!

Worse was to come, when I got a call to see George Thorpe. He tore me off a very large strip for driving the vehicle back in that condition, and then came the final insult.

'That's as close as you're getting to the continent, young man. We do fertiliser and sugar beet here, and I don't want to hear any more about this foreign rubbish. Understood?'

Obviously I'd been set up and there was general hilarity

[1] Cooked brakes: when the brakes are used too much and overheat, thereby glazing the surface of the brake shoe, rendering them virtually useless and requiring replacement.

back at the yard at this young whippersnapper getting his comeuppance. I admit I was stupid to drive the truck back like that, and I could have caused a serious accident, but back in those days the industry was changing rapidly and lots of stupid things were done.

Needless to say, in the not too distant future we started picking up foreign trailers from Felixstowe, and I quickly found my way around them, at the same time building up a stock of the varied equipment required to pull them.

In truth the company shouldn't have sent me down to Dover without making some enquiries, but maybe they were as innocent of the requirements as I was. The joke was the thing, and the joke was on me.

And when the time came, Bob Carter still gave me a job.

7

Middle East Here I Come!

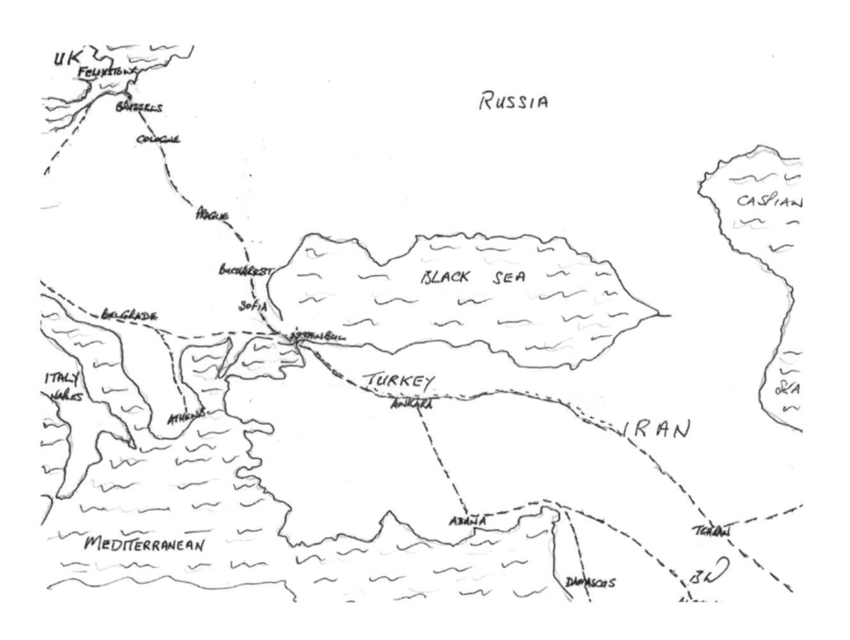

In the middle of July 1974 I went on holiday to British Columbia to stay with my Canadian cousins for seven weeks but before I left Keith had laid down the law.

'Your entitlement is only two weeks, so don't expect there to be a job here when you come back.'

I had taken that with a pinch of salt; I was indispensable!

Seven weeks later I returned from my holiday, and soon realised I wasn't quite as indispensable as I had thought. When I turned up at the yard Keith was standing by the diesel pumps.

'Hello young Paul, good holiday was it? What can I do for you then?'

'Can I start back Monday, Keith?'

'You're a lucky lad. Bert has just left and you can have your old Atkinson back if you want.'

'Aw come on Keith, stop winding me up. Where's my truck?'

'Sorry Paul, you were told before you went that it would be deemed you were leaving. What do you expect after seven weeks away? Did you think we'd just park it up and wait for your return? Don't be ridiculous. If you leave, you lose all your seniority.'

Mr Thorpe had taken my beloved Guy off me. I was heartbroken. That might have been a bit of an exaggeration, but I was still a bit aggrieved. I was slowly learning that my confidence wasn't going to get me through all life's obstacles.

'OK Keith, I'll take it.'

He must have sensed the disappointment in my voice.

'Don't worry lad, you'll soon be back up the list.'

It was good of them to offer me a job at all considering I'd ignored company rules on holiday entitlement, and since I had been there George had been very good to me.

Still, I'd made up my mind. As soon as I could I was going to get some proper continental work, hopefully on a ferry leaving Dover to go to Europe and wherever the load/road might take me.

For the next few weeks I worked on Fison's Fertiliser out of Cliff Quay, Ipswich, with the odd trip out of Felixstowe. On one of these trips I dropped in to see Bob Carter, who was by now sharing a yard with C Shaw Lovell by Dock Gate 1.

'Any jobs going Bob?'

'As a matter of fact I have, if you fancy driving an F86.'

Yes I did. If Bob was going to start doing continental sometime, the best place to be was working for him. So I handed in a week's notice at George Thorpe's, and left on good terms. They knew I wanted the adventure of driving abroad and wished me well.

The following Monday I started with Bob Carter on Trans UK Containers. For a couple of months I happily did container work out of Felixstowe, often with Sealand containers, and then one day, out of the blue, Bob caught up with me in the yard and spoke those words I had only dreamed about.

'I'm starting Middle East work in May and we're sending four trucks down to Iran,' said Bob. 'Problem is Paul, I only have one of my own going down. The rest will be subbies.'

'Who are they?' I asked, almost in disbelief. Could this be my big chance?

'Well, likely one will be a Mitchell-Rowlands truck. Another will be a subby who has a bit of Middle East experience, and the fourth, not too sure about at this stage. If you want to go, and I know you do, I'll put a word in with Mike Mitchell-Rowlands[1] for you. It would mean you working for him for a while though. When I buy a few more trucks suitable for Middle East work you can come back and work for me again.'

True to his word, Bob had a chat with Mr Mitchell-Rowlands, and within a week I was driving a Fiat 619T, one of the first such trucks in the country. I remember it now, UBJ 911M. It was different class. I was still doing the same sort of work, hauling Sealand containers on a sub-contract basis, mostly for Trans UK, and just occasionally for Loadwell Transport.

Often when I wasn't away I'd park up outside my mother's house in Gainsborough Road, Stowmarket, ready for an early start the following morning. One night about eleven o'clock I had just gone to bed when there was a horrendous bang, almost like a bomb had gone off, outside the house.

[1] Mike Mitchell-Rowlands, no relation of mine.

'What the hell was that?' I exclaimed rolling out of my newly warm bed. I scrambled downstairs and opened the front door. There, under the street lamp was a Ford Granada embedded up to the windscreen in the back of my unit with steam hissing out of its mangled radiator. There was no sign of the driver, in fact other than the neighbours there was no sign of anybody.

Bill, from next door but one, said: 'I saw someone staggering off in that direction,' pointing down past the grammar school.

Someone must have called the police, because within five minutes they were on the scene.

'Did anyone see the collision?' asked one officer.

No response.

'Whose vehicle is this?' he said, referring to my truck.

'It's mine chief,' I said.

'Do you know it's illegal to park on a road without any lights?'

'What?' I said, 'I often park my car out here without lights.'

'Ah yes, but is your car eighteen foot long, sir?'

'No, what's that got to do with it?' I asked.

The officer proceeded to quote the law to me concerning lighting requirements for different types of vehicles.

'Anyway, are you aware who owns this vehicle?' He nodded towards the wrecked Granada.

'Haven't the foggiest,' I responded.

By now all the neighbours had done a vanishing act and I was left on my own.

'We have reason to believe it belongs to Mickey Johnson,' said the other policeman.

Mickey Johnson! Everyone knew of Mickey Johnson. A very tough local guy with a bit of a reputation.

'Could you pull your vehicle forward sir, so we can look at the damage?'

I fetched the keys and moved the unit forward. There was a

bit of grinding and squealing as I pulled away from the battered car, but after checking round the rear end, other than a few deep scratches, there was absolutely no harm done. That's the thing about the back end of a tractor unit: it's all heavy metal girders with a multitude of sharp bits.

'Well I don't know where he's disappeared but wherever it is I'll bet he's got one hell of a headache,' said the first policeman.

After a few more questions they let me go back to bed with no further mention of the need for lights.

A couple of nights later there was a knock on my front door. Guess who? Mickey Johnson.

'Hello mate, can I come in for a mo? Just need a chat.'

What can you say? He wasn't the sort of bloke to take no for an answer. I let him in and showed him through to the kitchen. Luckily, mum was out!

'Listen mate, if the fuzz come back, you didn't see me the other night; my car was stolen by some toe rag while I was visiting my sick gran . . . the bastard.'

He'd got a bloody great plaster on his forehead; apparently he'd walked into a door post!

I told him no-one had seen him as he'd been off on his toes too quickly. He seemed satisfied with that and made to leave.

'We'll keep this little visit to ourselves if you know what I mean. Paul innit?'

'Yep that's fine by me,' I said, trying to keep any sign of nervousness out of my voice.

With that, as quick as he'd arrived, he'd gone, and as far as I know that was the end of it. I met old Raspberry a few days later and related the story to him. He'd heard about it and reckoned on Mickey being as 'pissed as a newt', and as he was already banned he could have gone down for it.

In the very early days Mike Mitchell-Rowlands had the franchise for Fiat trucks, and when a few weeks later the Middle East job was confirmed for May, Mike brought home a brand new Fiat 619T sleeper cab especially for the work. I felt like 'king of the road', 240 horses, twin bunks and an exhaust brake that worked; essential for the type of work we were going on.

I was all excitement and wobbly knees while the plans for the trip were finalised. How I managed to keep any interest in driving on the roads of Britain I've no idea.

We were going overland to Iran, 8,000-mile round trip, four weeks. *8,000 miles!* I couldn't believe it.

The convoy was to be Lenny in a Trans UK truck, Bob Crofton-Sleigh, a sub-contractor, in his own truck, me in Mitchell-Rowlands's truck, and the guy who was going to show us the ropes, Terry Blakesley, another subby, in his truck.

As it was the maiden voyage, Bob Carter and Tony Waugh the Middle East manager, were going to drive down in Bob's Humber Sceptre to suss out all the potential pitfalls.

Lenny and me were off to Abadan, where Iran, Kuwait and Iraq meet at the top of the Persian Gulf. Bob C-S and Terry, the experienced Middle East trucker, were going to Tehran.

This was it, something I felt I was born to do!

8

The Day is Nigh

First, a simple potted history of why the overland route to the Middle East grew so quickly in the 1970s, and it was mostly as a result of the oil crisis of October 1973.

For those of you who remember, this happened initially when OAPEC, the Organisation of Arab Petroleum Exporting Countries, embargoed the export of oil to any country supporting Israel in the Yom Kippur War. OPEC, the Organisation of Petroleum Exporting Countries (thirteen countries) used this as a way to stabilise prices at a higher level. In fact, by 1974 the price of crude oil had almost quadrupled.

In simplistic terms, the outcome was that oil-producing nations, especially in the Middle East, suddenly found that they were awash with cash. With billions of pounds filling their coffers, they went on a massive spending spree.

Initially, all the goods and machinery purchased were transported by sea, but within a year or so Middle Eastern ports couldn't cope with the volume, and very quickly massive congestion built up offshore. Cargo ships had to 'park up', sometimes for weeks, before they could get quayside to discharge.

Other alternatives were sought, and it soon became obvious that an overland route was the only other viable option.

Hey presto! The Middle East overland phenomenon!

Trans UK's plans went into overdrive. Trailers were hired from Rentco, and boxes were welded on to the chassis to carry food and other 'necessities' such as truck spares, tools, chains and any other paraphernalia we couldn't fit in the cab.

Each driver had to have anti-this and anti-that vaccinations. Cookers, gas bottles, plus ancillary equipment were bought, and international driving licences were obtained with translations into virtually every known language on the planet.

Here I have to give credit to the management team at Trans UK. They were faultless in their efforts to do the job professionally, and virtually every potential problem was resolved before the trip started.

The fact that Bob and Tony drove down with us on the first trip spoke volumes about their commitment to getting it right, and I have to say that the paperwork side of the operation was always spot on. All the i's were dotted and all the t's were crossed, which any Middle East driver will tell you was more than half the battle.

On 15 May, Lenny and I went down to London to load our trucks, ready for the off three days later and we had to strip out our trailers for the machinery to be loaded through the roof.[1]

[1] Most of the trucks that went overland to the Middle East were hauling forty foot tilt trailers. These were basically flatbed trailers with an eight foot high metal framework/superstructure built on top of the flatbed. The whole was covered by a fitted rubberised type of sheet with holes punched in the bottom. These holes fitted over rings around the bottom of the trailer. Then a plastic covered cable was passed through all the loops and rings, both ends gathered at the back of the trailer. The customs would attach a seal or plomb to the joined ends of the cable thereby proving to the customs at the next border that the load hadn't been tampered with.

Our loads were then nailed in place to the bed of the trailer to stop any movement in transit. To make doubly sure that the load didn't shift the two largest crates were tied down with wire cable and bottle jacks.[2]

The whole process was very exciting, and the anticipation was almost too much to bear. I was struggling to sleep properly. The following day we all went to Nurdin & Peacock, a local cash and carry, to stock up on food. It was a real dietician's delight: beans, instant mash, beans, tinned minced beef, beans, rice pudding, beans, tea bags, powdered milk, beans, cornflakes and other bits and pieces deemed necessary for a four week trip. Oh! Did I mention beans? Beans were a staple for me and I got used to, and loved eating them, warm or even better, cold!

The morning of 18 May was gloriously sunny and warm, and I felt it boded well for our trip of a lifetime. The plan was to meet up mid-morning in Trans UK's yard, and make final preparations ready to go down to the quay later in the afternoon.

We were all dressed in our 'continental gear'. Anyway I was, with my Green Castrol racing jacket made out of fashionable shell suit material, jeans, a denim cowboy style hat, a Zapata moustache, and the obligatory furry clogs, soon to be ditched in favour of something a little more convenient, and a lot more comfortable. Sadly, image and posing seemed important at the time. Bit sad really!

Also, we had the all important plastic bucket hanging from the towing hitch in the front bumpers. This was a badge of honour for continental drivers, or so we thought, as I had seen pictures of other trucks with buckets hanging from the

[2] Bottle Jacks are a mechanism that allow the driver to tension down his load to prevent slippage. Wire cables are looped through a retaining ring in the floor on either side of the trailer and passed over the load and attached to hooks in the end of the bottle jack which is then screwed up, which in turn tensions the cables.

front and it looked cool. The idea was that we would use the buckets for washing and stuff.

They were certainly used for 'stuff', so this idea didn't hold sway for very long. Within a couple of days the buckets were full of other people's rubbish, and before the end of the week regularly used as a urinal by any passing drunkard, which didn't predispose any of us to wash in them!

The ferry was due to leave early evening on 18 May for the eight hour crossing to Zeebrugge in Belgium. Other than Terry, who had done the trip before, the rest of us had had little sleep due to the tension and excitement. But none of us were in the remotest bit tired, and adrenalin would keep us going for the next few days.

Back then, other than 72 Park and the Sealand compound, both of which were container based operations, most of the port of Felixstowe was based around the old dock basin, where much manual loading and unloading of trailers took place and their cargoes were stored in various warehouses or sheds.

Nowadays, the huge majority of Felixstowe Dock's operations are containerised and based at Trinity Terminal, the development of which has turned Felixstowe into one of the world's biggest container ports.

About 4 p.m. we made our way down to the quay and parked opposite Boomers Café outside one of the old World War Two hangars,[3] which was now used as a dock warehouse, and awaited the arrival of the Townsend Thorensen ferry at 77 berth.

A few photos were taken for posterity, and at 6 p.m. we crossed the loading ramp and drove on to the ferry together with the many other trucks and holiday makers in their cars.

'We're off to the Middle East, Lenny!'

'I know Paul; I'm nervous and excited at the same time.'

We had an uneventful crossing, and berthed at Zeebrugge about 6 a.m. Belgian time.

The vessel was discharged and we parked up with the other trucks near the customs offices. As we were walking over to the hall Bob C-S's briefcase fell open depositing all his documentation over the terminal.

'Oh s...t, hang on lads,' shouted Bob.

We turned to see bits of paper floating in the gentle morning breeze.

'Hang on,' said Terry, trotting back to help.

We all turned back to help.

'Well done,' said Lenny to a sheepish looking Bob, 'someone had to be the first to make a cock up!'

Unsurprisingly, in the customs hall we found ourselves at the back of the queue. You could tell we were new boys by our hairy clogs and spanking new leatherette briefcases. These were our most important pieces of equipment, to be guarded with our very lives! They were full of the multitude of documentation required for a trip to the Middle East, the

[3] During the Second World War, the RAF had a base at Felixstowe situated where the old part of the dock is now, and Sunderland Sea Planes were among the aircraft based there.

most important of which were our TIR carnets for the load and vehicle, often called Triptix by the drivers.

Compared to the way it is now, crossing international frontiers back in the 1970s was a vastly more complicated experience.

For example, just to get to Iran required you to follow custom procedures at a minimum of fourteen frontiers, two for each country. If you were going overland to Kuwait or Doha, anything up to twenty-two frontiers, especially if you were transiting the old Eastern Bloc and that was just one way. The same applied to coming back, though if you were leer,[4] things were usually much easier.

Each frontier post required a copy from your TIR carnet, and very often each border would add a new plomb, or seal, to the ones already affixed to your TIR cord.

Arabic countries required translations of your load manifest into their language, and many required permits allowing you to transit their territory. In the early days the Eastern Bloc countries only allowed you twenty-four hours to transit time, and theoretically it was on a nominated route.

The further East you went the more complex the operation at the frontier crossings became. That's why good experienced Middle East hands became a very valuable asset. Compare that to today's international driver, who might still get problems, but can drive virtually from here to Turkey through any European Union country, without having one frontier crossing to negotiate.

Over the next few years I was lucky enough to do this trip many times and through many different countries.

My memories of that first crossing of Belgium are minimal as I spent most of it looking at the rear end of Terry's trailer while concentrating on driving on the right. I know it took

[4] Leer is a Dutch word that came into common usage, and was accepted and understood internationally as the word for empty among drivers and border personnel.

about four and a half hours, *after* we'd eventually found our way around Brussels. Back in the 1970s it wasn't bypassed and the best it could offer was a kind of convoluted North Circular route, similar to London.

Leaving Brussels behind as you climbed back on to the E5 motorway heading for Germany always brought back romantic thoughts of those early days for me when, between trips, we might be asked to do a 'local' to Italy or Germany.

One trip that especially engendered those memories occurred in 1976 when I took a girlfriend with me on a trip to Essen. The road was almost traffic free and in gentle rain we climbed out of Brussels on to the E5 at around 2 a.m. With the engine purring away we watched the neon lights reflecting off the glistening tarmac, late night music was playing on Radio Luxembourg, and in the warm cab my girlfriend was relaxing next to me with her head on my shoulder. For just a little while it felt perfect; those memories are magical.

But back to that first crossing. By the time we reached Eynatten Truck Stop a mile from the border my stomach was having a discussion with my mouth about starvation. This was our first visit to a European style Truckers Café.

'What do you reckon Lenny, bit different isn't it?' I said, taking in the relaxed continental atmosphere.

'Quality mate, it'll do for me, puts our old truck stops in the shade don't it?'

'Obviously a bit better thought of here than back home,' concurred Bob.

After croissants and coffee, we confirmed our plan which was to catch the train in Cologne that evening, and then sleep while it roared south through the night to Ludwigsburg in southern Germany.

But first we had to deal with the border post at Eynatten/ Aachen.

The Belgian side we despatched pretty quickly and then walked down to the German customs at the other end of the same building. With typical Teutonic efficiency everything was well organised, with orderly queues and numerous forms to fill in, though for us new guys it seemed like pandemonium.

As we were virgin soldiers, so to speak, and didn't understand what we were doing, poor old Terry was continuously bombarded with things such as: 'What's this form for? . . .What does this say? . . . What do I write here? . . . How do I fill this in?'

What, who, how, where, why? A thousand questions and it seemed like a thousand queuing drivers.

'Bollocks! I've made another mistake. Get another form.'

'Terry, give us a bloody hand, mate!'

'Don't forget to complete the Tankschein form,' he shouted through the mass of drivers.

Eventually Terry steered us through the paperwork carnage and we were able to make our way back to our trucks.

'Did you complete the Tankschein form? That's next,' he said.

We'd been warned about the Tankschein!

German diesel was more expensive than anywhere else in Europe at that time, and on your first trip you were only allowed to carry fifty litres of diesel into the country. The Tankschein check was done as you left the customs to enter Germany proper. A group of officials might pull you over and dip your diesel tanks. Should you have fuel in excess of the allowed amount, a hefty fine was incurred and duty had to be paid.

Thereafter whenever you left Germany, however much you signed for as having in your tanks was the amount you were allowed to enter the country with the next time.

Now we needed diesel desperately, having entered the country with fifty litres of fuel, we only had enough left for about seventy miles. As we joined the autobahn to Koln we came across our first German motorway service station, Propsteier Wald, (now called Achener Land). It was a Shell garage and boy, this was a new experience, one that I had never seen the like of before.

Walking into Propsteier Wald's shop was like visiting a Santa's grotto for truckers. It sold everything an aspiring international driver could wish for. Stickers for every country in the world, which I promptly bought, and stuck on the side of my truck. I hadn't even been anywhere yet! There were ribbons full of flags to be hung in the front windscreen, hats, clogs, fancy leather belts, waving hands and the men's magazines! Proper men's magazines, if you know what I mean.

'Hey Lenny look at these, are you going to take some home for your wife?'

'I daren't look Paul; if I do she'll get to hear about it.'

These magazines were the real deal and back home they would have only been sold from under the counter in brown paper bags, yet here they were, on open display in a garage forecourt shop - unbelievable! Like most young men my age I surreptitiously bought the odd one or two, just to use for research purposes you understand. In fact, we came to realise that these 'medical books' would be good currency in times of difficulty or hardship further down the line.

Propsteier Wald, like all the service areas in Germany, was a treasure trove of goodies for the 'discerning' trucker.

On our first trip, each day had an edge of excitement to it. We were on a journey that three of us had never attempted before. Everything was new, and would never be new again. We had a huge amount to learn and it was on the job training. This was our big adventure, and we were intrepid explorers!

Arriving at the commercial train terminus on the outskirts of Cologne we had to drive our trucks on to the flatbed railcars and sleep in a passenger carriage kindly provided by the German rail authorities.

There was no provision for grub, as there were no buffet car facilities. One or two of the more enterprising and experienced drivers took small Calor Gas stoves into the carriage and cooked up a mess of beans and stuff. The rest of us starved to death, and they held a 'wake' for us in the morning. Not true, but by then, we were more than a little peckish.

Most of us settled down in our sleeping bags and tried to get a bit of shut eye, which by now I certainly needed. I'd run out of adrenalin and was running on empty.

We arrived at Ludwigsburg around 6 a.m. starving, and once back in our trucks had to have a brew and a bowl of cereal to resuscitate ourselves before we got moving. By 7 a.m. refreshed, we were out on the autobahn and heading for the cobbled streets of Munich, then on to the Austrian border at Salzburg.

The first time at any frontier point meant new procedures to learn, and Salzburg was no different. As it had been at Aachen, the customs procedures on both the German and Austrian sides operated like a well oiled machine. It is the Germanic way.

Meanwhile Me, Lenny and Bob Crofton-Sleigh, being non Germanic, and coming from the planet Muddle and Blunder, were operating in our own less well oiled and less Teutonic way, pestering Terry, or anyone who would listen and understood English, about how we should fill in this and that form.

'Don't forget the Tankschein,' said a slightly irritable Terry.

Eventually calm descended, the paperwork was completed and we were released from the Salzburg border ready to tackle Austria. Back then the Austrians were only just beginning to develop a motorway network so the majority of the infrastructure was made up of single carriageway road, and as beautiful as it was, the going was slow, as we climbed mountains and crossed valleys heading for Graz in southern Austria and then onto the Yugoslavian frontier at Spielfeld/ Sentilj. We were more than a little apprehensive.

9

Big Women!

'This has a scary feel,' whispered Lenny.

It was our first visit to a Communist country.

With a sense of trepidation and apprehension we entered the Yugoslavia customs hall in Sentilj. It was late, 11 p.m., pitch black and compared to Spielfeld on the Austrian side, the lights in the building shone very dimly; a real metaphor for the differences between East and West. The fittings were very spartan, and silence hung in the air. It was an almost ethereal experience. We could have been extras in a John le Carre film.

For years we had been brought up on a diet of anti-communist film and propaganda. In politics, spy novels, and

Bond films, they were our sworn enemy. All that negative information probably instilled in us an uneasy sense of foreboding. It was almost as if we were expecting a troop of soldiers to arrest us *just* for being there. Of course it hadn't helped that as soon as we reached the barrier to enter Yugoslavia, we were confronted by a soldier carrying a machine gun. Back in the mid 1970s communism, politically, was at its most aggressive.

Once you'd crossed the frontier into any of the Eastern Bloc countries, it was like stepping back fifty years in time. Everything looked tired and drab, and there seemed very little impetus to life, almost as if people were going through the motions of living.

Yugoslavia was probably the least hard line of the Iron Curtain countries, but by our standards things were still pretty basic, including the road network. The main road between Zagreb and Belgrade was about 420 kilometres long and it was to be our first taste of the type of atrocious surface we would be driving over from here on. Underneath a thin layer of tarmac, much of which was missing, lay an old cobbled road that had most probably been put down by the Romans!

Holidaymakers know the Dalmatian coast as a very beautiful part of the country, but the central spine from Zagreb down through Belgrade to Nis is very dull and dreary.

Interestingly, when driving through countries like Yugoslavia, you were rarely aware of any discontent bubbling beneath the surface. I had no idea there was a large Muslim population in some parts of the country.

Over the years I loaded bicycles from Sarajevo on numerous occasions, and travelled back through Tuzla, Banja Luka and many of the other towns and villages that became embroiled in the Balkan War and ethnic cleansing of the late 1980s and early 1990s. It is only in recent times that I came to realise what a strong leader Tito was to keep a lid on this boiling pot of a country.

However, there were exceptions to the continual drudgery and perpetual greyness of the 900-kilometre trip through Yugoslavia, and they usually surrounded places where truckers from Western Europe made their stops.

Having spent the remainder of the previous night on the outskirts of Maribor, the three of us, bleary-eyed and tired, followed Terry out on to the main road at 6.30 a.m. heading for Zagreb. Eventually we found our way around Yugoslavia's second city, and on to the infamous stretch of highway that linked Zagreb and Belgrade.

Terry was leading the way and three hours later, about 220 kilometres north of Belgrade, we pulled into one of these 'bright spots,' a restaurant stop we came to know as 'The Trees', near Slavonski Brod.

This place was often frequented by West European drivers, and not just for the food! Actually, the food left a lot to be desired (it was atrocious), and came a very distant second to the main attraction.

The fact that European truckers stopped here had attracted some of the local girls on to 'the game'. These were women who had at one time worked on the land, pulling ploughs with their bare hands! Everything about them was of an agricultural magnitude; they were *big*, and I mean *big*, with *big* hands.

The loudest and brashest of them we called Queenie. She was humungous with a large lipsticked mouth and broken teeth, quite attractive if you like humungous women with large lipsticked mouths and broken teeth. She and her entourage of only slightly less fearsome acolytes would clomp around the parked trucks dressed in their brightly coloured tents, sorry frocks, propositioning all and sundry for '*fiki-fiki*'.

One of their favourite tricks was to reach up and grab hold of one of your windscreen wiper arms and haul their massive bulk up onto the bumper. Then they would lean against the cab and whip up their tops, plastering your windscreen with their vast, hairy, globular breasts, blocking out the sun, all the time cackling away like demented hens. '*Fiki-fiki, fiki-fiki*'.

I remember one of the girls doing this, only to pull the wiper arm right off and end up flat on her back in the dirt, ready for work I suppose!

Lenny and I locked ourselves in our cabs once we saw these fearsome 'women' approaching.

The main stopover point for drivers going the Yugoslavian route was 200 kilometres further south at the National Hotel, Belgrade. This became a major focal point on the long haul, as drivers met up, used the telex, and exchanged stories over a '*Pivo*' or many.[1]

Originally this would have been a middle-ranking hotel, but as soon as West European truckers started to arrive with their higher standard of living and larger wallets, the National became almost an international truck stop. Every one of the staff was known as George. George the receptionist, George the wine waiter, George the chef, and at least three George the waiter. There was even a Georgina, the waitress.

However on our first trip Terry didn't stop there. He took us through Belgrade to the other side of the city where we parked overnight in a huge lay-by amongst a large number of East European trucks, all cooking their food out of their trailer boxes. It wasn't till we were on our way back that Lenny and I 'found' the National.

This was the last we saw of Terry. Being mother hen wasn't his thing and we weren't going fast enough for him. The following morning at about 5 a.m. as we were making ready to leave, he pulled out and headed south. That left us three 'virgins', plus Bob and Tony in the Humber to make our own way to Iran. It was disappointing but just added to the

[1] Pivo, Serbian for beer.

challenge. Our plan was to be at the Turkish border at Kapicule by the end of the day.

At 5.30 a.m. I pulled out in front and we had another bone shaking drive down to a town called Nis in southern Yugoslavia. On this infamous stretch of road hundreds of religious icons littered the roadside, the majority left in memory of Turkish *gastarbeiters*[2] who over the years had died by the hundred in their single-minded quest to get from Germany, back home to Turkey in one hit.

Between Belgrade and Nis, as fatigue set in, their old Opels and Mercedes, usually loaded to the gunwales with goods, furniture and passengers, had accident after accident.

Here at Nis was an important parting of the ways, straight on was Greece and to the left Bulgaria, Turkey and far beyond.

For us it was left, heading for the Bulgarian border at Dimitrovgrad/Kalotina, about sixty miles away.

Arriving at the border post, the building looked as if it had only recently been constructed and surprisingly for us the whole customs procedure was pretty efficient.

As there were no other vehicles waiting, we were cleared within half an hour, only to find there was also a compulsory money change requirement to be completed up at the state bank. Here we received 15 leva in exchange for £10 which equates to one and a half leva to the pound, at the official rate. On the black market the rate was 7 leva to the pound, so who was being ripped off? We also had to purchase Naphtha (diesel) coupons in Deutschmarks, as officially it was illegal to buy fuel with cash. This was a law soon to be ignored when we realised that garage attendants throughout the Eastern Bloc were more than happy to 'do a deal' in foreign currency.

[2] Gastarbeiter, a foreign national e.g. Turkish workers allowed to come and work in Germany for a period of time, but not allowed to settle there.

Once we were able to unscramble some of the Cyrillic language on the signs we were on our way.

The drive across Bulgaria, even though it is a scenically attractive country, was an even more depressing version of Yugoslavia.

Everything was the same colour, a dirty battleship grey, the sky, the roads, the trucks and the people, the only way of differentiating one thing from another in this amorphous stew was that everything had a different number painted on it in a dirty white Cyrillic script.

In terms of progress this country had been totally left behind by everyone. Even by communist standards it was dreary. I don't think I saw one private car from Kalotina to Kapitan Andreevo, where we joined the queue to enter Turkey.

10

Turkey!

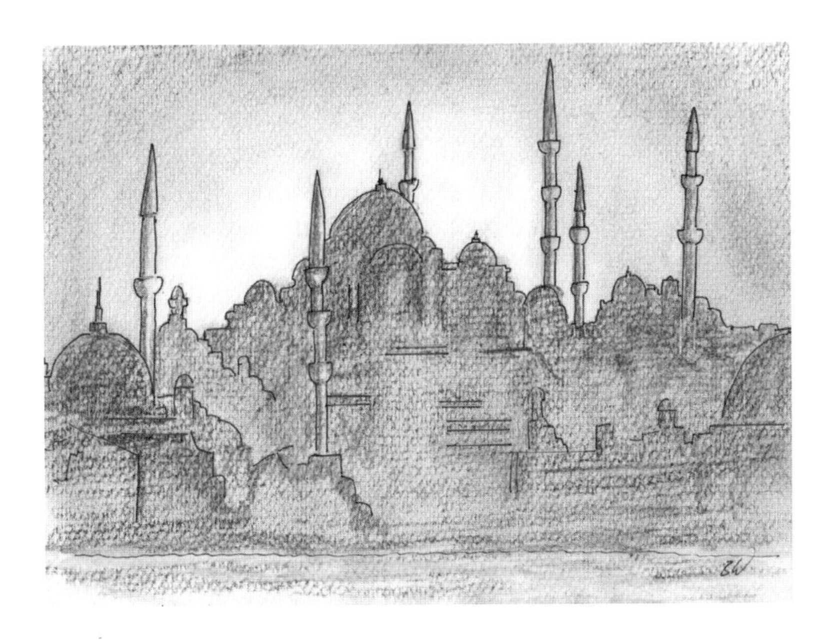

'Well, we're here Bob,' I said. 'This is what all the fuss is about.'

Bob C-S, Lenny and me were standing by our trucks having joined the back of a very short queue at Kapitan Andreevo. In front of us the road opened up on to a large square on the Bulgarian side that contained massed ranks of trucks waiting their turn to be allowed through into Turkey.

'Yeah,' retorted Bob, 'I feel quite nervous about it, as if I've got butterflies in my stomach. I suppose it's the fear of the unknown.'

Arriving at the Bulgarian/Turkish border was an experience not to be missed! For most drivers, making their first acquaintance with Kapicule did not instil any sense of confidence or well being as normally chaos reigned.

Kapitan Andreevo on the Bulgarian side was reasonably well organised, Often you joined the queue maybe as far back as two to three miles, and slowly worked your way forward, usually following the truck in front.

Mind you, woe betide any driver who fell asleep in the queue, as everyone behind would overtake without a second thought if a gap appeared. No polite knocking on the cab and 'excuse me driver would you like to move forward,' type of thing. Oh no, it was everyone for themselves. If sixty wagons came by you, that was half a day lost at least.

Many times I've watched drivers, in a panic, struggling to pull on their pants and getting tangled up in their trousers while trying to start their trucks, build up their air, and get it into gear all at the same time, while dozens of wagons pull past. Trouble is you have to sleep sometimes.

Within a couple of hours we'd reached the front row of the square awaiting our turn for the barrier to lift. I was extremely excited at the prospect of getting to Asia; another 170 miles and we would there!

Half an hour later we were being directed through the 'sheep dip' and into the mayhem and mud bath that we came 'affectionately' to know as 'the a. . .e of the world' – Kapicule.

All the trucks were fed off to the left and round the back of the customs area, where the ground, having been churned up by hundreds of truck wheels, was a quagmire. There were loads of young lads shouting agents' names. They were agents' runners, though we didn't realise this for a while.

Eventually we heard the name 'Young Turk' being shouted as a young lad waded through the mud past our trucks. 'Young Turk' was our agent, so we shouted to the youngster, who sloshed his way back to us through the morass.

'Collega, Young Turk?' he asked quizzically.

'Yes,' I said and held up three fingers and pointed to the two trucks behind.

'Ok collega, carnet TIR ... passeport ... CMR.'

We were a bit dubious about giving up our passports, but we saw other agents' runners with passports, so we handed ours over as well.

'Parking collega ... after office Young Turk,' he said, pointing somewhere.

We were still in the queue of slow moving trucks, all slipping and sliding our way to an area where hundreds of other trucks were parked in a totally haphazard way. There didn't appear to be any organisation at all; it was a case of everyone for themselves. Everywhere you looked there were broken down and wrecked lorries, many British. You could have been forgiven for thinking we had driven into a mud-filled scrapyard.

Bob and Tony, in their car, had of course been allowed straight through the border on the main road.

Having parked our trucks in among the wrecks, and ankle deep in glutinous mud, we had to try and find 'Young Turk's' office. This wasn't too difficult as everyone knew him. His office was with the many other agents, in a ramshackle cover all wooden structure intermingled with stalls and bars selling tea, coffee and food etc. The whole operation at Kapicule was one of disorganised pandemonium and reminded me of a noisy market day in a rundown seaside resort where all the stalls are in a state of disrepair.

As the volume of transport going overland to the Middle East grew over the next few years, the lack of organisation at Kapicule filled you with dread at its inability to deal with the increasing number of trucks wanting to transit the country. Many times when exiting Turkey on the return trip we would measure the length of the queue on the Bulgarian side waiting to access Kapicule. Sometimes that queue stretched back four or five kilometres or more.

In 1977 a large part of the truck parking area was concreted over. Mind you within a few weeks it was so covered in mud as to be indistinguishable from the surrounding fields. Cleanliness and tidiness were not on the agenda.

When we at last found the office of 'Young Turk', Bob and Tony were already ensconced round a table with the man himself, Suleiman. Young and disarmingly charming, he already had a thriving business, with one very useful bonus I was told - his father was the chief of police at the frontier!

Suleiman very kindly sent one of his minions to fetch us chai (tea) and asked us to be patient, as one of his men was, as we were speaking, organising our papers.

Two hours later we were done, and struggling to extradite ourselves from this morass of mud and humanity. I'd already realised that this was a massively different world; a massively different culture, where East meets West in geographical terms only.

Now, we were on the road to Istanbul - only 258 km distant.

At Edirne, Turkey's first large town, we had to stop at a single track bridge for oncoming traffic, and spotted our first minaret. Four hours later we were running into the outskirts of Istanbul and looking out for the Londra Camping truck stop.

Londra Camping, also known as the Mocamp, and the Harem Hotel across the other side of the Bosporus, were the two main stopover places for European drivers.

We pulled into the Londra at about 4 p.m. and parked up among the most eclectic mix of trucks and nationalities you could ever hope to encounter: British, Dutch, French, Swedish, Norwegian, Danish, German. Austrian, Hungarian, Belgian, Swiss and I'm sure there were others.

Many of the lads slept in their trucks, but Bob always allowed us to have one night a week in a hotel if possible, and tonight was that night. We booked into the motel and after a shower and a change of clothes, joined other drivers in the restaurant and what was known as Efes Kontrol, an excuse for a general piss-up, Efes being the only drinkable beer in Turkey.

Between the main building and the cafeteria was the green 'swimming pool', on which were growing more 'chemical cultures' than you would care to hazard a guess at and I reckon under the correct medical supervision would have resolved all the world's illnesses. Not that I was going to dive in!!

The following day was to be a day off for a visit into the bazaar and other sightseeing activities, so alcohol intake was limited only by our ability to consume it.

Around 8 p.m. a few of the lads suggested a visit to a club across the road called the 'West Berlin'. We didn't know it, but in fact it was a 'knocking shop' posing as a restaurant/bar. The three of us went upstairs to the restaurant area and sat outside at a table on the balcony overlooking the main road.

By 9 p.m. we *knew* what it was. One minute we were sitting quietly on the balcony and enjoying our beers; the next a load of girls came into the room and started mixing with the guys. Two headed our way and descended on us, one sitting on my lap and one on Lenny's.

'*Collega Anglia?*' said one of the girls.

'What's *Anglia?*' said Lenny.

'England,' I said. 'These buggers are on the game.'

'WHAT, you're joking,' said Lenny, 'you mean prostitutes?'

'*Fiki Fiki Anglia*,' said one of the girls to Bob.

'I'm not fiki fikiing anyone,' said Lenny. 'What if my missus finds out?'

'*Anglia, fiki fiki*, 60 liras, *on dakika*,'[1] said the not very pretty one.

'Why not?' said Bob, 'could be a laugh.' He, like me, wasn't married.

'I might catch something and take it home to the wife.'

'*ANGLIA, FIKI FIKI*,' said the even less pretty one, getting annoyed at our lack of enthusiasm. After all time was money.

'What are you expecting to catch?' said Bob. 'A fish?'

'Smells like I might,' said Lenny.

'Come on,' I said. 'What harm can it do?'

The girls were doing their best to encourage us, and the one on Lenny's lap had her hand down his trousers inspecting his artillery.

'No I can't do it, I'd be too embarrassed, and as soon as I walk indoors she'll be bound to know.'

By now the girls had got bored with all this discussion and were up and off looking for better prospects.

'Well done Lenny, you've frightened them off,' said Bob.

'She's rearranged my chronicles and now I'm all flustered. I wouldn't mind us all doing something together though, you know?'

'No Lenny, we don't know. What did you have in mind, mate?' I said.

'How about a . . .?' and Lenny whispered in our ears.

'LENNY, for crying out loud,' said Bob, 'let's not go there.'

[1] 60 liras = £2, on dakika = ten minutes.

'Look guys, let's just enjoy the spectacle. We've got plenty of time and there'll be plenty more opportunities.'

With that we settled down to a pleasant evening and were only bothered once more.

The girls were something else mind you, and quite a few seemed to have deformities or body parts missing. One had one and a half legs, another a hand missing, and there were the odd missing fingers and toes, a few had scars, and another, only one eye. In fact 'One Eye' became quite well known and accompanied a number of drivers on their trips down south.

On the Sunday we all took a taxi down into Istanbul city centre and did the tourist abroad thing. We went to a leather shop and got measured up for leather jackets and waistcoats, which we would pick up on the way back from Iran, in two weeks. We visited the vast bazaar, a huge maze of a place, and were pestered the whole time. We tried the ruse of pretending not to be English, but whatever nationality we claimed to be, the traders knew the language. Bob C-S found a jeweller called Danny, down one of the back alleys. He was an excellent goldsmith and I came to use him quite often on my travels.

I found the 'Pudding Shop' with the help of a couple of Canadian hikers. It was an interesting place and almost like a pre-European Union ex-pat community, mostly of youngsters, and some not so young, looking like relics from the 1960s, all searching for lifts either back to the UK, or east to India. All the overland buses put up their 'schedules' there. It was a great place with a great atmosphere.

Istanbul is where East meets West. It's a boiling pot of cultures and life and is most probably always destined to live on the edge. As one half wants to move west, the other is firmly entrenched in the history of its forefathers.

It was a remarkable day and opened our eyes to the type of cultural life we were soon to be driving into.

The following morning Bob and Tony had us up early to have a good run at the day. By 7 a.m. we were running on to the Bosporus Toll Bridge, which had only been open for eighteen months and there we were across into Asia. We made good progress throughout the morning running along by the Sea of Marmara, through the cobbled streets of Adapazari to the first decent climb in Turkey - Bolu, which is getting on for 6,000-ft high and a low gear pull to the top.

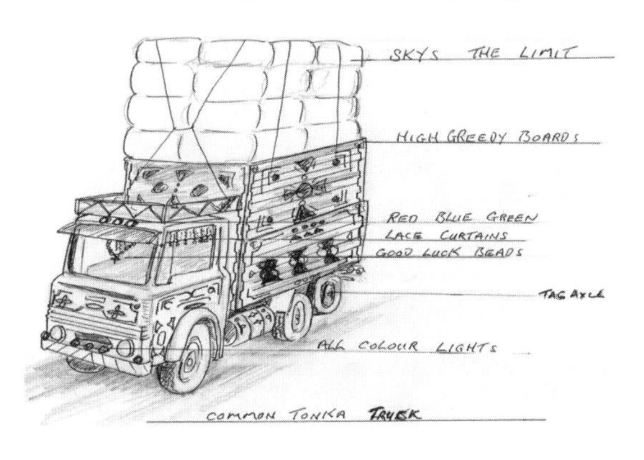

Even though we made slow progress on the climb, the local Turkish trucks, often loaded to the gunwales, were *so* slow as to make us appear very rapid.

These trucks were called Tonkas by most European truckers, named after our kids' tin toy trucks. Most were four or six wheel petrol engine Dodges, Fords, BMCs etc. with the occasional Mack, and all were painted in a fantastic array of colours and patterns. Windows were festooned with rows of flags and religious icons, and each truck was dedicated to Allah in some form.

In fact, painted on every truck in large script would be words such as Inshallah or Kismetse or some other Islamic phrase, all meaning God willing, or something similar which is how they drove, lived or died. Often when following, or being overtaken by a Turk, the question did cross your mind as to the level of ability of the driver, and who *was* the driver. *Was* it God?

This above statement can be applied to none other than the 'kamikaze' coach drivers, who I am sure were failed airline pilots, and considered themselves to be very important people and the world's best drivers. Dressed in their blue pilot-style uniforms, gold braid dripping from their epaulettes, shiny peaked cap with the obligatory dark sunglasses, and 'Corinthian' spirit, they would transit Turkey, double manned and virtually non-stop, a distance of up to 1,200 miles, week in, week out.

If they felt it was opportune, nothing would stop them overtaking. They would pull out to pass you with air horns blaring, and if, God help you, another vehicle appeared coming the other way, the second driver would have the escape door open at the back, and hang out on one arm at 60 or more mph, frantically waving you to slow down, sometimes beating your cab with a stick while his driver swerved in front of you. Woe betide you if you didn't accede to this gentle request. Turkey was littered with coaches, and sticks, where the driver had made a small error of judgement in an overtaking manoeuvre

Funnily enough on this our first trip we had trouble overtaking an overloaded Tonka on the climb over Bolu. The driver kept zigzagging across the road, like a galleon tacking into the wind.

These trucks were often so overloaded and underpowered that they couldn't make a direct climb, and had to reduce the angle of the hill by tacking across the road and back. Each time we tried to get past, the driver would reach the other side of the road and start to tack back and we'd have to drop back and try on his next tack. Eventually we got cheesed off with this game and on one of his tacking manoeuvres, instead of dropping back, much to his annoyance we all pulled through at the same time, waving and blowing our horns.

Near the top of the mountain we pulled into a large lay-by to have a brew and cook a 'special', beans, minced beef, and instant mash all in the same pan. Delicious!

Sitting in the shade under the trailer enjoying my cordon bleu meal, we watched and listened as the old bonneted Bedford 'Tonka' slowly hove into view, still tacking its way up the mountain. The driver was obviously still not happy with us, because as he crept past our lay-by, he had his head out of the window shouting at us while brandishing a gun! We all ducked instinctively and luckily no shot came our way, but it taught us a salutary lesson about driving in Turkey.

After our lunch we caught up with Bob and Tony who had eaten 'proper posh food' in the restaurant at the top of the mountain. Together, our small convoy headed down the other side through 'Death Valley', (known as such because of the number of trucks that didn't make it to the bottom in one piece), and on to Ankara, where Bob and Tony disappeared to find themselves a hotel for the night.

On this our first trip we hadn't realised there was a truck stop on the outskirts of Ankara, so we carried on through the city and headed for Kirrikale.

Between Ankara and Elmadag with dusk rapidly

approaching, we still hadn't found anywhere to park, so before it got *too* dark we pulled off the road on to a bit of rough ground adjacent to the main highway. Bob C-S set up his cooker and we had another - this time not quite so cordon bleu meal of I know not what - agricultural concoction from Norfolk, I believe. Bully beef and cloth cap I think it was. After clearing up and a chatting briefly about the day's adventures and the plan for tomorrow, we decided on an early kip.

At 9 p.m. I was well away when there was a loud banging on one of the cabs followed by strident Turkish voices. I scrambled into the driver's seat and pulled back the curtain. It was the Polis.

'*Park yapilmaz*.'[2] We didn't get a chance to ask, or respond as they shouted even louder.

'*PARK YAPILMAZ*,' waving their hands to shoo us away.

'*SIMDI GIT*.'[3] So *simdi git*, we did. They made it clear in no uncertain terms that we weren't stopping there that night.

It was a scramble to get into our driving seats in various states of undress and get out of there as quickly as possible. Being first trippers we were scared of anyone with a uniform who shouted at us.

Within a few miles we came across an old unused garage forecourt and pulled in there hoping not to be disturbed again.

'He called me a simdi git,' said Lenny.

'Well you are,' I said.

We never found out why they moved us on, but as I said we were first timers and in those circumstances we didn't argue we just followed orders.

The following morning broke hot and sunny again, and just as we were about to move off, Bob and Tony arrived in the Sceptre.

[2] *Park yapilmaz*, Turkish for 'no parking'.
[3] *Simdi git*, Turkish for 'go now', or something similar.

By now the car was looking decidedly dusty and travel stained and with its roof rack carrying extra supplies and tyres could easily have passed as a competitor in the London to Sydney marathon. It really had done remarkably well and hadn't missed a beat the whole way.

They had spent the night in a hotel in Ankara and were going to run with us for the next few days as we were now moving into wilder mountainous country.

We were also getting closer to the Kurdish part of Turkey which we had been given the impression of as being untamed, and as we noticed, the army here seemed to take a higher profile.

'Good morning lads' said Bob, 'hope you slept well, we certainly did.'

Lenny recounted the previous night's fun and games, at which Tony laughed.

'Didn't hear a thing, slept like a log. It was the most comfortable bed I've ever slept in, blah, blah, blah.'

'We're going to run with you today,' said Bob, as he and Tony jumped in the old Sceptre and pulled out on to the main road.

An hour later they were about 200 yards ahead of us descending a long straight road at about 60mph. At the bottom of the incline as it started to level out, the road was bisected by a railway track. Vision was good either way and no trains were in view as Bob hit the crossing. It was like watching a *Carry on* film, as in slow motion both Bob and Tony left their seats and hit their heads on the roof. The boot lid flew open, the roof rack came off and everything flew up into the air landing far and wide.

What Bob hadn't realised was that the gap between the rails wasn't flush and that there was a drop of about three inches on to timber boards. Fortunately we were far enough behind to slow down and take the crossing at a sensible speed.

Laughing hysterically, we pulled over and once we'd come to our senses helped to collect all the stuff that had fallen off the roof rack and out of the boot. How the car didn't suffer any serious under-body damage I've no idea, but after a quick check it all seemed OK and we even managed to straighten the mangled remains into something that resembled a roof rack and refit it to the car.

Slowly we resumed our journey with Bob's Humber in between us. From here on the 'roads' became extremely variable in surface quality and the dirt road through Kirrikale was so bad that we actually had to drive round a number of the potholes. Some were so deep and wide you could have sent a caving expedition to explore them, and had we tried to drive through them we would have done more harm than good to our wagons.

Once through the crater-strewn road of Kirrikale, things improved. Much of the surface was reasonably flat and the road to Yozgat had recently been sprayed with tarmac.

It seemed to be an annual ritual in late spring to fill holes in the road surface with dirt and then spray a thin layer of tar to 'renew' it. All well and good, but if the weather was hot, which in the summer it was, this film of tarmac was prone to melting and if you were unlucky, great chunks would stick to your tyres causing a very uncomfortable ride.

By now we had already realised that this part of Turkey was desperately poor and very little investment was made in improving the infrastructure. As if to prove this point, approaching Yozgat we came across a half-hearted attempt to build a dual carriageway through the town. But like a lot of things here it hadn't been completed, leaving you to manoeuvre around the piles of rubble that were left behind.

For the next 150 miles across the rise and fall of the Anatolian plateau the landscape was arid and featureless, with scrubby bushes as the only sign of vegetation. Even though this was mountainous country, it was difficult to get any feeling of great beauty. It was mile upon mile of shades of intermingling grey and brown, almost lunar in appearance, which didn't allow for any definition in the stark background scenery.

Reaching the outskirts of Sivas, a large city of about 220,000, we were diverted away round the southern side of the town, following the river in a large arc, and for another thirty miles we followed this angry ribbon of water bubbling along the wide valley floor. You could sense that this was a wild harsh country, inhabited by hard, hard people.

Finally the road moved away from the river, back up into the mountains towards Zara. Here, on the edge of town we stopped for lunch, the ubiquitous truckers' stew, while Tony went and bought a few bottles of Efes beer at a local shack.

This is where the real hill climbing was to begin and as we saddled up after dinner we only travelled about half a mile before having to turn sharp right in the village centre for a very long and steep 1 in 4 climb out of town. Now we were heading for the true peaks of northern Anatolia, and for the next few hours it was a non-stop battering for the gearbox as we slogged our way up, down and through the mountains towards Erzincan.

Eventually, as dusk approached, we dropped out of the hills on to a plateau and down towards Erzincan where for a change the road was reasonably flat. On the outskirts of the town we had to pull into the official police checkpoint for a document appraisal, and as we had come to find out a general request for fags, just to keep everything sweet.

That night the three of us parked up near a railway line twenty miles east of the town. Tomorrow we'd be in Iran!

In the morning Bob and Tony again caught us up, having spent a night in a not so good hotel and joined us for breakfast before setting off for Erzurum and the infamous crossing of Tahir. We were already in a state of trepidation at the stories we'd heard of the kids and their rock throwing antics.

At Erzurum we had to negotiate another police check, and this time 'lost' a couple of our German girlie mags to our new found Polis friends, who inferred that they were disgusting while flipping through the pages, then rolling them up and pocketing them, obviously to check how 'disgusting' they were later!

It was now only fifty miles to Tahir and other than the climb out of Erzurum, the road for the next forty miles to Horasan was across mainly flat land and the road surface was reasonable.

Horasan was the start of the climb over Tahir and here we hooked up with a Land Rover full of youngsters heading for India. They wanted to know if they could run between us over the mountain having heard all the horror stories about people being held up and stripped of all their gear.

So we left Horasan in our hotchpotch of a convoy, me in front followed by the Land Rover, followed by Lenny, then Bob and Tony in the Sceptre and finally Bob C-S. Initially we had a trouble-free climb up the lower slopes, eventually passing the old Guy Big J and Euro Rental trailer still lying on its side as it was in the *Daily Mail* photograph taken a year previously, but as the road got steeper the surface began to deteriorate badly, until it was just a wide boulder-strewn mountain track scraped out of the rock surface.

As we approached the bottom end of Tahir village I was down to second gear at about 10mph, and spotted about ten to fifteen kids all dressed like urchins, running to the edge of the track. Their ages ranged from four or five to twelve or so. It was difficult to say. They all had one hand to their mouths making smoking signs, with the other hand behind their backs obviously clutching a welcoming present should we not oblige them with a fag.

I had about a dozen in my hand and threw them as hard as I could over their heads. They turned and descended on them like a juvenile pack of hyenas. This gave me and the youngsters in the Land Rover the opportunity to get about thirty yards further up the hill before the kids congregated at the roadside again. This time Bob threw out a load of cigarettes.

Then we were gone, over a rise, down into the centre of the village and away from the kids. In a few more moments we had escaped and were climbing up the steep little slope that took us out of Tahir and away from those stone-throwing little darlings.

We arrived unscathed at the top of the mountain where we all stopped to gather breath and look out over mountains as far as the eye could see in all directions.

Next to where we had pulled over was a sight that anywhere else in the world would have seemed incongruous. At the top of this 9,000-ft mountain, unable to tell its story, stood a German lorry and trailer. The front half had gone over the edge and flipped on its side leaving the trailer still standing, like a sentry guarding an injured soldier. We had a look round and everything seemed intact except for a missing wheel.

Who was the driver? Where was he now and what was his story? Legally he wouldn't be allowed to leave the country without his truck, as on entry into Turkey the vehicle details were always stamped in your passport. However, many drivers did manage to get out by hiding under bunks or even lying on the top of tilts, just using their ingenuity when in desperate straits. This wagon's ending was like a metaphor for the life of a Middle East trucker. There were hundreds of vehicles in a similar situation the length and breadth of this wild country.

For a little while longer we all stood looking out over the Anatolian peaks, thinking our own thoughts. I took a few photos for posterity, and then grateful that we had sustained no damage ourselves, started our descent to Eleskirt.

All we'd been warned about had come to pass, and Turkey was all we were expecting it to be, but having been prewarned we were prepared for it.

11

900 Miles to Abadan!

Lenny, Bob C-S and I, together with Bob Carter and Tony were coming closer to the end of our epic adventure. We had reached the far end of Turkey in eleven days, just three more to go to the finishing line.

So far it had been a wonderful experience. Across Western Europe on wonderfully smooth autobahns, then the contrast of the mind numbing length of Yugoslavia with its rough, bone jarring roads, untidy scenery and roadside religious icons. Then, west again across the Bulgarian hinterland to Turkey, a country of incalculable contrasts, with a history as old as civilisation itself. Here we saw our first minarets and listened to the muezzin in his metallic voice calling his flock to prayer five times a day. It was a country of massive extremes, where the West wants to be in Europe and the East doesn't. Here in eastern Turkey life has stood still for centuries, struggling for existence. It is hard in the extreme and the temperatures range from -40C in the winter, to +45C in the summer. The terrain is as harsh and demanding as anywhere on the planet but soon we would be out of it and crossing our final frontier into Persia, the land of the magic carpet!

We had just dropped down off the infamous Tahir Mountain in the Kurdistan region of eastern Turkey, and we could confirm all the tales about the kids lobbing stones at the trucks unless fed a constant supply of cigarettes. This was life at its most basic and it looked as if some of the village people lived in caves hewn out of the rocks, almost troglodyte-like.

But now we were down on the valley floor, driving through Agri, with its huge army encampment, heading towards Dogubayazit, and then the Iranian frontier at Bazargan. The weather was hot, our trucks had no air conditioning and you most probably wouldn't have wanted to be standing in close proximity. We had heard there was a Turkish bath in Maku, the first town on the Iranian side of the border, and that's where we were headed.

Leaving Dogubayazit for Bazargan, we could see Mount Ararat soaring proudly into the sky in the near distance with its white domed peak proclaiming its supremacy over its hinterland. This was where Noah's Ark had come to rest all those millennia ago and whether we had belief or not, sitting in its proximity it wasn't difficult for us to visualise the spectacle. Remarkably the land in this area looks as if it could have been at the bottom of the sea at some time, and with Ararat standing in such proud isolation, soaring high above the other peaks, such belief wouldn't stretch the imagination to excess.

In this semi-arid wasteland by the frontier we joined a short queue and all walked up to the border to see our agent. Bob and Tony had slipped through and were heading to Marand for the night.

By now my truck needed some running repairs. The continual pounding from the atrocious Turkish roads had broken one of my diesel tank restraining straps causing the tank to shift slightly and opening up a small split at the base. I'd contained the ensuing diesel leak by scraping Fairy soap across the crack which restricted the loss of fuel to a gentle drip, though a constant rubbing of soap on the wound had been necessary. This was a wonderfully simple, though temporary, method of reducing the amount of fuel lost and would be used to good effect many times in the future.

Once through the border and down the hill, we headed for Maku and a garage that our agent had informed us could make the necessary repairs. It turned out to be a real backstreet job, and we had to leave the trailer out of town while the repair was completed.

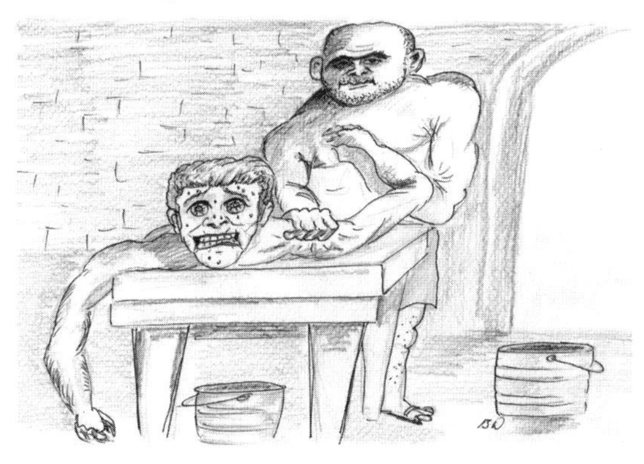

We used this time to good effect and got a lift to the Turkish baths. This experience was almost surreal. The building was very old and if you had never seen a Turkish bath before, but been able to imagine one, this would have been it. Tiled out totally in blue and white marble, there were a number of raised one-man baths alternately full of very hot and very cold water, and next to them raised marble slabs, where if you so wished, you could get manhandled and battered to death in an attempt to revive your aching bones. A gentle massage wasn't on the agenda. The choices were either agony or serious injury. I pleaded the plague and rejected any of the advances of these Machiavellian brutes. But after the pain of a boiling hot bath followed by a freezing cold bath and a scrub down with a loofer that was rougher than grade six sandpaper I felt wonderfully refreshed and lighter by two layers of skin.

Three hours later, truck repaired, and us cleaner than we had been for days, we were back on the road heading south, and *what* a road, gleaming black bitumen with a perfect flat surface. As you listened to the tyres humming on the warm tarmac you knew these roads were as good as any in Europe, and after the last 2,200 miles of rubbish this was like manna from heaven.

Next stop was the Oasis, on the road to Marand.

Iran is a *huge* country, with huge vistas. Every time we crested a rise, the next valley appeared, wide and long, with low mountain ranges on both sides stretching out into an indeterminate distance far beyond one's eyesight. Again this was another bleak and semi-arid land, with little but scrub vegetation. Just occasionally we spotted small groups of camels casually roaming through this inhospitable landscape.

One thing you quickly learned once you'd crossed the Bosporus into Asia was not to have an accident with man, vehicle, or beast, because the standard Middle East philosophy and mantra was:

'If you weren't here then there wouldn't have been an accident.'

This was an almost non-negotiable fact, and whether a bus had run up your rear or a goat had walked out in front of you, the same response applied. Most of this I believe was a cunning plan to extract compensation from the usually innocent driver.

There was possibly an apocryphal tale, of a trucker from Europe, who while driving down through Iran, had collided with a camel at some speed. The cab was badly damaged as was the camel. In fact, it was dead!

As is always the case in the Middle East you might think you're alone in these vast expanses of semi-desert, but when you stop, within a few moments, someone usually appears from the folds of the land, followed by someone else, and then before you know it you're surrounded by a whole host of chattering tribesmen. Where *did* they come from?

According to the story, this is what happened to one European driver after he stopped.

The poor old camel was lying prostrate by the roadside, and of course within minutes local herders had appeared as if from the very earth. There was the usual wailing, ringing of hands and gnashing of teeth, because they had lost a valuable commodity and wanted to heap guilt on the driver. By now a number of cars had also pulled up to give their 5p worth of advice.

Then came the hard sell: someone got down beside the camel's belly as if listening for something, then a second person got down to listen. After a few moments and a general conflab it was declared that this camel was in fact pregnant with three baby camels, which of course, would also be dead! Now came the totting-up procedure as to the total value of the four dead camels *and* the loss of the best brood mare in the whole camel kingdom!

Meanwhile, the truck driver, in this particular instance a little perturbed by the potential threat to his wallet, was having a closer look at the dead animal. When he had done so, he called one of the prostrated mourners round to have a look under the camel's tail – at the largest pair of testicles he had ever seen on man or beast. The tribesman shook his head violently while making a milking action with his hands, as he could see a large portion of his 'compensation' rapidly disappearing. According to him, these testicles were in fact the

udder! With that the driver managed to lift up one of the camel's legs to reveal the vital evidence: the camel's penile sheath. Pointing to the penis, he made the action of milking it, thereby implying that they were in fact wankers!

The financial outcome, though not cheap, was much less damaging to him than if it *had* been a female. As well as receiving a cash payment, the tribesmen felt honour had been satisfied. Interestingly, in all these sorts of contretemps, if you can prove them wrong, there is no apology forthcoming, just a resigned shrug of the shoulders that they didn't get away with it this time.

We arrived at the Oasis late afternoon. A very welcoming sight it was too as we crested yet another rise to see a tiny matchbox down on the valley floor about ten kilometres ahead.

It was called the Oasis, not because it was it was surrounded by palm trees – it wasn't. But it felt like a real oasis as it was the only building or facility for many miles around and stood in splendid isolation as if waiting for our arrival. It was a regular stopover for drivers of all nationalities and provided reasonable food and alcohol.

As we pulled off the road in a cloud of dust to park up for the night, there were already numerous other trucks parked up, from big Macks sitting tall on their huge sand tyres, to little Tonkas, overloaded with goods for Turkey.

It was here at the Oasis, in the wee small hours of the morning, while lying in my bunk and looking out at the midnight blue, star-studded sky that I first tuned in to what became my comforter and travel companion.

From the BBC World Service shipping forecast, I learned the names off by heart: Dogger Bank, Fisher, German Bight, Rockall. Where were these places? This, followed by the national anthem and the chimes of Big Ben, played at the end of each day's broadcasting was like a protective arm around my shoulder. I was always struck by the incongruity of it, laying in my bunk somewhere thousands of miles from home, possibly in the middle of the desert, listening to the shipping forecast. For me, it was a piece of Britain in my heart.

Anyway enough of the emotion!

From here to Tehran was a long day's run, about 550 miles on good roads, and as long as you had an early start, and didn't miss the police checkpoints on the way down, then you could be in the Davis Turner compound before dark.

For me and Lenny it was going to be at least another two nights before we reached our final destination - Abadan.

The three of us were up and running at 6 a.m. the following day and in the bright early morning sunshine drove down past one of the major Iranian cities, Tabriz, and headed towards Zandjan, 200 miles distant. Today was going to be another pot boiler, and already, halfway to Zandjan, the air rushing past our speeding trucks was rapidly warming up. In another hour there would be very little respite from the intense heat.

Halfway down this first stretch, Bob C-S was desperate for a pee and pulled over to the roadside dirt. When *one* needs a pee you might as well *all* have a pee - saves stopping again. We cocked our legs against our cab wheels, and looking round, as men do, I spotted movement in among the scrubby bush.

'What's that?' I said, pointing in the direction of the

movement as I slid down the bank to have a look. There among the sparse vegetation was a huge tortoise sedately munching what greenery was available.

'Bloody hell,' I exclaimed, 'come and look at this monster.'

Bob and Lenny slid down to join me.

'It's not a snake, is it?' said Bob warily and then spotted the shell. '*Good grief*, look at the size of that thing.'

The shell was at least two and a half feet across, and it was the biggest tortoise either of us had ever seen. Of course we *had* to try and pick it up. It must have weighed getting on for a hundredweight or more. The poor thing totally ignored us and didn't even retract its head, but carried on merrily munching away while we were messing it about.

'Come on lads,' said Lenny, 'we haven't got time to mess about here all day.'

Within minutes we were back on the road, and with Karen Carpenter gently caressing the airwaves, we were soon approaching Zandjan, where all heavy trucks were diverted to the right and around the town.

I was the lead truck in our little convoy and followed the diversion sign. Luckily I wasn't travelling too fast as I was keeping an eye out for further signs, when all of a sudden my head and everything else in the cab hit the roof as I hit some sort of obstacle in the road. Oh bugger! Surely the load must have shifted with that hit, was my instant reaction, and then the trailer wheels crashed into the obstacle before I had a chance to get the truck back under any semblance of control. I pulled over and shaken up climbed out to see what I had hit and survey any damage.

Lenny and Bob were far enough back to see what had happened and pulled up behind me. Lenny had a grin on his face as he walked towards me.

'Bet that shook you up, mate. Didn't you see it?'

'No, what the hell was it?' looking under the cab. 'Whatever it was, it gave me a headache,' I said, rubbing my skull.

'You *really* didn't see it?' said Bob, pointing back up the road to the biggest, fattest, sleeping policeman I'd ever seen, before or since. It must have been six foot across and eighteen inches high. If I'd had a British flag on me I'd have planted it on the summit; it was that big!

Unbelievably there didn't appear to be any damage and looking round the outside of the trailer, nothing appeared to have fallen over. Obviously those old 'bottle jacks' had done their job. Very gingerly I pulled away keeping a wary eye out for any more of these man made obstructions, and followed the diversion route round the town.

There were no more obstacles, manmade or otherwise and finally, having virtually circumnavigated the town the diversion sign pointed off to the right and across what appeared to be a field of flattened corn. We followed the truck tracks through the cornfield and within five minutes were back on the main highway heading south to Takestan, another eighty miles away, where Lenny and I would split and head further south to Abadan, while Bob C-S with Bob Carter and Tony would head for Tehran.

That night we stayed over at a restaurant truck stop on the outskirts of Takestan and had a pretty atrocious meal, supposedly chicken, but it could have been any old faded bit of leather off somebody's shoe, it was that tough and stringy. If it was a chicken, it must have been a sixty-five-year-old one. I'm still trying to get the bits out of my teeth thirty odd years later!

In the morning Lenny and I said goodbye to the others, turned right at the intersection and headed south. The plan was that after unloading in Abadan, we would make our way back to the Mocamp in Istanbul and telex home for reload instructions. Anyway that was all a few days ahead, firstly we had to get down to the Persian Gulf and unload. Only 600 miles to go.

Our plan was to head for Khorramabad, in the Zagros Mountains, then see how we were for time.

This land is still very much 'Kurdistan'; much of eastern Iran is an extension of the Anatolian plateau in Turkey. The people look just the same and live in an equally harsh environment, with stark desolate scenery and many peaks reaching to over 9,000 feet.

The one major difference for us were the roads. They were a joy to drive on, and allowed us to make good progress through this mountainous region. Even though we were up at about 3,500 feet it was still very hot . . . what would it be like down on the flatlands? The last eighty miles to Abadan was at sea level.

We had a steady run through to Khorramabad and decided to push on. Within the hour it was dark and we still had about eighty miles to go to the next town, Dezful, but we were comfortable with this and kept going. It was much more pleasant driving at night as the temperature dropped by 10C up in the hills.

Somehow or other we found ourselves near a small town called Eslamabad e Gharb, seventy miles off route and heading towards Iraq.

I blamed Lenny even though I was in front.

'What have you done with Dezful Lenny?' I laughed, 'you're supposed to know where we're going.'

'Ha bloody ha, well done Mr Geography-Expert-I-Know-The-Way sir,' retorted Lenny.

By now it was 9 p.m. and we really should have been looking for somewhere to park up for the night. We had a little conflab, with Lenny taking full responsibility for his error of judgement, and decided not to go back the same way, but to head south to a town called Llam, and then run alongside the Iraqi border to rejoin the road to Abadan, south of Dezful.

It was a beautiful clear night, with very little traffic as we followed the road, twisting and turning, up steep inclines, then down sudden drops into valleys. The driving was superb, even in a fully laden truck and with a full moon casting its light and shadow across the spectacular scenery it was a memory I'll never forget.

South of Llam the road straightened out as we dropped out of the highlands on to a plateau. It was getting close to midnight and we were *still* going; at one point we were only a couple of miles from the Iraqi border. It seemed strange to think that Baghdad was only fifty miles away.

Lenny flashed me from behind and I pulled over on to the side of the road. He was getting tired, so was I. We couldn't park here, so we'd try and find something in the next half an hour. Looking at the map we were now moving away from the border area and as we continued south we came across the strangest thing as we suddenly found ourselves driving down an extremely wide road with faint lights along the edge every twenty yards or so. I knew it was wide because from the edge of the road to the white line in the middle was about twenty yards! A forty yard wide road, what was going on?

The lines in the centre of the road were absolutely huge, at least as long as the truck and three feet wide. In fact I became a little disorientated, and had to drive alongside the white lines to ensure we were driving straight, then just as quickly as it arrived, it disappeared, and we were back on the normal road. What was that all about? Five miles further on we were able to pull off on to some scrubland and I asked Lenny if he had noticed the wide road.

'You pillock,' said Lenny, laughing. 'That was a runway! You should know, you lived at Wattisham for a few years.'

'What?'

Thinking about it, so it was, being quite close to the border. It was most probably a temporary airstrip just in case of trouble, obviously unmanned, otherwise we would certainly have been stopped.

It was 1 a.m. and time for sleep.

The following morning the brightness of the sun woke me up.

A bath was urgently required. I was starting to feel very uncomfortable; the last decent wash had been in Maku, and the monthly bath that I'd had as a teenager wouldn't suffice now.

Over a bowl of cereal and a mug of tea we discussed the previous night's escapade. Len reckoned he'd enjoyed it too. The only downside was that we'd put an extra 180 miles on the trip. Better not tell Bob, although he most probably wouldn't mind too much as fuel was only 10p a gallon!

'You deed a bath, old sud,' said Lenny holding his nose.

'Is that me?' I said, sniffing the pungent air around my person, 'I can only apologise, obviously I'm aware that cleanliness is next to godliness and by the by, talking about godliness, when was the last time you were in church. I've heard the muezzin calling to prayer loads of times since we've been here, but never seen you on your knees, *mate*.' We both burst out laughing . . .

The last day of our incredible adventure was from Pasgah to Abadan.

Once again it was a beautiful morning, not a wisp of cloud in the sky and as we savoured our breakfast cuppa we luxuriated in the early morning sunshine up in the Zagros foothills. This wouldn't last long and already the sun was gaining strength by the minute. Today was going to be another pot boiler.

There was little traffic on the road, just the odd bonneted Mercedes truck, with its big sand tyres and grossly overloaded, making slow progress to wherever. These we easily dispatched and left far behind as we got ever closer to our destination. Eventually we started to drop off the plateau and down to the semi-desert of the Euphrates/Tigris delta, and as we did there was a commensurate rise in the temperature, till it was almost unbearable. With my arm resting on the edge of the open window the breeze flowing across it was hot air. There was no relief, boy, did I need a bath!

Little did we know, but our prayers were about to be answered.

Approaching Ahvaz we spotted a number of British and Iranian trucks parked about thirty yards off the road. Two of the British guys had their trailers completely stripped out, with a line of washing hanging between their trucks. What a good idea, I thought.

We pulled over, stopped close by and spotted one of the reasons they had parked there; the answer to our prayers so to speak!

Running across the desert from as far as the eye could see was a huge open concrete culvert, about twenty foot across and ten foot deep, although when you slid down into it, the water was about waist high. We needed no second bidding as there were a few drivers already enjoying the experience.

Armed with my trusty Fairy Liquid I jumped straight in. Bloody hell! The water was freezing. It seems that the culvert ran down from high up in the Zagros mountains collecting all the snow melt and rain, then ferried it across the delta to Abadan. Who cared, this was magnificent and I soon forgot the cold as I introduced my unclean body to the pleasures of Fairy Liquid.

A couple of Pakistani guys, who were driving the Iranian trucks, were most intrigued by the amount of lather the Fairy was producing, and asked to borrow it. Within a few minutes everyone had a head full of white bubbles, and they thought it hilarious.

Lenny and I stayed there most of the afternoon luxuriating in this fresh water Eden, then eventually, taking a cue from the other British guys who were doing internals,[1] we *also* washed a few of our well used clothes with the ubiquitous

[1] Internals. There was a shortage of Iranian hauliers to move goods around the country, so some of the European lads 'helped' out by sometimes doing a few local runs to help out customers. This happened in a number of the Middle Eastern countries. I only did this twice myself. Officially it was illegal.

Fairy Liquid. By the time they were dry, late afternoon was upon us and it was time to move out and down to Ahvaz. We would definitely be stopping here on the way back.

We parked up on a dusty restaurant forecourt at about 6 p.m. on the outskirts of Ahvaz, and actually had quite a decent meal. This time the chicken was only thirty years old! After a pleasant evening and a few beers in the company of the proprietor, Lenny and I agreed on a starting time that would allow us to be at our destination at the oil terminal at 9 a.m. We would be cleared on site apparently, and empty by tomorrow night.

In the morning, after a mug of tea, we were on the road as we'd agreed, and after passing the port of Khorramshah, we rolled into our destination at just after 9 a.m. We reported to the site manager's air-conditioned office and introduced ourselves. It was like being in a fridge compared to the heat outside, and when we looked at a thermometer it was reading 25C, though it felt more like 5C, such was the temperature differential between out and in. The staff made us very welcome and offered us all sorts of cold drinks, which we accepted enthusiastically.

Our carnets, CMRs and passports were collected and whisked away somewhere, presumably to the customs to organise clearance, and we were offered the opportunity to make ourselves comfortable in the office while this was happening, which we did.

There is a danger in excessive heat of flicking in and out of air-conditioned facilities when the going gets too hot. That in fact is not always the safest thing to do, as the temperature variation between the inside and outside might be as high as 25C, and that can play havoc with your body's thermostat.

At two o'clock back came one of the office staff with all the relevant paperwork and a customs official. The customs man had a quick look around the trailers and proceeded to break off all the seals we had accumulated on our 4,000-mile trip down here, and we were free to unload our cargo.

What do they say about mad dogs and Englishmen? Well, I can confirm it to be a fair and true assessment of the British psyche. There we were, out in the midday sun, admittedly with hats on, but very little else pulling out the TIR cords, clambering over the superstructure and rolling back the tilt. Mind you, we had a few burnt bits and pieces by the time the sheets were furled. The metal superstructure was really too hot to touch and the tilt material was so stretchy it was like pushing pizza dough. Eventually they were rolled far enough forward to allow the crane to access the machinery through the top, and within a couple of hours we were both empty.

This is what we had come over 4,000 miles for; the first half of our great adventure, successfully completed. We both shook hands and contemplated the fact that now we had to refit the tilts, easier than it sounds.

Back home in England in a colder climate unfurling a rolled-up tilt wasn't too difficult, as normally the material was pretty stiff, and generally speaking if you sat on top of the superstructure and slowly edged your way back it was possible to unravel it without to much effort.

Here in 115F, trying to pull a forty-foot square of pizza dough the length of your trailer and make sure it fitted in all the right places was a mammoth task, and we weren't finally strapped up till it was dark and gone 7 p.m.

We were both filthy and knackered, but couldn't stay there, so after a quick splash with our own water reserves we decided to head back up to the culvert and have a proper clean-up in the morning before heading back the 2,000 miles to Istanbul.

An hour in the culvert the following morning set us up for the day, and anyway we would soon be heading up into the hills and away from this searing heat.

Two days later Lenny and I were in the queue at the bottom of the escarpment waiting to exit Iran.

The Turkish side of the frontier, Gurbulak, sat at the top of this 300 foot high cliff, while Bazargan, on the Iranian side, spread itself all the way down the hillside alongside a tarmac road. Originally all traffic had crossed the frontier on this road, but as truck volumes built up, the congestion on this single track road became intolerable, so the Iranian authorities blasted a dirt track out of the other side of the escarpment just for trucks heading back into Turkey.

This new dirt road was about half a mile long, and in some places only one vehicle wide. Close to the top before the final short very steep incline through into Turkey, there was a vicious left hand hairpin bend where in the wet many of the trucks lost traction.

The majority of the time the surface of this track was dry, and access to the top was simple enough, very rough and bumpy yes, but not difficult. However, if it had been raining, or in winter, snowing, the climb up was much more challenging. In fact, this, our first time back at Bazargan, it had been raining for a couple of hours and the track had been heavily churned up, so much so that the police were only letting one vehicle up at a time.

In case of difficulty there was a tractor positioned at the top to assist, at a price, anyone who lost traction and got stuck. The surface was too rough for chains, as they would have surely been wrecked by the time you had reached the top of the escarpment; on top of that some of the surface had been turned into a quagmire by the sheer volume of trucks.

Lenny and I were well down the queue, and while we were waiting, had wandered up to our agent and cleared customs 'leer', ready to cross into Turkey. Having got back to our trucks, we moved forward towards the bottom of the dirt track and noticed that the queue to the top wasn't continuous. That in fact, the last couple of hundred yards was being kept clear to allow drivers a run at getting to the top under their own power.

It was entertaining to watch as all sorts of methods were

tried - from putting it in crawler gear and letting the truck make its own way up, to blasting up as quickly as possible, hoping to make it round the hairpin and that momentum would get you up.

At the top a large crowd were gathered, mostly drivers, who cheered, whistled or booed and gave a round of applause to those who made it on their own. Slowly the queue in front of us whittled down until it was my turn next. About half the trucks had been successful, and the rest needed the tractor.

This was all very competitive stuff. Getting up on your own felt like you had won a race. I even had butterflies in my stomach. This was for the honour of British truckers, don't you know!

Lenny and I decided that as we weren't that far from the Crimea we'd go with zero finesse and have a bash at the 'Charge of the Light Brigade' approach. The surface here was stable and it was around 150 yards to the left hand hairpin, which was extremely muddy. I dropped it into gear, second low, and accelerated away. I needed to get into third high by the bend, and doing about 25mph. After about 100 yards the surface became really rough and I was bouncing all over the place. Arriving at the hairpin, the drive wheels started to lose traction and I was slipping sideways, but the head of steam and momentum I had built up pulled me through on to the more solid surface of the last steep incline and then I was over the top, past the jeering crowd and parked up waiting for Lenny. I climbed out of my cab elated, just in time to see Lenny roar over the brow of the hill, as he successfully made the climb as well.

We were well and truly on the way back now and three days later we met Bob and Tony at the Mocamp, where the confirmed instructions from Felixstowe were to go to Helmut Heid in Graz and then load out of Weiner Neustadt near Vienna. Bob and Tony met us in Graz as Bob wanted to discuss with Helmut a future working relationship. Lenny and I loaded in Weiner and after successfully completing our first trip we both felt like seasoned Middle East truckers.

Of course we weren't, it would take a few more trips before we could truly feel that we were the Masters of the Universe!

Our first trip was all I could have asked, and driving off the ferry at Felixstowe on our return I felt as if I was a different person to the one that had left one month earlier. As with most things in life it is the first experience that stays in your memory with the greatest clarity. I had many more wonderful experiences during my time in road haulage, but you always remember the first girlfriend . . .

12

Any Chance of a Lift Mate?

'The next trip to Iran won't be for a couple of weeks,' said Mike. 'How do you fancy a quick run down to Athens while you're waiting? I've got twenty tons of milk to be delivered to the QE2 a week tomorrow.'

That's transport bosses for you, a quick 4,000 mile round trip!

'OK Mike, who's it for, Trans UK?' I said.

'No, Dennis Gould, he's got an office in the Routemaster at Felixstowe. You've to load in Luton tomorrow, I've got the address. Then, it's back to Felixstowe to get the paperwork.'

Well, why not, and anyway 'how do you fancy?' wasn't a multiple choice question. It was 'right, this is your next job.'

Greece was a comfortable twelve to fourteen day round trip and a popular destination with drivers because, generally speaking, they were pro-British, the roads were excellent, and it was more first world than third.

My route down was to be via France, Italy and Yugoslavia.

I didn't know it yet but this was also going to be my first experience with 'bent' permits. As I was delivering outside the European Union I was running under TIR carnet but required a permit to transit France and Italy. These permits were issued by the various EEC countries and consisted of a green and white copy stapled together. Genuine transit permits were like gold dust and there were never enough issued to cover the number of vehicles needing to use them.

So, you would be given a permit by your boss with the strict instruction and under pain of death.

'*Do not get the green copy stamped*.'

This of course was highly illegal, as one permit = one trip, and for EEC records the proof that the trip had been done was a customs stamp on the green copy which was then supposed to be sent back to the Ministry. Of course many weren't sent back but were used again and again, and this led to the often embarrassing scenario of drivers at French and Italian frontiers slipping 50 francs or 10,000 lire in among their paperwork to discourage the official from stamping the green copy. If you were successful, the permit could be used again.

To make things worse, on this trip I had been given a permit that had *already* been stamped. When I queried it with the contractor who we were doing the job for, the response was: 'you'll be fine, just slip them an extra few thou.'

I followed another driver with duff paperwork from Zeebrugge down to Halluin/Menin and we blagged our way into France with our 'bent' permits by pleading we were new to international driving and playing the simpleton. Sometimes the border personnel got so cheesed off with your antics and the continuous flaunting of the regulations that they let you go just to be rid of you.

Having got through, it was virtually non-stop down through France, stopping at the 'Bakehouse' near Macon overnight. In the morning it was a four-hour haul up into the foothills of the Alps and Modane, the French border control where my paperwork was stamped and given back with no questions asked. Maybe this wasn't going to be that difficult after all. Next stop was Mont Cenisio and Italy - what a beautiful climb! Most drivers used this route as an alternative to Mont Blanc as it was decidedly cheaper due to the cost of the Mont Blanc Tunnel toll.

I joined a queue of about ten drivers at the Italian customs office and as advised, slipped 5,000 lire in with the permit. I got to the front and pushed my paperwork through to the officer. He opened up the carnet, stamped it, then lifted the already stamped green permit and saw the money. Without a word, he neatly folded all my paperwork and shooing me away, handed it all back to me. *What?*

'Back of the queue mate,' said an English guy behind me. 'Try again.'

I took his advice, and red faced joined the back of the queue, this time slipping in another 5,000 lire note. I got to the front again and slid my papers through for a second time. This time they were stamped and handed back without a word. Checking the permit afterwards, the money had disappeared. How did he do that? I had watched closely the whole time.

The downside to this whole charade was that the regular drivers in the queue, who always had the correct permits, regarded you as a cowboy for running with 'bent' paperwork.

The guy Dave, who had told me to try again, had waited outside for me.

'I saw you with a carnet mate, where you off to then?'

So I told him Piraeus. 'What about you?'

Dave was heading for Baghdad. 'Don't worry about the permit thing, pal,' he said. 'I could see you sweating a bit, it's not very nice but you get used to it. These bloody EEC countries won't issue enough; they only do it on a reciprocal basis. The problem is more British hauliers want to come over here than Europeans want to come to England.'

'Thanks for your help.' I said, 'I'm bloody starving. Is there anywhere to eat around here?'

'Yeah, follow me there's a nice little trattoria in Susa.'

Dave was driving a yellow DAF 2600 and as he pulled out I tagged on behind as we dropped down the much steeper Italian side of Mont Cenis to Susa where we stopped for lunch at Dave's trattoria.

After a delicious due uova and frites,[1] we left Susa, and north of Turin picked up the autostrada which took us past Milan, all the way across the Lombardy Plain to the night's stop at an AGIP Area di Servizio near Padua.

In the morning we were up at the crack of dawn and after a quick coffee were on our way past Venice and on to Monfalcone. By 8.30 a.m. we'd completed the Italian side, the customs officers weren't the slightest bit interested in the 'bent' permit. But strangely, the money still disappeared .

The barrier was lifted and Dave and I drove through the 300 yards of wooded no-man's-land to Sezana. In 1975 no permit was required to transit Yugoslavia and as the border was quiet we wasted no time being cleared by the customs officials and in half an hour were heading for Ljubljana.

The main road from Sezana took us in and out of huge earthworks that were soon to be part of Yugoslavia's first autoput. It was possible to see the Italian engineering influence in the design of the new motorway. The new tollbooths being installed could have been stolen from the autostrada network!

Another ninety miles and we were trying to find our way

[1] Uova and frites . . . egg and chips.

round Zagreb and link up with the E5, now the E70 and 'relishing' the next 400-plus bone shaking miles to Nis. What a horrible road. I don't reckon it had been repaired since Roman chariots were cruising up and down looking for Queenie's great, great grandhag. At least in Turkey their atrocious roads had 'character', here there was no let up from the continuous crashing and banging of your suspension the whole 640 kms.

Dave and I pulled into the Trees for a break and looking for a bit of light relief, but for some reason Queenie and her entourage were missing, maybe at their day jobs. How sad, I was looking forward to a bit of theatre. As entertainment was off the agenda we didn't waste too much time, and after ice cold Cokes rolled back out on to the battered old highway heading for Belgrade.

At least we had a decent dinner at the National. Dave decided he was going to stay the night as he'd met a couple of mates who were doing the same, which was fair enough. I said cheerio and thanked him for his help; as far as I was concerned he was an 'old hand' as this was his fifth Middle East trip. I needed to be down at least as far as Nis, 240 kilometres south of Belgrade to give me a chance of getting to Piraeus in time.

Nis is a major point of divergence on the long haul. To the east are Bulgaria, Turkey, and the rest of the world, straight on and to the south is Greece, a lovely country with simpatico pro-British people and *excellent* roads. Mind you, there were the odd older Greeks who blamed my father for the German invasion in the Second World War!

At 11.30 p.m. I pulled into a lay-by just north of Nis and after a quick lick and gum brushing fell sound asleep on my bunk.

Piraeus, I'd made it! Five days after leaving the UK I had cleared customs and was directed quayside to the QE2 and pulled up alongside her. A large gang of dockers arrived and rapidly unloaded my urgent delivery of milk powder on to pallets, which were then whisked away into the bowels of the boat by forklift. A purser supervised the operation and thanked me for my efforts by slipping me a few bob.

'We wondered whether you'd make it in time,' he said.

'Why the urgency?' I enquired.

'It's not so much the urgency, it's the logistics,' he said. 'On these cruises we stay in each port for at the most two days, then overnight while passengers are asleep we move on to the next destination, so the window of opportunity is small. We knew our itinerary would bring us here today so it was a question of organising a delivery that would hopefully arrive at the same time; we didn't want you chasing us all over the Mediterranean.'

'Does this happen very often?' I asked.

'Occasionally, though it's not a very cost effective way to organise things.'

'Why are you short of milk then?'

Apparently there had been stock taking problems before they had left Southampton Dock, and half way across the Bay of Biscay the quartermaster realised they were going to be short of milk on this cruise unless the milkman drove 2,000 miles in his milk float to meet them!

Having tipped my load I had to go and find the agent in

Athens to use the telex and let them know back home that I was empty. The instruction came back to make my way to Rovereto in north east Italy and pick up a load of garments from a factory for the UK.

I tied back the rear corner of the tilt so that the border guards could easily clamber up and see that I was leer (empty), and left on the return trip making my way back up to Larissa for the night. The following morning I was at the Greek border at Evzoni for 9 a.m.

As I was empty I was able to clear customs quickly on the Greek side and drew through the barrier to Gevgelija in Yugoslavia.

Climbing down from my cab, I was accosted by a couple of English lads who were hitchhiking back to the UK. I told them to wait near the truck until I had completed my paperwork, then I'd see. Twenty minutes later, my paperwork done, I returned to the truck. The guys were still there, and so were another dozen hikers, boys and girls.

'Any chance of a lift mate,' was the general request.

'Sorry guys I've already promised two blokes a lift, I've no more room.'

'Aw come on mate, some of us have been here three days already, and we were here before those two.'

I should have just jumped in my cab and gone.

'As you're empty driver, any chance we could get in the trailer?'

For some reason I felt sorry for them, soft touch, especially as there were girls as well.

'OK,' I said. 'I'll take you to Belgrade, these two guys in the cab,' pointing to the couple of lads who had first approached me, 'and the rest in the trailer.'

There was a rush for the trailer, as if it was the last bus out of hell.

As well as English youngsters, there were also a couple of Dutch and Norwegians.

Once they were on board I jumped on to the back bumper of the trailer so I could see in.

'OK guys, just one thing, whatever you do, *do not*, I repeat *do not* look over the backboard, I've got a feeling this may not be too legal.'

It was a beautiful day, and the sun was high overhead as we pulled out from Gevgelija heading through the western end of the Rhodope Mountains towards Nis. Things were going really well, when about fifteen miles before Titov Veles, ploughing through the tunnels up in the hills we rounded a bend and found ourselves up behind a Yugoslav police car doing about 20 kph. Bugger, now what to do?

I couldn't really stay behind him at that speed, and he didn't seem inclined to go any faster. So, on the next short straight I pulled out and overtook him.

I kid you not, within twenty seconds he came past me, blue lights flashing and with the second policeman hanging out of the window waving his lollipop at me. I knew straight away what had happened. Those silly pillocks in the trailer just couldn't keep their noses in.

He pulled in front of me and slowed down to twenty again and with blue lights still flashing stayed in front until we reached a section of road that was wide enough to pull me in.

Then it was both of them out of the car with guns out doing the old threatening bit. I always found the best recipe for trying to defuse the situation was to get out of the cab quickly and walk towards them with hand outstretched ready to shake theirs, and they did!

'*Collega, problem*,' said the driver of the police car just lifting his head in the direction of the trailer.

What a pain this was going to be!

Of course, everyone was made to get out of the trailer, and for the next two hours the police went through all their gear, generally giving them grief.

I was waiting for mine.

There was a lot of bickering among the hikers, all fault finding and blaming each other.

Eventually the police came to me with another, '*problem collega*,' which *I* knew meant it was going to cost me, and it did, 500 dinar, all official with a receipt!!

All the hitchhikers were standing around hoping to get back in the trailer, and in fact one did. The police soon spotted him though and made it clear that no one was getting a lift in *this* trailer.

Here we were in the middle of nowhere, up in the hills and the nearest town about twenty-five kilometres away, and they were all going to have to walk, might still be walking for all I know.

The police allowed the two guys to ride in the cab, but that was it and I had wasted over four hours trying to do someone a favour!

The two lads were not very popular with the other hikers, especially as they wouldn't change places with any of the girls.

'This is my seat and I'm keeping it, with a girls, what girls?' attitude.

I took them to Belgrade as promised and even though one of them was hoping for a lift back home to the UK, I'd had enough of them both by then: non-stop moaning and they were going to eat me out of house and home. They were the sort of travellers who gave hikers a bad name. Never again!

Having left them both at the National Hotel I headed north towards Zagreb, stopping off at 'The Trees' late that night. Strange, there were still none of the 'pretty' ladies about, bloody good job actually; I might get a little bit of shuteye. Mind you, it was a little bit, as in the morning I was up at the crack of dawn and cleared the border at Monfalcone around midday.

My plan was to head for the town of Schio in northern Italy, where I hoped to visit friends I'd known from my time holidaying in Elba ten years previously. They owned a bar in the main square, and it would be nice to see them for the night. Then the following morning I would cross the Vallee di Pasubio Pass and drop down into Rovereto to load.

Not so, the bar was closed, Franco and Christina were away on holiday.

Then I made a rash decision, a really rash decision, I decided to go straight to Rovereto that night.

I had been over the pass in a car ten years previously and remember the scenery as being dramatic, with overhanging rocks, and numerous tight hairpins.

View from a car, view from a truck - totally different!

As soon as I started the ascent and hit the hairpins I knew I had made a mistake. On some of the bends I had to shunt the unit as they were too tight to get round in one manoeuvre, and the trailer axles seemed to spend more time hanging out over cliff edges than on the road. Eventually I made it round the final bend on the climb only to have to deal with the huge overhanging cornices running up to the pass itself. It was getting dark and fortunately very little traffic was coming the other way. I had already noticed a distinct lack of trucks on this road!! Reaching the summit in near darkness I realised the scenery opened out a bit. Hopefully, the descent would be a lot easier.

At the top I stopped in a lay-by for a cuppa and a bowl of soup, into which I dropped a packet of crisps. Now you know why truck drivers are slim, svelte figures, and are to be admired!

Half an hour later, feeling a little less hungry, I was ready to roll. A quick look at the map showed there were no hairpin bends on the way down, just a tunnel on the final approach, so looking forward to the descent, I pulled out of the lay-by. Things could only improve, couldn't they?

The descent *was* a lot easier, until that is on the approach to the tunnel I spotted a sign that brought me out in a cold sweat. Bridge, 3.80 metres, 400 metres!

'Oh bugger this could be tight,' I thought out loud.

My trailer height was about 3.80 metres.

As I approached the tunnel, about 300 metres before the bridge I spotted a side road off to the right.

'Oh well, if I get into trouble I can always turn round and go back.' That thought only flashed across my mind for a fleeting second as I realised I'd most probably not get round the hairpins again. This hadn't been such a good idea after all

I gently manoeuvred up to the tunnel entrance and slowly put the unit under it, and with my head out of the window looking up at the hand hewn roof, oh so slowly I edged the front of the trailer into the mouth, only to come to a resounding halt within ten yards as the top of the tilt-covered headboard collided with a piece of the roof.

'This could be a disaster,' I thought as I reversed before anyone came up behind me.

Sitting at the entrance to this 400-metre long tunnel, in a daze, without a clue as to what to do other than dismantle the trailer and somehow cut down the top of the headboard, I realised that I had an audience as one or two cars started to arrive from the opposite direction. There was much shaking of heads and negative Italian speak, and I soon understood that trucks were banned from this road. I must have missed the sign back at Schio!

'*Non possibili*,' said one bloke, followed by '*molto difficile*' from another. It was all positive stuff . . .

Then I had a brainwave, I reckoned if I was able to drop the trailer back down the fifth wheel runners it would lower the height by four or five inches. This part of the tunnel was sloping gently downhill so the idea might work.

'Scuzi,' I said, and then asked in my 'best' Italian whether the road through the tunnel was downhill all the way. After ten minutes of trying to get them to understand, one of the women on the scene had a blinding flash of understanding and said '*Si, si, si*.'

With that, I said I needed someone at the other end of the tunnel to blast their horn as soon as it was clear and to stop anyone else coming through. There was another five minutes of deliberation until understanding again dawned and the plan was on.

I disconnected the red air line that provided air to the trailer brakes and then wound down the legs till they were about six to eight inches off the ground, pulled the pin to release the unit from the trailer and very gently I pulled forward until one of the locals shouted '*basta*' (stop). I jumped out to have a look, and it was perfect. The trailer was now sitting on the guide rails about three feet back down the ramps and some six inches lower than before. I reconnected the red air line, jumped back into the cab and released the deadman (handbrake). Very slowly with my foot shading the footbrake, the truck started to roll forward and ten minutes later having navigated round two shallow bends, I was out the other end, pouring with sweat, such was the tension.

I thanked everyone profusely, eventually coupled up and drove to the factory about a mile away on the outskirts of Rovereto, ready to load in the morning. It took me a couple of hours for the adrenalin to subside and in the morning instead of waking early as I was used to, I was awoken at 9 a.m. by a very pretty girl banging on the cab. The workers were trying to get into the factory and I was parked across the gate.

This was my lucky day; I was assisted in loading by a bevy of very attractive Italian ladies, whose sole ambition was to flirt with me. Not that I was complaining you understand! By midday I was fully freighted and had a goodbye session of snogging with the girls. Well, a peck on the cheek from each. It was a most enjoyable morning which in some way compensated for the previous night's trauma.

On leaving Rovereto I had to run down past Lake Garda and head for Milan. As I was pulling into an AGIP service area I was accosted by two spectacular looking Norwegian girls.

'Can you take us to Milan please?' they chorused, with their hands clasped together and a pleading look in their eyes.

I was going to say no, wasn't I? Whatever happened to that promise I'd made to myself only yesterday?

My enthusiasm in trying to say yes was constrained by the fact that my tongue was hanging so far out of my mouth I couldn't form the words properly, but I think they got the message. They were stunning.

'Thank you so much, how can we pay you, sir?'

How can *you pay* me? Did I *hear* that right? Wasn't this every truck driver's dream?

'Pardon,' I said with a silly grin on my face and still struggling to retract my tongue.

'My name is Niki and she is Madeleine, we are going to Paris.'

'Paris?' I said, then suddenly realised the potential implications.

'*IamgoingtoParisaswellifyouwantaliftiwouldlovetooffer youbotharidealltheway*.'

What was the matter with me? The sight of two beautiful blue-eyed blonde Scandinavians had melted my brain.

'Thank you sir, that is most kind. We can sleep in the seats and will not disturb you, I promise.'

Will not disturb me! I'd never been so bloody disturbed . . .

They were great company, and restored my faith in the hitch hiking fraternity especially the girls!

And did they sleep in the seats that night? Not a chance. A flutter of the eyebrow, a flash of cleavage and I slept in the seat while they each had one of my bunks. For this I was treated to a peck on the cheek and the curtains being pulled tightly together as they got ready for bed. I had a disturbed night, a very disturbed night. Was it just me, or are all men suckers for a pretty face and a self-supporting bosom? Over the years I have come to the conclusion that we are pathetic in the face of wishful thinking.

As you might guess I was as uncomfortable as hell and had practically no sleep, so when the girls woke up I was still struggling with the land of nod. It was then they obviously decided to give me my thank you 'present' as Madeleine changed her T-shirt while sitting on the bottom bunk. There for a fleeting moment I was treated to a vision of perfection as her naked chest flashed in front of my eyes.

'Sorry,' she said.

Sorry, did she say sorry? Don't be sorry, let me wake up properly and then you can do it again. I wasn't drooling was I?

After a cup of coffee and a bowl of cereal we were back on the road to Paris. I have to say that once I'd got the sex out of my mind we had a pleasant day's drive. They were great company and I was sad to say goodbye when I dropped them off near the Porte de la Chappelle.

It was an eventful trip to say the least. Mr Sensible would not have picked up the first lot of hitch hikers, and nor would he have tried to cross the bottom edge of the Alps without first checking the route, but there you go, obviously not me mister.

13

Water Melon Man

During August 1975, while still working for Mitchell-Rowlands, I had been down to Salonica (Thessaloniki) with a pair of bean harvesting machines that were going out from the port to one of the Greek islands. The trailer had to be dropped in the customs compound for a couple of days while the paperwork for the machinery was cleared.

I booked into the Afton Hotel, in the suburbs of Salonika, for two nights with Andy, another English driver, who was also delivering machinery. The Afton was to become a regular stop, as it was clean and reasonably priced, with pleasant staff and of course a decent shower.

While we were there Andy and I spent a couple of days on the beach at Michaniona. It was one of the benefits of this job that on reaching your destination it usually took at least a couple of days to clear customs. Often that allowed you the opportunity to drop your trailer in the customs compound and use the tractor unit as a taxi if you wanted to visit places – such as the beach.

And we did! It was summertime, the weather was superb and so were the girls, so for those two days we whiled away the time down by the sea ogling the ladies.

On the third day I had a call from my agent telling me to go to customs and supervise the unloading of the harvesters and afterwards to call into his office and collect the carnet and CMR. The unloading took all afternoon, mainly because it was what we called a full strip out, which meant rolling the tilt all the way to the front of the trailer, then dismantling the superstructure to enable the harvesters to be lifted out through the top. All very well except that it all had to be rebuilt afterwards. Still, I had to take the rough with the smooth. Two days down the beach, half a day unloading, not a bad exchange!

After discharging the load in the port it was off to the agent, George Giannopoulos, not far from the Afton to collect the paperwork and see if he had any news on a reload.

He had, and I couldn't believe what it was.

'Hi Paul Rowlands, how are you? You want a drink? Ouzo and water, maybe some food?

He was a really nice guy and so proud of his English sports car, a Triumph TR6, that he had a photo of it on his desk. To own something like that in Greece must have cost him at least double the UK price because of the crippling Greek import duties.

'Thanks Mr Giannopoulos, have you a reload?'

He handed me my carnet/CMR and raised his eyes to the ceiling.

'Have you a frigo, my friend?' he said.

'You know I haven't George. Why?'

'I need frigo trailer for water melons.'

'Sorry, just got a standard forty foot tilt.'

'I know my friend and you must load melons and hurry back to England.'

'You're *joking* George, its 35C, it won't work. Nobody carries fruit in a tilt.'

'This I know, but is the end of the season and there are no frigo trailers available, so you must go to Trikkala and load at the farm. Maybe you are lucky and there will be snow somewhere.'

'You have a sense of humour,' I said. 'The water melons will be very ripe but what if the load doesn't arrive in good condition?'

'There will be not a problem my friend.'

He gave me the address, and I was to load the following morning just outside Trikkala. I knew this was a potential disaster in the making. Melons had to be kept chilled to have any hope of a successful trip.

The following morning I was up early for the 250 kilometre trip to Trikkala, and arrived at the farm at 9 a.m. The farmer didn't seem at all fazed at the arrival of a tilt, and after lifting up one side, loading started.

Basically the water melons, of all shapes and sizes, had been put into old fashioned style apple trays, which had slightly higher sides than the ones back home. The trays were then passed up on to the trailer and stacked one on top of the other.

It was a complete joke. Some of the melons were as big as footballs and sat proud of the boxes. All the stackers did was rest the next box on top with a slice of cardboard 'protecting' the melon from the wooden base of the box above! When I commented, they just shrugged their shoulders.

The temperature inside the tilt was bordering on 40/45C. What would it be like when I closed it up?

These were the big green water melons with the bright red

flesh, and tasted absolutely delicious, but already some of their skins were beginning to crack because they were that ripe. The stacked boxes looked decidedly higgledy-piggledy, and I'd got to drive this load in a hurry through Yugoslavia, which had some of the worst roads in Europe!

The first half of the trailer was loaded out of the warehouse, and then a manager came out and told me the rest had to be loaded off the field, about two kilometres away. They would leave four of the staff in the trailer to keep the stacks from falling over. I was to 'drive very slowly please.' The whole episode was like a scene out of Fred Karno's army.

Most of the short trip was fine, but the last 200 yards were on a raised dirt embankment that was hardly any wider than the truck, and certainly not flat, with a drop down into the field at the end.

Somehow the farm labourers had managed to keep the stacks from toppling over, but they looked a lot less tidy than when I left the warehouse.

Labourers were scurrying all over the field like ants, collecting water melons, putting them in wooden boxes, then placing the boxes on a pallet for the tractor to pick up and bring to the trailer.

Very little care was taken. They just wanted to finish the field and call it a day. It was the end of the water melon season, and melon fatigue had set in.

The action of the tractor carrying the pallets across the bumpy field wasn't exactly beneficial to the melons' health, and by the time the trailer was fully loaded I could see quite a bit of damage had already occurred, with split fruit and juice trickling down the sides of one or two boxes, and I hadn't even turned a wheel in anger yet. Wait till we hit the 'angry bouncy' road in Yugoslavia, I thought.

In my formative truck driving years I had carried many loads of boxed apples, from all over Suffolk, up to Aldeby in Norfolk, and I can honestly say that not one of the loads I transported looked remotely as unprofessionally stacked as this one.

Already some of the boxes, which were supposed to sit on the corners of the one below, had fallen into those boxes and were squashing the melons.

The loading was completed, and I finished off by boarding up the sides, then pulling down the tilt and lacing it up ready for the customs to apply a seal.

I had to drive back up on to the embankment and proceeded very slowly back to the highway, with the rear end lurching around like a drunken trailer!

Once back on the tarmac road I drove back to the farm to get the paperwork. The farm agent was there with an agricultural inspector from the local authority who signed the load off as being free from plague etc. Also there was a customs officer, who attached a plomb to the loose ends of the cord and handed me my carnets.

Everyone shook everyone else's hand and I was ready to roll, 1,800 miles back to the UK, as quickly as possible, without any further damage to my immaculate load of water melons. As if!

Not only was the load poorly stacked, but the temperature inside that tilt was going to exceed 50C during the day. I reckoned there was going to be a little fermentation taking place in there, what with the heat and the movement.

It was 3.30 p.m. so I decided to make a run for the frontier at Evzoni and see how I felt when I got there.

Greek roads are first class and very hard wearing due to the amount of quartz based material in them, all very well until it rains when they can become lethal, like driving on sheet ice. They also double as runways in an emergency and the roads have markings already painted on them in case such a situation might occur.

On one occasion I had a particularly unnerving experience on these infamous wet roads. I had delivered a load of potatoes to a warehouse about ten miles outside Patras. It was pouring with rain and too late to unload so the owner had phoned up a small hotel on the outskirts of the town to book me a room for the night, chance of a shower and all that. I wound down the legs and dropped the trailer intending to take the unit to the hotel. I'd got about halfway there when I decided to light up a cigarette.

Silly me, I dropped the lighter! Now those of you who remember the old 619 Fiat will also remember that the handbrake/dead man was situated on the right hand side of the driver's seat. I reached down to pick up the lighter, my sleeve caught on the handbrake and pulled it on. Within the blink of an eye I was sailing down the road virtually sideways. In this rain it was like an ice rink. Fortunately nothing was coming the other way as I realised what had happened and still sliding down the road released the hand brake keeping my foot on the foot brake. Ever so slowly I came to a halt in the middle of the road, having travelled the best part of 100 yards.

Anyway I was at the border about 9 p.m. and decided to get through to the other side. I completed the Greek customs fairly quickly as no agricultural inspector was required, and pulled through to Gevgelija on the Yugoslavian side. The customs weren't too concerned about the load other than to be surprised it was in a tilt. They stamped the carnet and I was through.

What to do now? It was 10 p.m. and I felt good. I'd had a couple of days off, and they *had* asked me to get the load back to the UK as quickly as possible.

I thought I'll head for Nis and then see how I feel.

Other than a few west European trucks heading in the opposite direction, you could always tell by the extra lights and lighted headboards, there was virtually no other traffic on the road. I made good time through the mountains; one moment headlights shining out over deep gorges into the inky blackness, the next against damp shiny rock faces as I wound my way through the night, with Andy Williams crooning out on the eight track.

Nis was about 100 miles and I rolled in there around 12.30 a.m. stopping for a brew up and a can of cold beans.

I daren't think about what was happening in the trailer, so put it to the back of my mind and decided as I still felt wide awake to head on towards Belgrade, another 140 miles to the north. By the time I got there dawn would just about be starting to spread its tentacles across the western edge of the sky, and maybe I could have a couple of hours in the National.

Around 4.30 a.m. having gone through the 'low point', when the effect of sleep deprivation sets in for a while and where your mental and physical processes are at their least effective, I dropped down off the hill on to the dual carriageway that ran through Belgrade.

These times can be very dangerous and if you are exceptionally overtired can lead to almost hallucinatory experiences.

I had knocked off almost 400 miles since leaving Trikkala, and decided to keep motoring on towards Zagreb while it was still cool. The sun was starting to throw its rays into the sky, promising another fine, hot day.

Now I was heading up 'boring' road towards Slavonski Brod, and needed to fill up with diesel. Another 100 miles had passed beneath my wheels, the sun was up and getting hot and suddenly I was starting to feel very tired. I pulled into a service station at Zupanje to fill up, have a break and 40 winks.

Having filled up, I pulled off the pumps on to a bit of rough ground that doubled as a truck park and got out to check on the trailer.

Oh great, this was unexpected! As I walked along I could see juice dripping through the floorboards of my trailer. Not a huge amount, but a steady drip, and already enough to have blown back on to the axles and suspension, which were all starting to look a bit sticky and grimy. On top of that there was quite a sweet aroma drifting around the truck. I'd only done 500 miles, and already the load was starting to disintegrate. With 1,300 miles to go, it should be fun.

I was too tired to care; all I needed was a kip. I climbed up on to the bunk and instantly fell asleep. It was about 7 a.m.

I was awakened by someone tapping on the cab door. I stirred a little groggily and reached over to open the door.

'*Collega, problema rimorchio*.' Blimey, was he Yugoslavian or Italian? *Rimorchio* was Italian for trailer.

'*Si, si kapische, melone*,' I said in fluent Yugalian.

So just to please him I got out of the cab and had a look. The juice was still dripping merrily away through the floor, and had formed a small puddle under the trailer, which had attracted a number of wasps. It was 10 a.m.

I made myself a strong cup of coffee, splashed my face with cold water, lit a cigarette and pulled out on to the main drag, heading north to Zagreb (now the capital of Croatia).

Five hours later, I was through Zagreb and heading for Ljubljana. I flashed the headlights at Pete Ransome, one of Trans UK's drivers heading south, but Pete wouldn't stop, never did, so I didn't bother turning round to say hello.

I stopped in a lay-by near Postonja to cook up some grub. Cordon bleu cooking: a saucepan with a tin of minced beef and a tin of beans mixed together and a bowl of instant mash. How nutritious is that, and I still love it to this day. And in this lay-by occurred the first part of a most curious coincidence.

I ate my meal outside the cab, sitting on the cab steps, and when I had finished, cleaned the utensils and put them away. I clambered up into my seat, and as I leaned back against the lambswool rug, I felt a sharp pain in my left shoulder. Bugger! I'd been stung by a bloody bee.

The next trip down I stopped in the same lay-by, and after a similar dinner, as I sat there leaning back against the same lambswool rug I was stung in my left shoulder again by another bloody bee, most probably his brother!

By now, the juice was not exactly pouring out, but certainly dripping heavily along most of the length of the trailer, and the whole of the chassis was coated in a sticky mess.

Next I would see what response I would get at Sezana/ Monfalcone, the Yugo/Italian frontier. At 6.30 p.m. I arrived at Sezana, to find they weren't the slightest bit interested. I pulled through to the Italian side and went into the customs office with my carnet.

'*Doctore Agricola?*' I said.

'*Perquai?*'

'*Melone Aqua*,' was my limited response.

'Ah! *Melone Aqua. Domani matina arrivata Doctore*.'

It wasn't what I wanted to hear. In the morning the *Doctore* would be much more interested in my load of disintegrating melons. So in for a penny in for a pound, I slipped 20,000 lire into the carnet.

It was quite a common occurrence for drivers with bent permits to slip the official 5,000 or even 10,000 lire, but I didn't know what the response would be to this offer.

He didn't bat an eyelid, pocketed the money, stamped my papers and handed them back. I was through and on my way to Venice before you could say boo to a goose.

Tiredness was again taking a hold. I really needed a good few hours' sleep. I struggled on to Padova where I pulled into an AGIP service area, and tried to park out of the way near the exit. I was too tired to bother checking the trailer and just fell into the bunk. I was quickly asleep.

Next morning I was awake at 5 a.m. Quickly trotting into the service area before the place got too busy, I managed to have a docchia (shower) and put some fresh clothes on (could be the last ones before I got home). Then I went into the restaurant area and ordered a café latte plus a ham and mozzarella bake.

As I walked back to the truck in the early morning sunlight, I could see liquid dripping from all points of the floor. The tarmac under the trailer was covered in this wet sticky goo. It was time to make a fast exit.

Next stop was Mont Cenisio, the Italian border with France, about 250 miles away across the Lombardy Plain, past Vicenza, Verona, Brescia, Bergamo and Milan, then north to Susa and Mont Cenis.

All the while the constant drip, drip, drip of damaged melon was getting worse, coating the whole of the underside of the trailer with a thick gelatinous mess of dust and juice.

Around 11.30 a.m. I was close to the border. I had been worrying for the last few hours how I was going to deal with the situation if the agricultural inspector rejected the load.

It was a fair old climb up to the Italian border at Bardonecchia. The frontier itself is on a slope and I pulled up behind a couple of other trucks then climbed down from the cab. A quick glance at the trailer showed that the situation hadn't improved and already there were rivulets running down the hill.

'*Bonjuorno chef, Doctore Agricola?*'

'*Perquai?*'

'*Melone Aqua, chef.*'

This was *déjà vu* . . .

He stamped my carnet, turned and called into the back room, while the 20,000 lire in the permit magically disappeared.

'*Doctore, un'altro camion di Melone Aqua.*'

Obviously, there had been quite a few loads of melons passing through here.

The inspector came through and looked at the paperwork.

'Why is no signature from Monfalcone?' in broken English.

'*Non lo so*. I don't know, it was very late,' I said.

He shook his head resignedly and stamped the authorisation. He wasn't going to bother checking.

I think I've realised now why they didn't bother. Virtually all loads of fresh produce come through in reefers (fridge boxes), so they most probably only check a tiny amount, if any. As a load of chilled fruit is ensconced in a forty foot tin box set at -5 degrees or more, they most probably assumed mine was the same, and who was I to disabuse them.

Another border cleared, I was off and climbing through 'the steps' to the top of the mountain, all hairpin bends and steep angles.

I'd only climbed for about a mile, when I rounded a hairpin to find myself being waved down by a Dutchman standing by his car which was hooked up to a small caravan. I pulled up in front of him and jumped out. Before I could say anything he said in perfect English: 'Your trailer is leaking.' Juice was dribbling down the road in lots of little rivulets.

'Try not to stand in it,' I said. 'It's melon juice, very sticky.'

'Oh, OK, can you help please? I have VW Golf and the clutch it is slipping badly, I think I have overheated it. If I can get to the top it should cool down and it maybe OK.'

'I have no rope,' I said.

With that, he produced a professionally made length of tow rope with clips on either end.

'OK,' I said. 'It is very steep and the hairpins are very tight so you must follow where the back end of the trailer goes, you must not try to cut across the corners, otherwise your car will be dragged across the road.'

'OK, no problem, thank you.'

I dropped the truck back enough so that we could hook up the tow rope to the sticky rear bumper of the trailer. Then I asked him to let off his handbrake and roll back to take up the tension.

This should be fun and games, an artic, grossing thirty eight tons, towing a car and a caravan up through the Steps Hairpins. Well if he was up for it, let's go.

And we did, without any mishap. At the top, by Victor's

Restaurant we parted company. He thanked me profusely and gave me 100 guilders (£30), then, slowly drove off heading for Grenoble, another satisfied customer. As I was already at Victor's I pulled over on to the dirt area near the café, went in and had dinner. Hopefully the dirt would soak up the dripping juice.

After lunch it was on down to Modane on the French side. I managed to park between two French trucks and wandered into the customs office. Unbelievably, the reaction was the same as before, a distinct lack of interest from Le Docteur who again signed me off, and I was away down through the foothills of the Alps to St Cyr and the 'Bakehouse'.

The 'Bakehouse' was a well known watering hole for British truckers back in the 1970s, and part of the attraction were the owner's two daughters, the more attractive one being Francine. I don't remember the other sister's name: says it all about me really, doesn't it?

The food was typical Les Routiers fare, good quality and well presented. It was a great rambunctious place to be at night, with steamed-up windows, cigarette smoke laying heavy in the air and curling slowly up to the ochre-stained ceiling with tables groaning under the weight of wine and beer bottles. Very, very Gallic, even though full of Brits.

It was an old French farmhouse. The shower block was outside across the yard in what seemed like a converted cowshed and the cubicles were ranch style, half door, so when the wind swept in during the winter months it took a very brave man to venture out there '*pour un douche*'.

I managed to get into the lay-by in front of the café even though time was getting on. Luckily it was dark, and a quick glance under the trailer with a torch confirmed that things were getting worse.

There were a number of Brits there and a pleasant night was had by all, with tall tales told and plenty of alcohol imbibed. The more we drank the taller the tales. It was 2 a.m.

when I retired to my bunk and fell sound asleep until 10 a.m., which for a truck driver is almost halfway through the day. I had a quick shower, stuffed a 'croque monsieur' (cheese on toast) sandwich, down and said my goodbyes to anyone that was left.

Already it was a very warm day and there was a distinct sweet smelling aroma in the air.

I climbed into the cab, fired her up and pulled out on the last leg of my 1,800-mile journey, to Zeebrugge. What the hell will my load of water melons be like when I get there? It was certain to be lacking a bit in the way of water, as most of that had been deposited across Europe. Maybe I had created a new type of fruit, the dry melon!

I headed into Macon, across the River Saone, turned right at the lights and headed north towards Tournus. There were a couple of British trucks still parked by the river near the bridge; they'd obviously had an even later night than us!

Around 5 p.m. I hit the Paris Perepherique. Rush hour, great! Bloody stop start, stop start. I soon noticed people in other vehicles pointing at my vehicle. There must have been puddles of melon liqueur all the way round the ring road.

Sensibly, I should have stopped on the south side of Paris till about seven o'clock, by then I would have had a clear run through. However I eventually worked my way round to the Porte de la Chapelle exit and was off and heading up the N1 to Chantilly and Arras, with 350 kilometres to go and another three hours' driving time left.

I just about managed to scrape into the outskirts of Bapaume for the night within my driving hours, and pulled off the road on to an area of hard standing, behind a Dutchman. Beans, mince, mash and a cup of tea, for a change. Absolutely wonderful!

A splash of water on my face and a rub of the gums and I was in the land of nod, dreaming about beautiful undamaged water melons and how after a heroic drive across Europe I managed to deliver the whole load to market without the slightest damage to any melon.

Today was the critical day. I awoke and peeked through the curtains. Rain, fantastic just what I needed. This was a bonus. The sky looked grey and overcast so it might stay around for a while.

I was booked on the 11 p.m. ferry out of Zeebrugge to Felixstowe which gave me plenty of time. Even though it was raining it was still warm, so I braved the rain to have a quick check of the lights and trailer. Underneath it was dripping heavily along the whole length.

I made myself a cup of coffee and a bowl of cereal, and after clearing up, moved off, heading towards Arras then Lille. Just past Lille I turned off the motorway at Ronq and headed north to the small border at Halluin/Menin. This was a frontier I used many times over the years. It was virtually a one man and his dog border when I first passed through, but over the years it eventually became as busy as any other. Drivers were always looking for alternative crossings that might be a little quicker and a little less fussy.

I pulled up at Halluin on the French side in the pouring rain and trotted across to the office. There were only two officers present. They noted that the load was fruit and one of them made a phone call to what I presume was the Inspector d'Agricole, and after a couple of minutes of conversation, he came out to the truck to check the seal. I had my heart in my mouth.

Was this the end of my trip? He turned to me and said: 'Bon' and walked back to the office. The rain was beating down on his peaked cap, but did he trot, or walk fast? No, he just casually strolled back as if the rain wasn't there, even though it was dripping off the end of his Romanesque nose. Then it was back in the office and on the phone again to the inspector, for a short exchange. Then my paperwork was stamped and handed back to me.

It was a short walk to the other end of the building, so I left the truck parked where it was. The Belgian customs man I recognised from a previous visit and he wasn't the slightest bit interested in coming out and neither was the Belgian inspector, who was apparently at the Armentieres border crossing and wasn't coming down. The paperwork was stamped and handed back to me.

I ran back to the truck as by now it was bucketing down. The barrier was lifted and I was through and heading home. Last stop Zeebrugge. I stopped for lunch at Torhout Les Routiers and even had a nap for an hour. No point in getting to the port too early.

At 7 p.m. I rolled in to Zeebrugge in a drizzle and joined the queue of trucks waiting to load. There were quite a few cars and coaches too. Collecting my documents, I traipsed across to the customs office to do my paperwork for the last time. These guys spoke perfect English and asked me to confirm the load, which I did. No further questions! So they stamped the carnet and took out the last but one sheet. Then it was back to the wagon to wait patiently for loading to start after the ferry arrived and discharged its incoming load.

It was still drizzling when the boat arrived, and embarcation started three-quarters of an hour later. I ended up about a third of the way down the loading deck on the right hand side, stuffing my rucksack with passport, wallet, wash gear and clean clothes. I then headed for the stairs and the purser to find out which cabin I was in.

I could just imagine what was happening on the loading deck. If the gangers said anything when they were chaining down the trailers then they could make me get off, but would they do that? Because then they would have to unload all the vehicles behind me. Nothing was said. Maybe as the deck was wet from the rain, the juice escaping from my trailer hadn't been noticed. I'd deny all knowledge!

I had my dinner in the drivers' cafeteria with a few of the

other drivers. There was a bit of desultory conversation about trucking, and those 'bastard French coppers' at Arras, who always checked you for fags and confiscated any extras you had over and above 200. They always had a field day with us Brits.

Then it was off to the cabin for a shower and a few hours' kip.

The morning broke fine and warm, and I was up and ready by 6 a.m. for a quick breakfast and to get ready for docking at Felixstowe.

When the doors were opened to allow us on the loading deck there was the usual scrimmage to get down the stairs. As I made my way down there were one or two comments about the sweet smell permeating the air.

'What's that smell? Blimey bit rancid in'nit,' said a bloke a couple of steps down in front. There was general agreement as passengers' noses tested the air.

'You're right,' I said. 'Wonder what it is, smells a bit off.'

As we got down to the main deck the people who were getting into vehicles on my side of the deck were complaining about the sticky floor.

'What is this stuff, it's as sticky as hell, and it's all over my shoes.'

I had to agree.

'Look it's coming from that lorry there,' said someone else.

'Terrible,' I said. 'Shouldn't be allowed on the ferry with a load like that, people will ruin their shoes.' One of the gangers was waiting for me as I quietly let myself into the cab.

'There's going to be hell to pay for this mate. Have you seen the state of the cargo deck? What have you got in there anyway. Not chemicals I hope?'

'Water melons mate, I didn't realise how bad it was, as it was raining all day yesterday.'

'Bloody hell, *melons*! Is that what that sweet smell is then?'

An officer came along the edge of the deck keeping his feet out of the sticky mess surrounding my vehicle.

'Well done driver, that was clever. Look at the mess,' he said sarcastically. 'We'll have to wash the deck down before we can load up. Now get off my boat and report to the food hygiene inspector as soon as you do.'

I had to take the truck through the customs shed first, but they just moved me on. So I dropped the trailer in the trailer park for the agent to clear the load.

Guess what? The load was condemned. Can you *believe* it, all that effort and they *condemned* it.

Apparently the load was a shambles when the trailer was finally opened up, and resembled more a puree of wood and fruit than pristine examples of perfect water melons.

And they did have to pressure wash the cargo deck before they were able to reload.

As I said to Mike Mitchell-Rowlands: 'I did tell them!' But I was only the driver.

14

Irate Stowaways!

On my fourth trip in late autumn 1975, I met a Whittle's driver at 'The Trees'. He was a great bloke, whose name was I think Alan, and who was running his first trip to Baghdad, while I was on my first trip to Amman, the Jordanian capital. He had stopped for a tea break and to watch the antics of the 'girls', and I parked alongside him.

Nothing had changed and Queenie was still leader of the gang, wearing even more lipstick, and it looked as if she had lost even more of her teeth. How could anyone resist such immense beauty? Anyway we were having none of it and locked the cab doors before crossing to the restaurant. On the way we noticed that one of the other English drivers had managed to find room in his cab for one of Queenie's attendants. Rather him than me, I thought. He must have been a glutton for punishment.

Amman became my favourite place to go because the money was good; we were paid trip money.

For the purposes of wages, the map of Eastern Europe through to Pakistan was divided up by concentric circles. Amman just fell into the £800 sector and was a comfortable sixteen–eighteen day round trip.

Alan and I decided to run down to Adana in southern Turkey together, which was about five–six days. There we would split up, with him going to Iraq, and me to Jordan.

We had a good run down to Kapicule, the Turkish border, and then stayed at the Harem Hotel in Istanbul for a day finding time to buy some gold trinkets from Danny's and do some shopping in the bazaar.

It was just one of those trips where everything was perfect: good weather, good company and reasonably hassle-free frontier crossings - not a common occurrence.

The following day we headed off to Ankara, over Bolu, the first real mountain climb in Turkey, then down through the 'valley of death' on to the flatlands to Ankara.

Ankara is at a major intersection on the Middle East trail. According to some of the lads this is where the boys go south to Iraq, Saudi, Jordan and the Gulf States and the men go east to Iran, Afghanistan and Pakistan. This old tale is most probably based on the fact that the winters in eastern Turkey are usually worse than they are in the south.

Staying the night at the truck stop, we were away by 6 a.m. and heading south across the Anatolian plateau to the Taurus Mountains, then Adana in south west Turkey

Turkey is a very mountainous country, and the plateau itself is about 2,500–3,000ft high. Driving across this vast plain you can very often see the Anatolian Kharbash dogs lying by the side of the road. They are a giant breed that have now become part of the Western showdog world, but here in Anatolia are still used by Turkish sheep and goat herders for the reasons they were bred - to protect their flocks from the attention of wolves and bears!

After stopping for a bite to eat close by Lake Tuz Golu, it was on past Aksaray, to the Taurus Mountains. We were now entering what most call the cradle of civilisation, from where Paul/Saul of Tarsus originated, and there *is* a certain prescience about the region. The mountain climb can be dangerous with a narrow road, many blind corners and not a lot of protection to stop you from a very long drop over the edge.

We stopped the night at Adana and the following morning said our goodbyes as Alan headed west to Iraq and I turned south towards Syria and Jordan.

I had a lengthy but trouble-free border crossing from Cilve Gozu on the Turkish side of the border to Babel Hawa in Syria. I filled up at the gas station by the border. At 7p a gallon it was cheaper than water and spilled just as easily by the pump attendants who took no care when pulling out or replacing the nozzle, splashing fuel everywhere. From here I headed south and hit Damascus at rush hour, not a good idea. It must be one of the worst cities in the world to navigate through. It was a horrendously chaotic experience, with drivers attempting to drive at an angle down the relatively steep sides of the open drainage culverts in futile attempts to try and overtake vehicles in front. Even Tonka truck drivers would try it, and occasionally some of the loaded ones would turn over such was the angle of the descent.

I eventually scrambled my way through the mayhem and headed for the border at Ramtha. Customs clearance was once again a laborious process, but finally I was through into Jordan and headed to Amman where I parked up at the customs. The heat was intense and with no air conditioning, very uncomfortable.

Within two days I was cleared and tipped. The agent Abdul was a really nice guy and invited me and another driver to his house for a meal the night before I left, and it was a wonderful experience.

It's a strange feeling when you're invited into a family from another culture. How do you behave? What is the protocol? We must have behaved ourselves because on future occasions I was invited back.

I left for Ramtha and the Jordanian/Syrian border the following morning and was cleared and ready to go in a couple of hours.

All the continental truck drivers know that when running leer (empty) with a tilt, we always tie back the rear corner so that the border guards can have a look in and wave us on. This is exactly what I had done and within a few minutes of getting my papers back I was being checked by the border guard and on my way back up to the Syrian/Turkish frontier and hoping to reach Adana that night.

It was a glorious day; one of those where you feel life is worth living. The eight-track was bashing out Olivia Newton-John and I was at peace with the world.

After about ten miles I became aware that something was not quite right but couldn't put my finger on it. I kept checking my mirrors and all seemed fine. I was aware of something waving at the rear of the trailer, but thought it was just a torn piece of tilt flapping in the breeze. It was difficult to make out because the offside mirror arm was vibrating quite badly.

I drove on for another five or so miles and when I glanced in the mirror once more there appeared to be a length of wood sticking out at the back.

It was one of my trailer side boards. I rapidly pulled over on to a patch of rough land away from the road, skidded to a halt and jumped down from the cab. As I trotted to the rear I could hear a commotion and some Arabic 'swearing' coming from the back end.

Rounding the back of the trailer I was greeted by a very portly Arabic gentleman clambering over the tailgate while giving me a load of verbals. How he had managed to climb in I'll never know because he was more rotund than he was tall, with very short arms. I had to help him get his toes on to the trailer bar as his belly was too big to allow him to reach the bar with his feet. He was like a very large beach ball with an arm and a leg stuck on each corner.

As he got down to ground level he carried on berating me with his short arms, and then I was amazed to see a child climbing over the back, then another adult, a goat, another goat, another child, and three more goats. It was unbelievable. Who did they think I was? Noah with his fourteen-wheeled ark?

This wasn't the finish. A car drew up behind, while another elderly man appeared in the back of the trailer. He also gave me some abuse. Apparently, when I braked hard he'd fallen over and banged his head. He started passing down sacks and bales of straw.

The guy in the car had a grasp of English and was conversing with the short, rotund Arab. Then he turned to me.

'This man is not happy. You should have stopped twelve kilometres back, that is where you should have put them off.'

I was in a dream. 'This man is not happy, what about me? I'm not happy.' This was surreal; everything was passing me by as if I didn't exist!

'Why did they get in my truck?'

'It's normal,' said the guy. 'At the border they go with Syrian or Jordanian driver. Is like bus, but here is not bus.'

Apparently there hadn't been any suitable trucks at the border so they jumped in mine assuming I'd know the score.

While this conversation was going on, the plump guy was

across the other side of the road, having waved down a truck going the other way. Within a few seconds the Syrian Tonka had crossed over to our side, and this guy and his entourage were up on his backboard passing up goats and hay.

The man explained. 'It's usual when they want to stop. They bang on the back of cab, but I can see it is not possible with this camion.'

'Why didn't the border guard stop me?' I asked.

'Most probably friend,' he said shrugging his shoulders.

With that he shook my hand, jumped in his car and in a cloud of dust was off. There was a blast of air horns as the Tonka moved off back towards the border, and I was left slightly bewildered in the middle of nowhere.

In future, at all borders I checked the trailer before I left. It never happened to me again, but I know it happened to one or two others.

Looking back, it was quite funny and I've always been stuck with this vision of the irate, plump little Arab hanging off the backboard aimlessly waving his legs about, unable to get his feet close enough to the bar because of his belly.

Those early trips were a steep learning curve and you had to accept the fact that in that type of job anything that could happen would eventually.

15

Ekmek and Egg

Charlie Pennington, Brian Wales, and I were off to Antalya, a fishing port on the Mediterranean coast of Turkey; a little off the beaten track as far as normal Middle Eastern trips went. This was to take down three trailer loads of telephone cabling for the new international exchange that was being built for the soon-to-be, burgeoning tourist trade.

You have to remember that back in the 1970s Turkey still wasn't a major package holiday destination for the Brits. We were still drinking Watney's Red Barrel in Torremolinos, and Turkey would have seemed a *very* exotic location.

All three of us were driving for Mitchell-Rowlands and

instead of pulling for Trans UK, which we normally did, Mike, our boss told us we were doing this job for another local haulier, Gould's. Brian and I had already done a couple of trips for him, so as usual we went to his office in The Routemaster, Felixstowe to collect our paperwork, and as usual the permits were 'bent', and valid only for Menton/Ventimiglia, the French/Italian border just above Monte Carlo.

Going this far south added another 300 miles to the trip. It also meant another carton of 200 Marlboro for the lady customs chief at that border; a real battleaxe of a woman with horrendous body odour who could be a right tartar when she put her mind to it.

The morning of our trip we picked up our documents, and to my disbelief found on opening them that only the first two pages had been filled out on all three of our carnets. This allowed one copy for the customs at Felixstowe and the second one for Zeebrugge. Great! To get down to Antalya we needed another 12 copies each, one for each frontier. I knew what I'd be doing on the ferry crossing. By the time we reached Zeebrugge I'd filled in, in my best handwriting, thirty-six pages, twelve in each carnet and each page an A4 sized manifest of our loads.

Normally on that crossing we'd try to get a few hours' kip, but not for me. There'd be a bit of a ruckus when I got back, because this wasn't the first time.

This was Charlie's first trip and he was very excited by the prospect. After an eventful run down, which involved a heavy duty discussion with the French traffic police in the Alps concerning the quality of Charlie's driving, we eventually made it to Kapicule. Here his luck ran out, because when our agent 'Young Turk' took our paperwork away he quickly spotted that the carnet for Charlie's trailer was due to expire in three days.

As that didn't allow enough time for him to reach Antalya, unload, and get out of Turkey before the expiry date, he couldn't enter Turkey at all (poor bugger) which meant he had to wait at the border for a week until another truck brought a new carnet down from England. A week at Kapic was just what the doctor ordered! This job had enough potential for problems without your own people back home not doing theirs properly.

Strangely enough, the same thing happened to me a year later after I'd started back with Trans UK. I had arrived at Kapic on a Friday afternoon to find out *my* trailer carnet was due to expire in a couple of days; stupid me for not checking. I telexed back to the UK and was told to wait till Monday, then get a taxi to Istanbul and find the Turkish AA office and they would extend the carnet by three months.

The rest of that weekend I was parked up with numerous other trucks in a field away from the customs and spent the whole time playing 'international football'. Generally speaking it was the Rest of Europe drivers versus the Turkish drivers. Great fun and it was here I met and befriended a French driver called Sonny. We went on to become great pals, often crossing each other's paths in the months and years ahead and enjoying some interesting social action at various 'clubs' across this end of Asia.

In fact that first night we grabbed a taxi and went off to Edirne to have a look around, eventually finding a *sort* of club where alcohol was sold and there was plenty of belly dancing activity. I don't think we were too popular with the local guys though, firstly because I don't reckon they had ever seen a non-Turk in the club, but mainly because we were a bit too free with sticking money in the girls' skimpy tops! Luckily we didn't overstay our welcome; it was getting a bit fraught, and we made good our escape in the same taxi.

First thing Monday morning I was in an old Anadol taxi, a Renault 12 to you and me, and having a hair-raising 160 mile ride down to Istanbul. Didn't the driver realise I wasn't ready to die yet, God willing or not? Having found the Turkish AA office (properly called the 'Touring and Automobile Club of

Turkey'), the whole procedure took about an hour and then it was another mad trip back to the border.

For me this episode with Charlie's carnet was the final straw and I telexed Mike Mitchell-Rowlands from the Mocamp telling him I was handing in my notice when I got back. At the same time I telexed Bob Carter, explaining what had happened and asking him if there was any chance of a full-time job, now that he'd got a few more trucks on Middle East work. The response was positive which gave me good heart.

Anyway before we left Charlie we made sure he was OK for the essentials, then bade him goodbye. Brian and I left for the Mocamp in Istanbul and a decent shower followed by a few beers; it was another two days to Antalya so get a shower whenever you could was the policy.

The following morning we left for Adapazari on the Ankara road, where we turned south and entered new territory. We stopped for lunch at Bilecik and here under pain of death from his wife Maria, should I forget, I gave Brian the birthday cards from his family. Today he was forty!

From Boyucuk onwards we were up and down through the mountains; the scenery was similar to eastern Turkey, stark and arid. South of Kutahya we dropped down a steep valley into a small one-horse village and were preparing for the quick down changes and a steep climb out when I spotted a shop selling ekmek,[1] and pulled over to the side of the road. A piece of fresh ekmek would go down a treat tonight. When we got into the shop the shelves were pretty sparsely filled and reminded me a little of the old stores from the western films I used to watch as a child.

'Got any eggs, mate?' said Brian.

The ancient shopkeeper shrugged his shoulders.

'He's not going to understand that Bri,' I said, and started to

[1] Ekmek is Turkish for bread.

make the shape of a chicken laying an egg, while flapping my arms, squawking, and then turning round to pick up an imaginary egg. Suddenly his eyes lit up as understanding spread across his weather-beaten old face and a broad grin exposed his three teeth, one gold and two nicotine-stained. Guess what? He *had* got eggs. So that night while parked in an old river bed near Isparta we had a feast, an eight egg omelette, beans and ekmek. It just tastes so good when you're eating out under the stars.

In the morning we threw some water at our faces, made a cup of tea, and watched as a farmer walked up and down his field just as they would have done 2,000 years ago in biblical times, casting his seed by hand from a large bag at his waist. The field was full of very large boulders. No tractor could have worked it, and we marvelled at his patience as he slowly worked his way around them.

Around midday we started to make a steep descent from the mountains down an escarpment to the city of Antalya, squashed between the Anatolian plateau and the Mediterranean. In that short, sharp drop down to sea level the temperature rose 10C.

We found the building site and reported to the site manager. He organised the agent for customs clearance and suggested a small hotel where we might stay for the two days we were likely to be there. It was one of those old hotel rooms that come alive when you turn on the taps, as air locks roar around the building, vibrating pipes like an orchestra warming up their instruments.

In the afternoon Brian and I decided to have a wander around the town near the port. He was in need of a haircut and when we came across a Turkish barber's shop with a couple of available chairs he said: 'What do you reckon, shall we go for it?'

'What do you mean *we*?' I replied. 'My hair's perfect.'

'Come in with me then.'

So in we went. It was like a drop in centre for the males of

Antalya! There was a general hubbub of conversation hanging in the smoke-filled air with moustachioed men sitting round, drinking chai and playing board games. There were even a couple of barbers, one tall, one short, and when a chair came free the short one looked over and flicked his head to call one of us over. Brian got up, sauntered across and climbed into the old fashioned seat.

The barber pumped him up and climbed on to a running board behind the chair. He said something in Turkish. Brian didn't understand and shrugged his shoulders. The barber pointed at pictures on the wall of different styles. Brian pointed to the cut he wanted. The guy was brilliant and when he had finished, with an artistic sweep of his arm he slipped a tool from his top pocket and flipped open a cut throat razor.

'Blimey,' said Bri, 'don't like the look of that, looks like a weapon of mass destruction.'

The barber was flashing the open razor around as if he was Zorro's younger brother.

'What's he going to do with it?' was the nervous question as Brian tried to keep his eyes on the flashing blade. 'Are these guys pro or anti-British?'

The barber wrapped a hot towel round Brian's face and then lathered him up in the old fashioned way. It was like watching an artist, as he swished the blade round my mate's chin, leaving neither a mark nor a sign of stubble. How did he do that? Bri, poor bloke, sat like a statue in the chair and didn't move a muscle during the whole performance. It was worthy of a round of applause and was certainly a source of amusement to the locals as they watched their man play to the assembled audience. When he finished he gave Brian another hot towel to clean his chin while he expertly massaged his neck and shoulders.

Later, after he had fully recovered from the trauma, Brian reckoned that to have been the best haircut he'd ever had . . .

'What shall we do tonight Mr Wales? We'd better celebrate your advancing years somehow. How about a meal somewhere?'

'Good idea, where's the local fish and chip shop?'

'Yep OK, here we are in southern Turkey and we're looking for a British chippie. Not sure that's going to happen Brian.'

That evening we wandered down to the fishing port of Antalya, at least we might find some fish!

The harbour was ancient, most probably built in the time of the Crusades. It was protected from the sea by a fortress of a stone wall, with a small entrance for the vessels to enter and exit into the Med.

We found a nice little restaurant that looked down on the fishing boats bobbing up and down in the harbour. The local delicacy was a fish called '*boluk*'. I must be honest here and say, that's most probably what it tasted like as well!

Everywhere there were signs that this was a city waiting for the future – tourism. There were new builds starting all along the coast. I wondered what it would look like in twenty years.

Brian and I had a pleasant couple of days in Antalya, mostly down by the beach. On the second day we pulled down a couple of ten-foot long leaves off a palm tree which I tied, one to each side of my cab to 'show off'. I'd seen this in a Roman film somewhere, where the hero charioteer drove into the arena with two huge palm leaves strapped one either side of his chariot to the acclaim of the massed hordes. I was going to be 'The Return of the Conquering Hero' – Charlton Heston, eat your heart out.

When I returned to England with the palm leaves still intact, I too received a hero's welcome. 'You prat,' said Scotty, one of our other continental managers, when he came down to the ferry to clear our loads through customs.

On the morning of the third day our load of huge cabled reels were lifted off by crane and by midday we were heading north to Isparta.

Late in the afternoon we pulled off the road near a place called Sandikli. The area here was quite flat with a semi-arid desert look and we decided to stay the night before making a run for Istanbul the following morning. I was in my truck reading and Brian, in his underpants was lying down on his bunk wishing he wasn't forty! He'd left his trousers folded on the driver's seat and as it was hot the window was wide open.

Now, as has been said before, you could be sat in any of the vast expanses of this part of Asia with not a soul or animal in sight and think you were the only person for miles around, but eventually *someone* would appear, as if out of the very folds of the land and usually with a request for a fag or something. In this case Brian didn't spot him until he noticed his trouser legs slowly disappearing over the edge of his driver's door.

'Oi!' he yelled, scrambling out of his bunk just in time to see this guy, dressed in a tunic and the obligatory baggy trousers drop down off his truck and sprint with a bandy legged gait across the deserted landscape, Brian's trousers in one hand, wallet in the other.

'Come back with my bloody wallet you thieving bastard,' bellowed Brian, scooting out of his cab in his underpants while trying to pull on his shoes. He was not a happy chappy, and though not the world's tallest person, had a huge turn of speed when a potential loss of money was involved. He covered the ground like a young gazelle, well a forty-year-old gazelle, little legs twirling like Road Runner, and he was soon closing on the thief at a rapid pace of knots. The robber, realising Brian was intent on murder, threw the trousers in the air with a loud wail, hoping Brian would stop and pick them up. But Brian had the scent of money in his nostrils, *his* money, and he ignored the trousers. When he was within ten yards of the thief, the guy gave out another loud wail, and dropped the wallet, knowing that if he didn't Brian would have put his head where the sun doesn't shine. As soon as the wallet fell to the ground Brian came to a dead stop, picked it up, checked the contents, turned round and sauntered back collecting his trousers on the way.

'Cheeky bugger,' he said. 'Didn't he realise that me and money have a very close relationship, and how upset I'd be if it came to an end?'

With that he clambered back into his truck, lay down on his bunk and went to sleep.

Sadly, we didn't see Charlie for the rest of the trip, so could only assume he had got his carnet and found a different way down.

Brian and I were instructed to head back to Germany,

where we loaded out of Essen for Gunter Baumann, back to England.

Interestingly, though I've never been back to Antalya, I find it quite nostalgic *and* sad, listening to work colleagues thirty years later speaking of holiday destinations like Bodrum, Izmir, Marmaris and Antalya, as just *that*, holiday destinations.

Here, this coastline, once fringed with beautiful deserted beaches, is now littered with high rise hotels filled with the sound of tourists, and I sometimes wonder whether it still retains its ancient charm. I suppose not, how could it? These places are so easily accessible now, four hours on a plane for a trip that used to take us eight days each way.

16

Somewhere East of Plovdiv

'The Eastern Bloc,' I said, 'why's that then Tony? What's wrong with our usual route, down through Yugo?'

'Can't get the permits for Austria any more,' he said.

'What does the commie bloc entail then?'

'Dunno Paul, hopefully you'll let us know, we've done all the checks on the paperwork requirements, and I know the route. It's Czechoslovakia, Hungary, Romania, then into Bulgaria and you pick up the old route somewhere east of Plovdiv.'

'Who am I running with?'

'On your own to Tehran.'

'OK, is that shipping out Sunday?'

'Yep.'

Sunday night I was on the Felixstowe–Zeebrugge ferry as usual, docking in Zeebrugge at 6 a.m. ready for four weeks away and another huge learning curve, the Eastern Bloc.

The first part of the run down through West Germany went as per normal. I spent the first night at Geiselwind Truck Stop, then the following morning it was on to Nuremburg and into new territory as I turned west off the autobahn and on single carriageway headed for Amberg in the foothills of the Bohemian Forest. This was very attractive and picturesque countryside heavily wooded with low rolling hills leading to the border at Weidhaus. In Czechoslovakia these hills were known as the Sumava Mountains and were to become a major tourist destination. Nowadays this route from Nuremburg to Weidhaus and into Czechoslovakia is all autobahn. Thirty odd years ago it was single carriageway all the way from Amberg to Plovdiv and often it was bloody hard work.

The frontier at Weidhaus/Rozvadov was typical of all borders where Western Europe met Eastern Europe. The German frontier guards were, as always, immaculately dressed, and very efficient. By comparison the Czech border personnel, who were also very smart, required twice as many officers and took twice as long to do the job as their brethren on the other side of the barrier. Teutonic they were not.

When crossing into the Communist Bloc the first thing you noticed was the size of their frontier barriers; they were absolutely massive. I'm sure it was a penis envy thing. These mechanisms were too heavy to swing up vertically in the conventional way and had to be pulled round horizontally by two soldiers. Without a doubt they were substantial enough to halt a runaway tank!

Once through the barrier at Rozvadov you drove up the hill and parked in front of the offices. Now things became really serious. Everything was security based and thorough, including personal checks, cab checks, trailer checks, and on occasion load checks, though this was against the TIR convention.

Rumour had it that all border guards in countries that flanked Western Europe were in fact Russian, as they were the only ones that could be trusted to keep the locals in and the foreigners at bay. Finally when all checks were completed to their satisfaction, you were required to drive under a gantry while a soldier surveyed the top of your trailer looking for spies!

One occasion, in the middle of winter, I was at the Romania/Bulgaria border at Ruse and felt really sorry for a Turkish driver who had his seals ripped off and his trailer opened up, totally against the TIR convention. A gang of soldiers arrived and started unceremoniously to strip out his load, dumping it at the side of the truck. The snow, drifting gently down through the arc lights, was slowly covering the poor guy's load. Within half an hour the group of squaddies had completely emptied the trailer and found - nothing. Did they put the stuff back in the trailer? No! The driver had to reload the whole lot himself in the freezing cold and snow. Luckily the cartons weren't too heavy and while we were there we gave him a hand, but as soon as your paperwork was done, you were told to move, and move you did.

Anyway, once again I digress.

Having cleared Rozvadov after a three hour hold up I was eventually released from the frontier and as I drove through the beautiful hills and forests of the Sumava, about 10 miles from the border, I noticed, up ahead in the forest a brand new wooden building with a few trucks parked outside.

A restaurant! Hallelujah! I was absolutely bloody starving. It looked like an overgrown pine log cabin, and a bit incongruous compared to the multitude of dour and dingy concrete buildings I'd seen in the villages on the way. But it was a more than welcome sight. The owners, Hans and his wife, were very friendly and produced a pretty fair Wiener schnitzel. I enjoyed a pleasant evening chatting to them, and they were very interested in the gold jewellery I was wearing.

Hans offered me Deutsche marks to bring some gold jewellery back from this trip.

'Gold is better currency than money here,' he said.

I wouldn't take the money, but promised to do what I could to buy some gold for him.

'If you can make it pretty, so much the better,' whispered Hans, looking over at his wife.

Over the next two or three years we became firm friends and he always paid in marks for the numerous trinkets I brought back for them.

The following morning I had a coffee with them both and at 10 a.m. left for Plzen, the spiritual home of lager. I was making good progress on the old road and looking forward to seeing Prague. My good humour soon evaporated however when I got totally lost. Not because I couldn't follow the signs, I could, but nearly every bridge I came against was too low to drive under, even when marked as supposedly higher than my trailer. They often weren't and it got to the stage where even if a bridge height was marked, I approached it very gingerly to see if the trailer would pass underneath.

Eventually I ended up not far from Wenceslas Square, in the middle of Prague, and finally had to submit, having to ask two policemen, the route out of town. They were brilliant! Starsky and Hutch in uniform, and presumably said 'follow me' in Czech. It was hilarious, like a scene from the Keystone Cops as in their brand new Tatra police car, with blue lights flashing and sirens blaring, they took me through every red light in Prague to the outskirts of the city where they pulled over and pointed me in the direction of Brno. Judging by their smiles they had obviously enjoyed it as well. In the whole of my time driving abroad I met none better or with a better sense of humour. I offered them my undying thanks and slipped them 40 JPS.

The same thing occurred the next trip, but without the police assistance, so from then on I found an alternative route across country, from Stribro through Pisek to Jihlava where I picked up the main road for Brno and thereby missed Prague's infamous bridges. In general I didn't find Czechoslovakia to be a good place for bridges anyway, as very often the information on the height marker boards was incorrect.

That night I made it down through the border at Rusovce/Rajka into Hungary and parked at a service station on the outskirts of Budapest. What a fantastic place: Buda on the west bank of the Danube and Pest on the east. Where Prague and Vienna seem staid and formal, to me Budapest is alive and throbbing with vitality, and after Rome, is my second favourite city.

I did make one promise to myself that I was able to keep a number of years later, and that was to see Lake Balaton, fifty miles south west of Budapest and the largest lake in Western Europe, fifty miles long and five-six miles wide.

In 1989, Brian Wales and myself had the opportunity to take a truck load of medication and ancillary equipment down to Oradea in northern Romania at the end of Ceausescu's regime and just after the international furore broke out over the appalling state of their children's homes.

On the way back we decided to drive down to Lake Balaton, and very beautiful it was too. But the Germans were already there and buying up property, reminding me a bit of the old towels and sun beds syndrome.

Anyway, once again back to the tale ...

In the morning I was up and away early to beat the rush hour. Getting through Pest was OK but once I'd crossed the bridge, trying to find my way through the cobbled streets of Buda was a comedy show. Once you got tangled up with the tramcars you were a goner. Every few yards little tram stations, crowded with waiting passengers, lined the route, and the road out of Budapest seemed to be continuously criss-crossed by tram lines. Keeping out of the way of these squealing, clanking behemoths was the difficult trick. Many were driven by large women, whose time schedule didn't include getting baulked by a lone, lost foreign truck driver, and they soon let you know when you were in their way. These ladies were wonderful drivers may I add! Thankfully I eventually left the hustle and bustle of rush hour Budapest behind, found the Szolnok road and was off towards Romania, about four hours away.

Transiting the border at Artand was a slow and laborious event, not so much on the Hungarian side, but the Romanian customs were unbearable. It seemed that the deeper into the Communist Bloc you travelled, the more frightened of visitors they became and the more thoroughly things were checked. One of the problems was that Western European trucks and their drivers stood out like a sore thumb compared to the dreary grey and green little trucks from Romania and Bulgaria and I had the feeling that sometimes the brash bright colours of our vehicles rankled with them, almost if we were foisting our western arrogance on them.

Other than Hungarocamion, the national freight company of Hungary, who had a number of Volvo trucks and looked quite smart, nearly all haulage was done, as it was in all the old eastern bloc, by very underpowered petrol engine lorries that in design harked back to British and American trucks of the 1940s and 1950s. Trying to overtake them was a nightmare, especially if they were towing a trailer, as 30 to 35mph on the flat seemed to be the norm. Uphill, their speed could be registered in minus figures!

That first time at Artand I sat for five hours waiting for clearance, and I dreaded the thought that they might rip off the seals and demand to see the contents of my trailer. Finally, after a change of shift I was cleared to go and quickly headed to the first major town, Oradea.

Ask any trucker who went on that route in the 1970s what was the first thing that caught their eye and nose after leaving the border, and it would be the colour of the sky and the smell! How anyone could live in that environment was beyond me. Over the town of Santion Santion, draped like a garish paint-splattered cloak, was a permanent cloud of hazy red, yellow and orange smoke, and the acrid metallic smell emanating from the chemical and smelting works could be tasted for hours after you had passed through the area. It was horrendous. I often wondered what the life expectancy of the local residents was.

Of course in contradicting that, the long-term potential for tourism in the beautiful unspoilt rural areas of this country was immense.

The following day I drove down through the centre of the country, past Cluj, Sibiu and the oil fields of Pitesti, to the capital, Bucharest. In all the towns a sense of slapdash pervaded the newer architecture. The buildings all seemed the same, built down to a standard rather than up, concrete formed with the framework slightly out of square, lintels bowed, walls marginally out of perpendicular, and there was a general feeling of couldn't care less to these communist-built structures.

In the villages ... out in the countryside, away from the large towns and cities, the sense of dilapidation and deterioration was just as deep. Here most forms of transport were still stuck in the nineteenth century and were mostly performed by the ubiquitous horse drawn cart, consisting normally of a single horse, occasionally two, that would be pulling a twenty foot long V-shaped wooden trailer, usually with four bald pneumatic tyres. These 'vehicles' performed all transport tasks, from carrying goods, to people, to livestock. At night if you were lucky they might have an oil-powered single red light swinging from the back.

Rural lifestyle was very one paced, until that is, in autumn 1977, when one of our drivers, who shall remain nameless, one dark and dank evening, ran straight into the back of one of these horse drawn carts. The rear end was slightly damaged. I lie, in fact it was kindling, and the last to be seen of it was the horse bolting up the road, exceeding the speed limit, with the driver perched on what remained of his seat, pulling half of what was now a two-wheeled trailer. Damage was done to the truck, but as he was only thirty miles from the border, it was decided to get out of the country pretty damn quick!

From Bucharest it was only a short drive to Giurgiu/Ruse, the Romanian/Bulgarian border, where if the scenery was very similar, the language certainly wasn't. In Bulgaria the language is Cyrillic and impossible to read, but if you pick up a few of the letters it is possible to do a letter to letter translation into a form you can at least pronounce, even if you don't understand.

Once through another long and arduous frontier crossing I was into northern Bulgaria, another beautiful part of Europe, with mountains up to 8,000 ft and enough snow in the winter to make skiing a distinct tourist possibility in the future. Some of these places which we were lucky enough to drive through on our Middle Eastern ventures were absolutely stunning and only served to make me thankful for the opportunity I had been given.

Soon I was back on familiar territory when I dropped down out of the Balkans somewhere east of Plovdiv, into Harmanli, and back on to the old road to Persia.

From here on I had a trouble-free trip through Turkey to Tehran and arrived at the Davis Turner compound on the thirteenth day.

My God, those Turkish roads were rough!

There were a couple of lads at the compound who I recognised but whose names I don't remember. Sitting around waiting for customs clearance was often quite boring especially when there weren't many other drivers there. If there *were* enough of you, then you could have a kick about or spend time round the pool at the adjoining campsite, or even maybe in the afternoons go up into the city for a wander around. It's a pity that in my twenties I wasn't a little more interested in culture because there was a tremendous amount of Persian history to pursue. Problem was at twenty-seven, it was girls versus culture - a difficult choice!

On this trip there were a number of other British and European trucks already there, and on arrival I noticed one of the guys had pulled up one side of the tilt on his trailer and set up a table and chairs in the back.

Once I'd settled in I wandered over and said hello to all and sundry. In the trailer, the guys were playing of all things, chess, and while watching I noticed that one of them, a Dutchman, was a much better player than the rest. I also realised was that there was a joint or two doing the rounds.

Now I wasn't averse to having a draw on the odd social occasion, but *here* in Tehran, that was taking a chance, wasn't it?

Eventually most of the drivers that could play had been beaten by our friend from Holland and he asked if anyone else fancied sharing a board with him. I had played a bit of chess in my time, in fact I was lucky enough to have been taught at school, not that I was a grand master or anything, or even good, and I hadn't played properly for a long time. But I agreed to a game as long as he was gentle with me.

As we were setting the board up a joint was passed in my direction, and for some reason I accepted. What *was* I doing? In fact while ensconced in this 'international' game of chess I had more than a few drags, and do you know what, I played the best game of chess I have *ever* played. It was as if my thought processes were heightened to such a degree that I could see his moves miles ahead and I won. Kurt immediately wanted a rematch, so I obliged, I was Bobby Fischer. No I wasn't! Suddenly I couldn't see any of his moves and he thrashed me. In fact over the next couple of days we had a few matches and I lost every one quite easily.

What the hell were we doing smoking pot in Tehran? I don't know, even in the sanctuary of the Davis Turner compound it was a ridiculously stupid thing to do. I mean, there was an Iranian guy *guarding* the place, and anyone who has ever smoked the dreaded weed will tell you it has a most distinctive odour. Possibly the guard didn't realise what the smell was, because it was certainly hanging round in the air. Had we been caught it would have been a prison jobby for us.

A couple of days later I received the call to go up to Tehran customs for clearance and a load check of my flat pack furniture.

I know I said in a previous life that I thought Damascus was the worst city to drive in, and I stick by that. However Tehran comes a close second, and in many ways it was worse. There were no drainage culverts for drivers to use; all traffic was confined to the roadway and any hard landscape adjacent to it. Traffic lights were virtually ignored, and unless there was a policeman at a junction, the whole shebang became a free-for-all.

There was a rumour that the Shah, and the chief of police, had at some time asked the Metropolitan Police traffic commissioner and the New York Police traffic chief to send experts to Iran to help unravel the traffic problems endemic in the major cities. The rumoured advice also went on to say that the situation was so bad that the only way to resolve it, other than putting thousands of traffic enforcement officers on patrol, was to take everyone off the road and start again from scratch. Maybe that will give you some idea of how bad the standard of driving was.

It has to be remembered that only thirty years previously there had been virtually no vehicles in the country at all. It was only when oil was discovered that people ditched the camel in favour of the car, and not just any old car, but the Paykan, a Hillman Hunter by any other name. A huge factory was built in Iran to build this trusty steed.

Anyway, back at the customs, having given my agent a bottle of Johnny Walker to grease the right official's palm, I waited patiently for him to return with a customs officer to check the load and set me free of the bond.

It was a horrible place to have to wait around, and there were hawkers everywhere, a lot of them selling 'kilo' watches. These guys were like the Persian version of a spiv – an Iranian Arthur Daley. They often wore loose sleeved jackets, and if they caught your eye, would sidle up to you, pull back their sleeve and reveal an armful of spectacular looking watches, 'Rolax Oyster', 'Longgines', 'Omiga', 'Tag Hour', and many more that looked really authentic, but cost a pittance. They all had the obligatory number of quartz movements and were water resistant to a depth of five miles!

The reason they were called kilo watches was because that's how you bought them – by the kilo. A number of the lads bought four or five to take back home for their kids, and as long as they were kept out of harm's way, they might give you three months' usage, by which time the 'solid gold' casing would have tarnished and turned green, and the hands inside turned rusty.

I remember Smudger buying a few on one occasion when we were down there, and then diving into the pool with his new 'Rolax' on. There were more bubbles coming out of his watch than out of his mouth, and when he climbed out of the pool and looked at it, all the hands were floating round inside!

'Look at that,' he said, 'water resistant to 200 metres.'

17

600 Miles East of Ankara!

The winter of 1975/76 was reckoned by locals to have been the worst for fifty years. I don't know how true that statement might have been, but what I do remember is that I have never before or since been in such a cold place as at that time in eastern Turkey.

Taffy and I were running together again, and even though we had already done separate trips in October and December, nothing could have prepared us for a 'proper' Turkish winter.

If I remember correctly we'd shipped out from Felixstowe–Zeebrugge on 10 or 11 January and had a good run down across Germany into Czechoslovakia at Weidhaus/Rozvadov.

Border controls at places like Rozvadov on the Czech side were still struggling to deal with the new influx of west European trucks wanting to transit their countries. Until the Middle Eastern phenomenon, any border activity would have been almost non-existent. Of course the Germans, as usual, were organised with typical Teutonic efficiency.

Once clear of the frontier, our good luck continued down into Hungary and we only encountered our first heavy snow at Cluj Napoca at the top end of Romania. From then on through to Marand in northern Iran, a distance of 2,500 miles, the snow stayed with us or near us. The run down through a snowy Romania was steady and until we hit the Balkans in Bulgaria we were lucky enough to get away without using snow chains.

Climbing over Stara Zagora in central Bulgaria was the first time either of us had ever used them in anger. Neither of us had a clue, and in fact the first time we tried to fit them was a disaster. We laid them out on the road, in the snow, in front of the drive wheels on an incline, and then tried to drive on to them. Of course, as soon as the drive wheels touched them, they were unceremoniously spun out and thrown half the length of the trailer. Eventually we realised that this wasn't the best way, and that if you laid them *over* the wheels that at least looked as if it was correct.

'Taffy, how do you do these bloody things up?'

'I've got about as much idea as you boyo, which is none,' said Taffy.

We quickly learned the technique, and soon became dab hands at throwing them over the drive wheels. But it was always a filthy job, in the mud and slush, reaching round the back of the tyres to hook them up.

We had managed to get a good way up the mountain chain-free, but on the last stretch even with the chains on and diff lock[1] engaged Taffy couldn't make any progress, and in fact

[1] Diff lock. Short for differential lock, a mechanical method of engaging both wheels on the drive axle, so they both give traction at the same time.

had started to jackknife sideways as the drive wheels fought to gain a grip.

Pulling up behind him, I jumped out. It wasn't the safest place in the world; the conditions were very slippery and if another vehicle came round the corner behind us the situation could have been very fraught. We had a quick word and agreed that if I could get past him to the top, which we knew was only about half a mile, then I would drop my trailer, and come back down to try and help pull him up.

While Taffy walked gingerly back down to the bend to watch out for traffic I climbed back in my cab and after looking in the mirror I reversed carefully until I'd got enough room to pull out past his truck. Having more weight than Taff on my trailer gave me just enough traction to get past him and up to the top.

I dropped my trailer in a large viewing area at the summit and refitted the chains, which had become a bit slack. Very carefully, I crept back down the hill to witness Taff playing the good Samaritan and helping to push a car that was slipping and sliding all over the road. Twenty minutes later with the tow bar fitted, it was job done and we were both at the top of Stara Zagora.

The views out across the Balkans were magnificent and with all the trees heavily laden with snow, it was very much a stunning picture postcard scene.

As well as continuously snowing, the temperature levels were falling quite dramatically, and we were soon having problems with our air brakes not releasing properly. This was because with the very low temperatures, the water vapour and condensation in the air lines were starting to ice up, a very nerve-racking situation which could occur while driving. As you applied the brakes gently and then tried to accelerate away you could find your brakes were still on, and you would come to a halt in the middle of the highway. The only way to deal with this problem was to ensure all air tanks were drained daily, and that the alcohol (methanol) bottle, fitted in line with the air pipes, was kept full. If not, and your brakes did freeze on, it was out with the paint remover gun, heat the pipes and drain taps, which were all exposed to the elements, and not something you wanted to be doing too often when the temperature was down around -20C.

After that escapade we dropped down to the Turkish border at Kapicule quite quickly, and were through a very quiet border within three hours; some sort of record for Kapic, I should think.

We had a quick stop at the first garage in Edirne to pick up a few bottles of Tamyak, a fuel additive that reduces the freezing point of diesel from about -9C, when diesel starts to jellify, to about -20C or more depending on the mix. If it got even colder the last resort was to add petrol, which we did on numerous occasions, often up to thirty–forty litres per tankful of diesel. Often this gave a good fireworks display, especially at night when sparks were flying out of your exhaust.

There was intermittent snow all day, and that night we parked up at Luleburgaz as it was snowing quite hard and we didn't fancy driving through to Istanbul at night in those conditions.

It was amazing, the polis in Luleburgaz were conspicuous by their absence. Normally in fine weather in this town you could virtually guarantee to be pulled over for some trumped-up driving offence or other!

The following morning we woke to find a two to three feet deep layer of snow for as far as the eye could see, and we had to wait for a grader to come along before we could access the road. It was a bit of a sod getting the chain on the nearside wheel as the snow had drifted up to the top of the wheel arch but as an ex-Boy Scout of three months' service I was prepared, dyb dyb dyb and all that, eventually the snow was cleared away and we fitted the chains.

I always tried to get away without using chains unless absolutely necessary, especially on the flatlands, using the excuse that the more you used them the more chance of damage. That was actually quite true; snow chains *were* easily damaged if you weren't careful. It was most probably laziness on my part!

We made slow progress through Silivri until we reached the big hill at Kumburgaz. Here it was absolute chaos, trucks and cars everywhere, slip sliding all over the road, trying to get to the top of this long, steep incline. Somehow Taffy and I wormed our way through the carnage. I left her in second gear and let her make her own way up. Once over the top, it was plain sailing down to the Mocamp even though it had started snowing heavily again.

So far we had lost about a day and a half due to the extreme weather. We decided that if conditions were worsening we would have a clean up here and leave the next day but one.

We had a restful day in the Mocamp, and noticed there weren't as many wagons in as usual. Most of the day was spent in the restaurant with a few Efes and chatting to a few of the lads. One or two were on the way back home and said the weather had been atrocious further east towards Erzincan.

We pulled out the following morning with a couple of guys driving for McNeil's, who were going to Ankara, and then heading south to warmer climes. We had a reasonable trip through to Ankara, and other than chaining up for Bolu, and coping with a few snow showers, we were in the Ankara Motel that evening by six. What we had noticed though was that the snow wasn't clearing up during the day. The temperature was dropping back quite severely again and because it was so cold, even with the heavy traffic between Istanbul and Adapazari, the roads remained icy and rutted, with very little slush.

The nightmare started the following day after we said our

goodbyes to McNeil's guys and headed east straight into the jaws of a terrifying snowstorm. I won't bore you with the detail, but suffice to say it took us five days to get to Erzurum, about 400 miles. It was horrendous.

Snow, snow, snow, snow, snow!

We pulled into a garage forecourt twenty miles east of Erzurum early afternoon. By this time we'd lost track of the days, and were absolutely knackered from the exertions of the physical labour and the amount of concentration needed to keep a truck on the road in these extreme conditions. There are many web pages that show photos of some of the many accidents and road conditions that occurred that winter of 1975/76.

Taffy and I decided to stop here as there was already another Brit, a French truck, and a Romtrans, (double manned).[2] Later on another couple of guys pulled in, a Belgian, followed by another double manned Romtrans. They were so heavily caked in snow that it was difficult to recognise their nationality.

These Romanian guys were the bee's knees. Been there, done that, albeit very slowly, mark you, but they'd got the badges. Luckily for us as it transpired.

Garage was a very loose term for the place we were all parked up. Basically it consisted of a large wooden shed for the attendant to keep out of the weather, three pumps and a large hard standing area where we were all parked.

The garage attendant, Oktar, was a decent bloke, and gave us chai boiled on a wood burning stove. He had worked for a couple of years as a gastarbeiter in Germany and was able to

[2] 'Double manned'. All of the old Eastern Bloc countries sent their trucks out from behind the Iron Curtain with two men; the trucks had to be totally self sufficient for the period they were away as they had virtually no western currency to use. They carried all the spares necessary to virtually rebuild their trucks. Officially one was the driver and the other the mechanic. However in reality at least one of them would have been a Communist Party member, to make sure nothing went wrong, so to speak.

converse in German. The Belgian guy, Saul spoke French, English and German and was able to talk with Oktar, who told him that this was the worst winter he could remember, and according to the forecast that worse was to come over the next seventy two hours, and that it would be best to stay here.

No traffic had come past either way since we had arrived and Oktar, who lived in Pasinler, said the grader would be along in a while, and he was going home in the grader driver's cab until the weather improved. This didn't sound so good. True to his word, half an hour later, out of the murky gloom appeared the grader, all chained up, and off went our garage attendant not to be seen again for three days!

So here we were, nine guys, and seven trucks, with not the faintest idea what to expect, and judging by the fact that Oktar was leaving his station, what was coming, wasn't Father Christmas with a load of presents.

This is where the experience of the Rumos (Romanians) came in, and to think we always referred to them as *'F' Troop*, after the American comedy programme of the 1970s. Not after this trip! These guys had been used to severe weather in the past in central Russia, and knew how to cope, and more to the point had the equipment to cope. One of the 'assistant drivers' spoke a little German and told us that we needed to batten down the hatches for the next two or three days and the first rule of survival in severe cold weather, DO NOT SWITCH OFF ENGINE! In fact over the next eight days I never once pulled the engine stop.

The Romtrans guys organised us all. It was like a survival training course. Saul, the Belgian, had a Berliet truck and managed to squeeze five of us in there and four in one of the Romtrans' cabs. Saul interpreted what they said we should do when the weather closed in.

They had all the tackle needed to survive extreme weather and they said we should all keep an ear out during the nights, and listen for each other's engines cutting out.

If any did, we must all muck in to try and restart it.

If we weren't able to restart it within the hour, it would cool down so rapidly that in severe cold we would not be able to restart it. All this seemed more than fair and we were only going to survive if we helped each other.

Then it was all outside to help the Rumos set up their cutdown drums underneath the trailers. They had three each, cut to about a foot high. The idea was to half fill them with a mixture of diesel and petrol, then top them up with rags, bits of timber, and any other bits of rubbish that would burn, and pull them into place under whichever unit needed to be restarted. Of course F Troop had all the rags and we had none. None of us had the foggiest idea of how much equipment you needed to carry and how organised you really needed to be to do this job all year round in such extreme conditions. Later that night we were ripping up our own towels to add to the pile.

I have never been so cold, even wrapped up as I was. Once out of the cab it was mind numbing, I don't know -30C maybe, just a guess and by now I really didn't want to be there.

According to Stefan, one of the Romanians, the most important things to keep from freezing up if and when an engine stalls are the diesel tank, fuel filters and sump, to make sure the engine stays warm enough so that the oil doesn't thicken up and solidify! I had noticed that their own filters were swathed in rags.

Eventually that night we all went to bed. Taffy and Frank, the other English guy came and had a cup of coffee in my cab, and discussed what the hell we were doing here. I suppose in all honesty we were a bit scared: well I was. I'd heard talk somewhere that Erzurum was one of the twenty coldest inhabited cities in the world. I don't know the truth of it, but that night I could well have believed it.

Taffy and Frank went back to their respective cabs and I,

with extra jumpers on, climbed into my sleeping bag, a very good quality one, supposedly good enough for the Arctic. I wasn't sure about these conditions though, most probably good enough for a lunartic! I pulled out the hand throttle to a high tick-over, put the heater on full blast (no night heater then) and settled down for a fitful night's sleep.

Morning arrived, and as I pulled back the curtains it was as Oktar had said it would be. There was a whiteout, and it looked as if it was here to stay. Nothing came past all day, not that anything could have done in these conditions. There was most probably a two or three foot depth of snow covering the landscape as far as the eye could see, and where it had piled up against anything, it was much deeper. Mostly, we stayed in our cabs, sharing our food and drinks, and when called on by the Romanians, as best we could we cleared snow from around our trucks so that we had some access to each other should we need it. They had put covers on the drums to stop snow getting in, and when they opened one to check, it looked like a thick, not very appetising, grey gruel. Still I wasn't going to eat it.

It was a long, long day with very heavy snow squalls and an exceptionally bitter wind, interspersed with a depressing dull greyness when the snow abated.

That night we all went to bed and I fell into a fitful sleep again. Even though the cab heater was on full blast I could feel the bitter cold trying to sidle its way through the cab panels and air vents. It was as if these chill winds from Siberia and the cab heater were at war, and luckily the heater was winning - just.

I don't know what time it was, but there was a banging on the cab. I opened it to be faced by Saul.

'Camion stopped. *Vite, vite*!'

Give everyone their due; we were all out within two or three minutes. The Rumos were already trying to pull the drums towards the Berliet. Two of us began shovelling snow out of the way, and between us all they were set up in position. Rags, including our 'pristine' English towels were chucked into the gruel, and Stefan's mate fetched some strips of material and dipped them in the mush, while we with our paint remover guns set fire to them. These were fed slowly into the mixture until they caught fire: it wasn't easy.

Meanwhile Saul had been panicking, as would I and was frantically trying to restart his truck with his key. It nearly caught a couple of times but then lost interest and one of Stefan's mates had to tell him to stop before he ended up with a flat battery. This whole episode was happening in dream time, and even looking back, it remains such a surreal memory. We were all dressed up like we were going to be slung on the bonfire. One of the Rumos had even got on a sleeping bag with string tied round his chest, the bottom cut open and holes cut in the side for his arms. There was stuffing hanging out of it everywhere.

I cannot emphasise enough how good these Romtrans guys were; their knowledge and professionalism most probably saved our lives. All the time they tended the fires and made sure nothing got damaged. We just did as we were told.

Once the fuel filters had been heated up sufficiently I was told to wrap an old bit of sleeping bag around them - also provided by our communist friends - and then helped to pull the drum further under the engine. About twenty minutes later they told Saul to try and start his truck. First twist of the key and it was up and running. How good did that feel.

Many times I've looked back and wondered how we would have coped on our own, and the truth is I don't know. If our wagons had stalled like Saul's we'd have been in serious trouble.

One of the Romtran's drivers poured another ten litres of petrol into Saul's tank, and then we waited another ten minutes or so until they said it was all good now. We all mucked in to pull everything back under the trailers and the lids were put back on the drums to douse the flames. During the whole interlude the snow had virtually stopped, but as soon as we climbed back into our cabs, filthy dirty, but so pleased with the result, the blizzard started again. I was absolutely knackered, but Frank, a real Brummie, invited me into his cab for a brew up. Eventually I crawled back into my bed at 6 a.m. It was still pitch black, and so was I, but I didn't care and fell asleep. How much longer would we be stranded here? When was the weather going to break?

I have been stuck at the Drumochter Pass in Scotland overnight in a car transporter when the blizzards blocked the roads and cars disappeared in the depth of the snow. That was cold but not as as cold as this in eastern Turkey, where you felt as if it wanted to hurt you.

I did hear later from a reliable source, that temperatures had got down as low as -40C in eastern Turkey. True or not I don't know, but if you'd told me it was -100C it wouldn't have made a difference. It was a cold like no other.

These were experiences I would never have dreamed of having to deal with and I don't reckon they would have been on any job description when companies were looking for Middle East drivers. At the time it was difficult to cope with, but with a genuine group of fellow drivers around all supporting each other, I almost felt we had beaten the weather.

About midday Taffy woke me with a beaker of tea, and told me all the trucks were still ticking over. He'd had one hell of a job getting into the trailer box to get more tins of food out and had to use the paint stripper gun to heat the catches and hinges. Those that he had got out were frozen solid, so he couldn't pierce the tins of mince properly. He'd had to stand them in a saucepan of boiling water to defrost them first.

The weather had cleared quite a bit, in that the snow had stopped, the bitterly cold wind had eased off considerably, and the heavy grey overcast seemed to be lifting.

About an hour later we were shocked when a guy

stumbled into the garage in a bit of distress. We were able to get him into Frank's cab where me and Taffy were chatting. The poor guy was frozen and he was in a bit of a state as apparently his mate was up the road in his cab, which had stopped running early the previous night.

This bloke was a Welshman called Albert and worked for a Welsh company whose name I forget. In fact, they both did. According to Albert, his mate was in a bad way and needed help pretty desperately. Albert said that they had come past the garage an hour or so before we arrived there two days previously and had decided to push on for a while. It seemed they had only got another half a mile when they were forced to pull over to the side of the road as the trailer brakes seemed to be freezing on. Anyway they topped up the alcohol bottle, but by the time the brakes came free, it was getting a bit late, so they decided to sit it out overnight.

They had seen the grader, who stopped and asked if they were OK. Albert said yes they were, because at the time there was no immediate problem. Albert was parked close up behind his mate and wasn't aware that the weather was going to deteriorate so dramatically, and was as shocked as we were at the severity of it.

They had coped, like us, with the second day and were waiting there riding out the storm so to speak.

Albert wasn't aware of his mate's truck stalling until he struggled back through the snow to tell him. He told his mate to stay in the cab with him as the front of Albert's truck was tight up against the back of the trailer and as such afforded it a little more protection. His mate said he was OK as his gas bottle was on and keeping him warm, and he didn't want to leave it in case something went wrong.

This morning Albert had got up, his truck was still ticking over nicely, and decided to check how his buddy had coped with the night. Luckily the guy hadn't locked the door, because as soon as Albert opened the door he knew something was seriously wrong. The gas bottle wasn't on and his mate looked as if he was in a semi-stupor and not very coherent when Albert asked how he was.

'I then got very panicky,' said Albert, 'and realised without help he might not survive the day. I managed to get my cooker and bottle up to his cab and lit it. Then my idea was to drop my trailer and try to get back here in the unit. Of course I was parked up tight against the back of his trailer and with the amount of snow that has fallen couldn't budge it. I knew where the garage was and thought I'd try to get back here to get some help. I wish we'd stopped here ourselves now.'

While this conversation was going on we were also having a discussion about how we could help. According to Albert the snow depth was variable. Once the gloom had lifted it had taken him over an hour to plough his way through to us. Luckily, from where they were stuck he could just see the garage in the distance, and could see some trucks here.

It was decided that as I was closest to the exit I would drop my trailer and we would have a go at getting up to Albert's mate and if possible bring him back to the garage. By now, though still extremely cold, the weather was improving and a weak sun was trying to raise its head.

We decided four of us would go with Albert, so we chained up all four wheels and took a shovel each.

Luckily the road back to Albert's truck - not that you could see it - was virtually straight. Having chained up, me, Frank, Albert and the French guy whose name I can't remember, and one of the Romtrans drivers, pulled the pin with great difficulty and pulled out slowly. Two of the lads stood on the cab steps holding on to the mirror arms and the door with the windows wound down.

A couple of the Rumos had already been out to find out where the edge of the road was, and had shovelled two ten foot tracks for us to follow. Once out on the road we could see the outline of the two trucks further up in the distance.

We made painfully slow progress. The snow was a good eighteen inches to two feet deep and some of the crests were even higher, and once or twice we had to back up and make a run at a deeper drift. Run is a bit of a misnomer, but we had to reverse and have a go to breach some of the larger ridges. Eventually, with the help of the guys with their shovels we reached the trucks.

Everyone clambered out, and when Albert opened the door he was pleased to see the cooker still burning and the cab getting warmer. Albert turned it off, and his mate, though still very much out of it and shivering intermittently and violently, hadn't apparently deteriorated, but wasn't up to doing very much to help himself. He could have been in the early stages of hypothermia.

Between us we were able to manhandle him into my cab, and I must admit he didn't look too sharp. He was unable to talk without shivering uncontrollably.

It was fun and games trying to turn the unit round, but we did and following the tracks, returned to the garage far quicker on the way back. Saul had made up some Belgian soup concoction which he immediately gave to our invalid. We decided to let him sleep in my cab that night and I doubled up with Frank in his top bunk. Albert said he'd keep an eye on his mate in my cab and sleep tomorrow.

By the morning he was greatly improved, though still very ashen looking. That night hadn't felt anywhere near as cold though most probably still -15C to -20C. It seemed as if Oktar's forecast was going to be correct. Albert had left his truck running back where they were parked. It was going to be difficult enough to restart his mate's unit after another two or three days of freezing weather, without worrying about Albert's as well.

That night we all felt much better about the situation and even managed to defrost a few bottles of 'chilled', beer from the trailer. It had frozen solid in the extreme cold and pushed off the tops. Once they had defrosted you can imagine how flat the beer was. Still we didn't really care.

The following morning broke bright and clear, with a watery sun. The storm was over and by 10 a.m. the grader reappeared with Oktar, who had to borrow some water from us as his supply had frozen up. The temperature was still around -10C or so and it would soon be time to think about making a move. First though we would have to help to get Albert's mate started. That was going to be a game of soldiers, and another story.

Albert's mate made a full recovery, and I went on to meet Albert on a couple of occasions in the future when we had an alcoholic reminisce.

The final act I remember on that almost fateful trip was that there was also extremely heavy snow on the return trip out of Iran, and the Turkish authorities stopped us from even attempting to cross Tahir, and instead sent us north to Kars, then up to Giresun and along by the Black Sea, rejoining the old road near Bolu: a fair old detour.

As for *'F' Troop*, they were magnificent, and we could not thank them enough for their help and knowledge. They were never the fastest guys on the road, even when they got their new Roman trucks, but I always found them to be generous with their help, and certainly during this extreme situation their experience and assistance was invaluable.

The following winter we were much better prepared, but it was a little milder and even 10C less cold makes all the difference. I never again faced a winter anywhere near as severe as those three days, twenty miles east of Erzurum.

18

Ladas and Lollipops

Oh bugger! Here they come!

And why wouldn't they, we'd just flashed past them at the speed of sound ... well, 60mph anyway.

Taffy and I were on our way down to Tabriz in Iran, and had just slipped on to the only bit of dual carriageway in Bulgaria, the Sofia bypass.

The trouble was we were breaking the speed limit and had just passed a Bulgarian police car parked at the side of the road. As I looked in the mirror I could see that he had pulled out to give chase, blue lights flashing and sirens blaring.

I was trying to push my right boot through the floor and was flat out at 65mph. We had about fifteen miles of motorway to get away. I looked in the mirror again, he was closing with us slowly, then, next moment, Taffy pulled out from behind me and roared past. The old sod was going to leave me to it.

Taffy quickly disappeared into the distance pulling well over 75mph, and all the while the police car was slowly gaining on me.

A few minutes later the blue and white Lada was pulling past me, dark smoke billowing out behind him with the driver hunched over his steering wheel urging his beast to go faster. The passenger side window was down and the other copper had his arm out and was waving his lollipop wildly at me.

He didn't pull me over, but kept going in the hope that he would get us both. There was no chance, Taffy was flying.

The Bulgarian police with their Ladas and lollipops always seemed a bit comical to us because, with the large KAT sign they had on their roofs and the fact that the fuel quality was so poor, maybe 78/80 octane, they were fair game to try and give the slip.

We were terrible really, but we were young and this was our big adventure.

Their cars struggled to hit 70mph. So even though we were carrying over thirty tons of freight, once we'd got up a head of steam and a clear road, who knew?

This one did, because a few miles down the road he was pulled over on to the hard shoulder, flagging me down.

I had to stop this time. Then it was out of the cab trying to shake their hands, but they were having none of it. We'd made fools of them and now it was our turn.

'*Passeport collega, problema collega.*'

He spoke to his mate, '*Collega Takograf, problema,*' pointing his finger at me.

I had my hands outstretched, palms up while shaking my head as if I didn't understand.

'*TAKOGRAF*,' said the driver, crossing his wrists as if he was wearing handcuffs.

'Ah tachograph,' I said, nodding my head as if I'd had a blinding flash of understanding.

This was going to cost me. My tacho had been in the speedo since we'd left Germany and had been round the clock at least three times, so it wouldn't be that legible.

Still, it didn't need to be legible for them to extract money from me. This obviously wasn't their first time either.

I took out the tachograph and officer one took it from me and started to inspect it in minute detail. It didn't take him long to discover a high point on the chart that read 105kph. The speed limit here was 70kph.

The fact that the speed he'd read might have been anywhere in Europe was of no relevance in this drama.

He pointed it out to me. '105kph' in Cyrillic (Bulgarian language), and I knew then it was barter time.

'Fifty leva,' he said. That was £35 in official exchange, but of no value outside Bulgaria. It was most probably more than he earned in a week.

I pulled out my wallet and produced fifty leva in notes. He looked shocked, and shook his head open mouthed.

On entry to the old Eastern Bloc countries it was compulsory to exchange currency. In the early days it was fifteen leva for £10. There were very few places to spend it, and you were expected to change it back on exiting the country. I once conducted an experiment at the Austrian border when I offered levas for exchange into Austrian schillings and was offered a rate of seven to one. The official Bulgarian rate was one and a half to one!

I tried to hand over the levas and the policeman withdrew his hand rather rapidly.

'*Collega*, fifty leva?' He looked at me quizzically as if wondering where I'd stolen so much money.

His partner took control of the situation. 'Deutschemarrrrk ... dollaarrr?'

Here we were at the negotiating table at last. I pulled out ten DM and proffered that, at which they shook their collective heads. I then offered twenty DM which they declined, holding up three fingers ... thirty DM. I pulled out five DM to make it twenty five DM, which clinched the deal.

'*Factura collega*?' I asked.

Shake of the head ... *so* no receipt then, and they were twenty five DM better off, which they could change on the black market for considerably more levas should they wish.

They waved me off, wagging their fingers at me for being a naughty boy, and when I got down to Svilengrad and caught up with Taffy, he thought the whole episode hilarious.

Ah Bulgaria! The lowliest ranking in importance in the old communist Eastern Bloc, and continually fighting relegation with Romania to see who would qualify for third world status.

In the early days it was the only way we knew into Turkey and once you'd reached Nis in Yugoslavia it was left turn to Dimitrovgrad and Bulgaria.

19

Their Eyes are Everywhere!

WCCCHHHEEEEEEEEEEECCCCHH.

Well it's the best I can do, and it's the sound of my water pump giving up the ghost just south of Sebes in central Romania.

Perfect timing, it's the middle of winter and Steve, Pete Ransome, Taffy and I are on the way to Iran again, me to Shiraz, the others I know not where.

Romania was one of the alternative routes to the Middle East, down through Czechoslovakia, Hungary, Romania, and then rejoin the original route in Bulgaria.

The snow was laying a few inches deep, but we had been

making good progress. I was running second in convoy and flashed Steve up ahead while pulling over to the side of the road. The water pump, which had been rumbling for the past day and a half, had finally seized up .

I had been hoping to get down to Aydin's garage opposite the Mocamp in Istanbul for him to work his magic and repair it.

Breaking down here wasn't part of the plan and could cause us some grief. In fact we ended up having more than we could have expected. What now? That was the next question.

Steve had spotted us pulling over and reversed. It was decided to put me on a bar and tow me down to the next big town called Sibiu, about fifteen miles to the south. Taffy and Pete went ahead to find a suitable parking place for us all.

Luckily, I was able to keep my engine on tick-over, which made towing a lot easier, as it meant I had power steering and brakes. The temperature was about -15C so overheating wasn't going to be a problem on that short trip. We had a slow tow down and an hour later pulled into a large parking area on the edge of the town.

Little did I know that this would be home for the next fortnight.

We decided to find a hotel that night as it would be bloody freezing in my cab. So I took a small holdall with the essentials, and we stopped the first local we met and asked for directions.

'Hotel, chief?' This drew a blank expression.

'Otel?' I said, clasping my hands together by the side of my head sleeping fashion.

'Ah!' Points finger up towards the town.

'Well done Paul, perfect Romanian. You'll have to teach us the lingo,' said Steve 'as you're so fluent.'

'Yep, I've never believed in the shouting louder method. Just speak to them in their own language . . . instant response. Otel, see.'

We headed up towards the town. It was bloody cold and getting dark. Once on one of the main streets we started looking for this 'otel'. All the buildings looked grey and dreary but you could see that under the decades of grime that the older architecture was of a very grand design, obviously pre-communism, most probably nineteenth century.

There was nobody about to ask so we trudged on through the icy slush until we came to a building with a Romanian flag hanging outside; climbing the steps we squeezed through a revolving door to find that this was the otel![1] What a bit of luck.

The four of us walked over to the reception desk only to be blanked completely by the receptionist. How very rude! Then a few moments later a small, sharp featured besuited man appeared from a side door and stood in front of us with upturned hands and shaking his head in a questioning way.

'We would like two rooms please,' said Steve.

The small man repeated his gesture.

'*Sprachen ze Deutsch, parlez vous Francais, parliamo Italiano*?'

A small light shone in his austere face. '*Si, poco Italiano, collega*.'

We were standing by a large square pillar which had full length grubby mirrors on each of its faces.

Pete whispered: 'Don't look now but were being observed.'

'Bloody hell, where did they come from? Are we on a James Bond film set?' There had appeared, as if from nowhere, four or five blokes dressed like extras from a Bond movie, in full length leather coats and fur-lined leather hats.

Looking around there were numerous pillars in the entrance hall, all with mirrors on them, and these guys were

[1] The hotel we stayed at is now a popular tourist hotel called the Imparatul Romanilor.

watching us in the mirrors. The whole thing would have been scary if it hadn't seemed so incongruously funny.

Obviously Ian Fleming and Michael Crichton had done their research, because these guys could have had a starring role in any of their books.

Other than the frontier crossing this was to be our first encounter with the Securitate, or secret police.

It seems that no foreign tourists or visitors ever stay at these hotels, and they were only used by party members for functions or to bring their girl friends away for the proverbial dirty weekend!

To have four foreigners asking to stay had obviously thrown a major spanner in the works.

Still we needed a bed for the night, and the guy spoke a little Italian.

Eventually, we made ourselves understood, but the little guy kept glancing at the leather-clad ones as if for approval.

They'd obviously got a spy fixation, and because these were such 'closed societies' with virtually no freedom of movement anyone who was different was to be treated with suspicion.

After a prolonged discussion, which included us querying the price of 70 lei, when the tariff board clearly said seven lei, we were shown to our rooms, which were quite pleasant and had a certain faded elegance.

Apparently seventy lei was, '*turistic* price, *collega*'.

That night was hilarious. We had asked if we could eat in the hotel restaurant, a service which they seemed quite eager to provide, and when we got down there, around 7.30 p.m. the restaurant was already half full of these cloned Securitate guys, now without their long coats and hats. Weirdly, in a restaurant catering for about twenty-five people, not one woman was present.

Within five minutes of us sitting down, a young guy of about twenty-five stopped at our table and introduced himself as Flavius, a lecturer at the local college. He spoke good English and wondered if he could join us for dinner.

This whole charade was too obvious for words and the whole evening was spent with him questioning us about everything. What, why, where, who?

It was a litany of information gathering, and *then* we got on to politics ... not such a good idea as we'd had a few drinks by now, and I in particular, being interested in the subject, was a bit outspoken. Steve and Taff kept telling me to lay off or we'd be getting into trouble. Flavius was more than happy to encourage the conversation as 'this is a free and democratic country which prefers to vote for communism and the equality of all'. Roll the drums and blow the bugles!

Flavius, a very Italian name, but that is Romania, still loosely tied to its history as part of the Roman Empire and the Romanian language still has its roots firmly lodged in a Latin base.

We parted on good terms having had an unusual night to say the least, and made our way back to our rooms. The question was: were there spy cameras in the rooms?

The next morning we asked if they had a telex and were directed to the police station. We had to let Trans UK know what had happened and get instructions on forward planning. The response was that Steve and Pete were to leave straight away, and Taffy was to stay with me in case further assistance was required.

The police directed us to a Romtrans[2] service depot on the other side of town to see if they could provide any assistance. They were as good as gold and came and dismantled the water pump and took it back to their workshop but to no avail, it was a write-off. So it was back to the police station to

[2] Romtrans was the national haulage company of Romania ... similar to British Road Services in the UK.

let Tony know back home. Later in the day the response came back.

'We'll get one sent down through the Foreign Office in London to the British Embassy in Bucharest in the next diplomatic bag ... about a week. All our love and best of luck, Tony Waugh.'

The next week passed so slowly; there really was nothing to do. Once a day we wandered down to our trucks to check them over and Taffy started his every day to keep everything working. We'd need to use his unit to taxi us down to Bucharest when we got the say-so, meanwhile mine was getting covered in more and more snow as it stood cold and idle.

This was a nice town and it was interesting watching how these people struggled on through life's adversities. Compared to the things we took for granted back home, like personal transport, food in the shops, in fact any shops at all, these stoic people made do with very little. Most walked everywhere, with grim, tired faces.

The most common form of transport seemed to be horse-drawn sleighs, often with numerous people sitting on them, and the pace of life seemed very lethargic and lacking in enthusiasm. Maybe it was the continuous cold weather.

The hotel personnel had lightened up a bit though, and the James Bond extras had also disappeared, though we felt quite sure we were being kept an eye on.

Then on Friday morning came a call from the hotel manager to say that a telex had been received at the police station that the 'machina' was on its way from England and we should go down to Bucharest to collect it.

We paid our bill, said our thanks and walked down to the trucks.

'Better take two sets of snow chains with us,' I said, 'just in case'.

We uncoupled the trailer and stuffed the chains in the passenger footwell. We were going to try to get to Bucharest tonight. This wasn't going to be the easiest of runs; it was about 150 miles with the first 100 through the Carpathian Mountains and the last fifty a dual carriageway from Pitesti to Bucharest.

On reflection, it would have been easier if we had taken the trailer with us.

There had been intermittent snow since we had been here, and the roads were very icy. Little attempt was made by the authorities to keep the main highways open.

At least with the trailer behind we would have a lot more traction and maybe we could have got away without using the chains quite as much. As it was, it was zero traction, and chains on, chains off, chains on, chains off. In the end we left them on and pootled along at 20mph. On the whole trip we only encountered a handful of vehicles.

Up in the hills it snowed heavily for a while, and at one point the wipers were only just able to keep the screen clear. It was a really dry snow that stuck to everything and compacted at the edge of the windscreen.

We arrived in Bucharest at 11 p.m. and were so tired Taffy just pulled over to the side of the road and parked up. We were filthy dirty from the continuous chaining up, but too knackered to care.

Taffy made a brew for us both, and then retired to his bunk, while I struggled to make myself comfortable in the passenger's seat, trying to fall asleep to Taffy's snoring and the gentle vibration of the engine as it ticked over through the night keeping us both warm. But as to actual sleep, I had virtually none. It was a horrible night, and by the time morning broke I wasn't in the best of humour.

Anyway after a cup of tea and a tin of beans I felt marginally better and we decided we'd better try and find the embassy, which we did quite easily. But of course, it was bloody closed for the weekend, and we were turned away by the duty guards.

Really we hadn't thought our plan through, and we should have stayed in Sibiu for the weekend.

We weren't going *back* to Sibiu, *that's* for sure so it was a question of finding a hotel for a couple of nights. This wasn't the problem it had been in Sibiu, as a number of European companies did business in Bucharest.

We found a reasonable hotel near the embassy and settled down for the rest of the weekend. At least we could have a shower. And we both tried caviar for the first time. I can't see what all the fuss is about, basically it's fish eggs. Do I sound like a philistine?

Monday morning we were at the embassy gates at 10 a.m. and were allowed through to the main building where we were met by a member of the embassy staff, Nigel. How can anyone talk like that with their mouth full of so many plums and marbles?

'Hello cheps, how jolly nice to make your acquaintance, hwa hwa.'

We shook hands and exchanged names.

'Ny ... you're here to collect some dratted piece of machinery from the diplomatic beg, is thet correct?'

'Yup,' said Taffy, 'it's a dratted water pump for my friend's Velvo.'

'Right, demned nuisance, the old beg won't be here till the morrow, old bean.'

We almost felt like asking for a translator, but Nigel was a genuinely decent bloke and his next statement made us like him a lot more.

'Look cheps we're orf to the American Embassy tonight and you're more then welcome to teg along as you're Brittish. It's usually a good besh and plenty of the old grog available.'

And teg along we did. What a fantastic time we had and treated so well. We were also privy to the first showing of the film *Duel* before it went on general release. Those 'Damned Yankees' just know how to do it.

There were a couple of British businessmen there as well, and after the show was over and we had said our goodbyes to our American hosts, all four of us wandered along the street back to their hotel singing rugby songs at the tops of our voices. The English guys invited us in for a nightcap and the offer of some extra curricular at a place they knew ... which of course we turned down!

The following morning, bleary-eyed, and regretting the previous night's activities, we met one of the consular officials, Tim, who came with us to the airport to supervise collection of our water pump.

Two hours later we had the precious water pump in our possession, said goodbye to Tim and were on our way back to Sibiu.

The drive back was just as slow and hazardous as our trip down, and we rolled into Sibiu about 10 p.m.

Taffy didn't bother coupling up to his trailer. We just got our cases and struggled up to the hotel. This time they were pleased to see us back as we had become sort of minor celebrities, very minor ... in fact, miniscule. They provided us with a late night meal and beer and we stumbled into bed at 1 a.m.

Late the following morning we drove Taff's truck round to the Romtrans depot and asked for their assistance again. They couldn't have been more helpful, and by mid-afternoon their fitters had the replacement pump on, vehicle defrosted, air lines unfrozen, and we were ready to roll.

Strangely enough they didn't want paying, so we gave them a carton of ciggies and a bottle of Johnny Walker, with which they were more than happy.

We decided to return to the hotel, have a shower and a meal, then come back and sleep in our trucks ready for an early start the following morning.

At six o'clock we were away, and with the extra weight of our trailers made much better progress across the

Carpathians, down to Pitesti, past the huge gas terminal and on to Bucharest. It was only forty miles further to Giurgiu, the frontier with Bulgaria, and by 3 p.m. we were parked up at the border.

Collecting our briefcases, Taffy and I walked over to the custom shed and joined the queue. Eventually, when we got to the front desk and before I could hand any paperwork over, the official looked up at me and said: 'Ah hello Mr Rowlands, your camion, it is fixed?'

The shock was palpable. 'Yes,' I mumbled.

Their eyes, they *are* everywhere!

20

Poo Bare!

This is a delicate subject and a delicate tale of how basic life is when travelling through the less well developed parts of the world.

Taffy was a non-aggressive, gentle type of guy and one of Trans UK's early employees. He was a little older than the rest of us, about forty and consequently had been brought up in a more austere time in the valleys of South Wales where the Baptist ethic was still very strong and toilet humour was frowned upon. The sorts of activities involved in this short story were considered very private and not discussed, even in humour, down at the men's clubs. Trouble was that in the type of work we were now engaged, privacy wasn't always possible, and toilet humour was the norm.

He was running down to Tabriz with Steve (Hercules) and they had got as far as Yozgat, central/northern Turkey. Here civilisation, as we understand it, struggles to come to the surface. Every 100/200 miles you will come across a large town, and in between, hidden away from the road there are small villages, but little else, other than a barren, mountainous landscape.

As you can imagine there were a distinct lack of toilet facilities of any sort. Many a time I have washed in a beautiful clear mountain stream. For the rest you make do and mend.

Now Taffy wasn't too keen on make do and mend, so to speak, and when it came to the more personal stuff, he struggled.

The lack of toilet facilities meant you kept hanging on, and hanging on until desperation finally set in and you had to prise your white knuckled hands off the steering wheel. You'd park as far off the road as possible, jump out of your cab and scramble up on to your diesel tank, drop your kecks, hang your bum out over the edge and hope everything ended up missing the truck, which was sometimes difficult if you were having a power poo!

The more stylish way was to plan for a more sensitive and relaxing session in between the rear axles of the trailer, maybe taking a magazine and a cigar to while away the time and remind you of home. This procedure was called a 'spread axle', on account of the axles being far enough apart so that you could back into the space between the trailer wheels, crouch down and proceed with business while surveying the surrounding landscape in a state of utter bliss.

Now Taffy, as already inferred was a bit of a shy guy and liked a bit of 'privacy', *so*, when the need arose he would drop his shorts and instead of reversing into the space between the axles, would in fact shuffle forward and, facing the trailer, grab hold of a chassis ring and do the business. Why he preferred this style of celebration of the poo, we never knew, and we always kept well out of the way. Not really a spectator sport!

Anyway, one day on the far side of Yozgat heading towards Sivas and in the middle of nowhere, Taffy became desperate for a poo and pulled over on to some wasteland. Having ensconced himself comfortably between the wheels of his trailer in his customary position, pure white bum on display to the central wastes of Turkey, what should come along but an inquisitive dog that took offence to Taffy's rectum, which was in explosive mode, and took a bite out of it. The hound obviously didn't like the taste, yelped and buggered off. There was a horrendous scream from Taffy, who was trying to wipe his bum, wipe away the blood and reverse out from the wheels at the same time. Bit of a horrendous mess really and not a vision I'm totally happy to share with you!

The whole episode was worthy of a *Monty Python* sketch. The downside was that poor old Taffy had to be driven back to Ankara Hospital to have an anti-rabies injection, which according to him was even more painful than the dog bite. It meant a few days recuperating on one cheek of his behind, and though a full recovery was made, scar tissue remained. Thereafter he always carried a large builder's type bucket with him for those more personal moments.

21

Tahir Village

We'd had our week off, and now Taffy and I were off together again. Anyone would think we were married or something.

It was March 1977, and we were heading for Abadan again, right down on the Persian Gulf. Having just got back from a nightmare of a trip that had taken getting on for seven weeks, Tony must have thought we were gluttons for punishment, and instead of sending us to the Saudi sunshine, was sending us back to hell!

We had a good trip across Europe and into Turkey, where our progress was slowed considerably, not so much because of the cold, this time it was unseasonably warm, -10C! It was more to do with the amount of snow that was falling; it was virtually non-stop. We had a couple of days at Imranli, and Zara, and on the odd occasion managed only fifty miles in a day.

Eventually we reached Horasan on a very cold and snowy morning, only to be stopped at the back of a queue of thirty odd wagons by army personnel. Maybe they were going to let us use the military road around the base of Tahir Mountain, instead of having to climb over it. I think not! It would require a national emergency of earth-shattering proportions to let us anywhere near that road. No, it was far better that we Europeans were made to climb this dreaded 9,000-ft plus mountain than offer us a safer alternative.

Horasan was a town at the base of the mountain on the western side of Tahir and Eleskirt was the town at the base of the mountain on the eastern side and in between was Tahir Mountain, 8,500 feet and fifty-six kilometres of dirt and rubble-strewn road, with narrow hairpins, very steep inclines and, close to the top, the infamous Tahir, a village which almost seemed hewn out of the very rock of the mountain itself.

This corner of Turkey did not seem to have much in the way of policing as you and I would understand it and all the duties you normally associated with the police appeared to come under the remit of the army.

Of all the 4,000 miles from the UK to Iran, these thirty-four miles were the bit that caused trepidation among us all. It was always the fear of the unexpected . . .

This was Kurdistan, and the Kurdish people are without a doubt some of the hardiest people in the world. It was as nothing to see these men walking along the roadside, in the middle of winter in freezing temperatures, with just a shirt, trousers and an old jacket on, while you sat shivering in your heated cab.

Nearly all Kurdish men have moustaches, and there was

once an occasion when I was parked by the roadside having a cuppa one very cold winter's morning, psyching myself up to get back among the snow and ice, when a middle-aged Kurdish man came up to the cab wearing just this garb. He raised his hand in the time-honoured way to make the smoking action, obviously looking for a cigarette. As he raised his hand to his mouth his jacket sleeve caught the edge of his moustache and snapped a bit off. It was actually frozen! He went ballistic and blamed me for his distress, on the basis it's got to be somebody's fault because as sure as eggs is eggs, it ain't his. This damage to his dignity and reduction in his manliness cost me forty B&H to salve his pride, and I'd done nothing!

It was not unusual to see horses trotting across the mountainside ridden by men looking like bandits, with bandoliers full of bullets and rifles draped across their shoulders. This was like the wild west of Turkey, an untamed landscape and an untamed people.

Apparently the track conditions up towards Tahir village and beyond weren't too good, so the soldiers were only allowing trucks to leave Horasan in groups of four at fifteen minute intervals. By the time it came our turn, about two hours later, the snow had stopped.

While we were sat in the queue waiting, Freddie Archer had come across the top from Eleskirt on the other side and stopped to have a brief chat. He reckoned that the run up to just this side of Tahir Village wasn't too bad - very slushy and muddy, but once into the village and above, it became quite icy.

We thanked Fred and decided to try it without chains as mud, rocks and chains are not a good mix. Taffy had a step frame trailer with about twelve tons on board and his beloved Volvo F88 290. I had a standard spread axle trailer with fifteen tons and the old F88. As I was pulling a normal forty foot trailer, I was carrying the snow chains for both of us.

Finally, our turn came, and we were paired up with a couple of Bulgarians pulling Dapsofia trailers for Willi Betz. They both had brand new orange Mercedes 320s, with huge black air intake pipes sprouting out of the front corner of their cabs. These trucks were designed mainly for desert work.

Of course the Bulgy guys with their 320s, and double manned as always, left us for dead within three miles, and Taffy with his more powerful and lighter truck also left me behind. We were going to meet at the café in Eleskirt later.

The climb up wasn't too bad as Fred had intimated, and traction was good; the graders had been up first thing in the morning and done an excellent job. The snow at the side of the road was five to six feet deep, but the only bit I was worried about was in the village itself. The climb up to Tahir village was quite steep, then on the approach the road levelled out before entering the 'built up' area, and dropping gently down round a right hander before a very steep little incline about thirty yards long that took you up and out of the village the other end, whereupon it settled into a slow and steady low gear climb to the top.

The temperature was so cold that even the kids, who often gave us grief, were nowhere to be seen.

In the better weather when traversing the mountain, the Tahir village children, some as young as three or four and dressed like extras from an *Oliver Twist* play, would congregate by the side of the road at the steepest point, and as you approached, in their own appealing way, usually with a boulder in one hand while making the motion of dragging on a fag with the other, would try to persuade you to dispense with a cigarette or two. If you were uncharitable enough not to throw out any largesse, then they took immediate offence and you'd find a barrage of missiles aimed at your cab. Many a driver had the misfortune to have his window smashed in this way.

I used to buy cheap Romanian ciggies, about 5p for twenty, and as I approached the kids I would brandish a handful of loose cigarettes at them out of the window so they could be seen, and then as I drew alongside would hurl them as far as I could, and watch as they scrambled around fighting among themselves. This gave us enough time to get a few more yards up the road and hopefully out of reach of the stone throwing. This part of the mountain was so steep that we were normally down to second or third gear and doing about 10mph.

Approaching the village, I felt good, and was pleased that we hadn't put chains on. It really was the last thing any of us liked to do and if we could maintain momentum that's what we did, sometimes across the most horrendous terrain.

Then it was up into the village, around the first bend, drop down the gentle right hander and get ready for a bit of power and momentum then up the short steep incline out of Tahir.

But the next thing wasn't meant to happen. There was Taffy at the side of the road at the bottom of the steep incline. I pulled up behind him and jumped out. Not the best place to stop, I was thinking! I stumbled through the ice and snow to his cab and as I got there he clambered out. His face was as white as a sheet; in fact I thought he'd taken ill.

'*Where's the chains, where's the chains?*' he was shouting at me in a trembling vibrato voice.

'I've been bloody held up, bloody Turkish bandit had a gun in my face, threatened to shoot me, *the bastard*.'

'*What!* Where is he?' Suddenly, I wasn't above being scared either.

He *really was* badly shaken up.

While we were getting the chains sorted - because we both needed them now - he tried to tell me what had happened.

According to Taffy, he had been making good progress and had kept the Bulgarians in sight all the way until he reached this point in the village, and he pointed out a path that had been cut into the snow bank on both sides of the road. A little lad had shot out of the path and across the road in front of him. Taffy had stamped on the anchors, lost control and ended up half jackknifed, but luckily missed the boy. He had managed to straighten out the truck and no damage had been done. The trouble was he had no momentum to get himself up the steep little incline and out of the village. He tried three times and each time ended up back where he started.

'It was no good mate,' said Taff. 'After the third time I just sat here waiting for you. That was about ten minutes ago, and then this bloke came out from the track over there.' He pointed to the track on the other side of the road.

He climbed on to the cab step, grabbing hold of the mirror arm and seemed friendly enough. Then he said to me: '*Problema collega*?'

'No problem friend,' I said. '*Collega* come soon with chains.'

He sort of became insistent and repeated: '*Problema collega?*'

'Nix problem,' I said again, and with that he pulled out a bloody gun and waved it in my face, saying: '*Problema collega*,' in a threatening sort of voice.

'Then he whistled, and out of the gully came the same youngster I think, struggling to pull this snow chain, which he obviously expected me to buy. What could I do?' said Taffy.

By this time I was beginning to get worried myself, but then, as if on cue, in the distance I could hear the faint noise of more trucks climbing the mountain.

'Where's this chain then Taffy?' I said, and he showed me. I'd completely missed it in the excitement. Apparently the guy who had held him up had even given Taff a hand to lay it over the drive wheels; the only problem was it didn't fit. The bloody thing was a snow chain off a grader, I reckon, which had huge tyres, and even though it had been laid over the top of the wheel, that was the only place it touched. The rest of it hung down in a heap on the ground either side like an old pair of worn-out breasts! It was no use to us, so we left it there by the side of the road for him to sell to someone else.

By this time a couple of Swedish trucks had turned up behind us. We felt safe enough now, and after finishing off chaining up, waited for the Swedish guys and together we all climbed up the bank out of the village, up to the top of the mountain and headed down to Eleskirt.

Sadly, this wasn't the end of our drama for the day. As we dropped down the mountain towards the town of Eleskirt we found we were driving along on a thick layer of ice.

This often occurred when the snow graders levelled the road. The operators didn't drop the blade close enough to the actual road surface in case they damaged their ploughs, which was easily done on these 'roads' and left an inch or two of snow cover which then froze. Then when more snow fell, and over a period of time when more grading was done the actual road surface ended up a few inches below the ice.

In fact by the time we hit the middle of the town we were driving along with our wheels sitting in four inch deep ice ruts. It was as if we were in guide rails and had no option other than to stay in them. This was all very well till we came to the main crossroads in the centre of the town and approached a set of ruts crossing ours at right angles. Where the two sets crossed I misjudged the ice junction, and my front wheels hit the corner of the ice, throwing them out of the lanes on to virgin snow. I suddenly found I had no steerage, and as all the rest of the vehicle's wheels were still happily trundling along behind, firmly ensconced in the ice tracks, I found myself being jackknifed around in slow motion until the cab gently collided with the trailer and I was facing the wrong way. Sliding down the road I came to a halt thirty metres past the junction.

What a palaver! Here I was blocking the main highway

across Turkey. Fortunately there was no traffic because it took another three hours to get me straightened out finally with a tow bar fitted between my trailer and Taffy's cab and him dragging me backwards till I got straight.

We got ourselves sorted, parked up at the café and had a few Efes beers to put life into some sort of perspective. When I asked Taffy how much he'd paid for the grader chain, he couldn't remember, but said he would have paid anything, as he'd never been as scared in his life as when that gun appeared over the edge of the door. Anyway he'd rather talk about me jackknifing *my* truck, thank you very much!

22

Charioteer?

'Hallo.'

Who was that, I thought.

Again: 'Hallo'.

'Hello,' I said. 'What's up, chief?' I said walking round to the other side of my truck.

Steve, Pete and I were away on the long haul again; it was late summer of 1978. Pete was off to Kuwait, Steve to Dammam, and me to Amman. We were going to run down to just north of Amman together, and then the other two would split off towards Turayf. We had not long parked up for the night at the railway sidings on the southern outskirts of Brno, when I'd heard this voice calling in an urgent whisper.

It was an elderly guy, maybe in his sixties, not very tall and quite nondescript to look at. He was dressed in an old raincoat, and was leaning against his dilapidated old bike, close to the truck.

Surprisingly, when he spoke it was in a determined whisper, as if he was a little afraid of being heard. His English was excellent and he asked if we were going back to Britain. It was all a bit secretive and even edgy. He had made sure that our trucks were between him and the road, so that he would not be seen by anyone passing by.

It turned out that this bloke wasn't quite so nondescript after all and for the life of me I can't remember his name. However his story was amazing. He told us that he had been a minister in Alexander Dubcek's Czechoslovakian Government when it was overthrown by the Russian invasion in 1968, and until 1977 he had been in prison for his part in the 'weakening of Soviet authority in Czechoslovakia', and by default, potentially subverting the strength and unity of the Communist Bloc Alliance. He had been released eighteen months previously, given a job in a heavy industrial plant in Brno and warned to keep a low profile.

He had stopped to talk with us because he had recognised the GB stickers on the back of the trailers and hoped that we could take a message out of the country for him. His story was that he had very good friends in London who worked at the British Library. Since the 1968 uprising and his imprisonment they would have had no information concerning his whereabouts, and possibly even thought he was dead. Could we please pass on a message to them that he was alive and well and living in Brno? I gave him a sheet of paper to write down the relevant information and promised to do what I could when we returned home. After writing down the details of the contact, he handed back the sheet of paper, thanked us profusely, then mounted his wobbly old boneshaker and very slowly cycled off back towards Brno.

(When I got back from that trip I contacted the British Library, and left a message for the person named on the sheet of paper, but never heard anything back.)

After he'd gone we looked at each other in amazement; this job threw up everything.

'Did you recognise him?' said Steve.

'Not me,' I said, 'I know about the Russian invasion and all that, and you'd assume all the senior people would have been sent off to a gulag in Siberia or somewhere.'

'Maybe he was,' said Pete, 'he didn't look all that healthy.'

That was a bit of excitement to start the trip and kept a buzz of conversation going till we went to bed. Tomorrow was going to be a long day; if possible we were hoping to get to the National at Belgrade which meant a silly 4.30 a.m. start the following morning.

It was a beautiful morning as the sun broke the skyline and washed over the countryside like a wave, but dropping down off the new dual carriageway into Bratislava around 6.30 a.m. we were all pulled by the police for doing 100kph in a 70kph zone. They could have only caught Steve with the gun but charged us all as we were running together. Luckily we each got away with a fifteen Deutschmark fine, and no receipt, and we only lost twenty minutes. It could easily have been an hour.

At Rajka we had a quick clearance. Mind you on the Hungarian border weighbridge Pete was close to being overweight on the front axle of his trailer, which would have been costly. That weighbridge could be such a pain, and we all reckoned the scales were dodgy. Individual axle weighing was always a dubious exercise even back home.

Other than lunch by the Danube in Budapest it was a non-stop run across Hungary to Subotica, the Yugo border. Here we got held up in a tedious bit of theatre, watching a whole host of security police dragging a young Hungarian woman, kicking and screaming off a bus.

This wasn't the first or last time I saw this sad act. Back in the 1970s it was virtually impossible for residents of any of the communist bloc countries to move freely from one country to the next. Special permits were required and these were only issued to trusted party members.

Interestingly, when the Iron Curtain collapsed and the cold war ended in 1989, it wasn't long before there were vast queues of overloaded, smoky, stuttering old Trabants and Ladas, all waiting patiently to visit relations in other countries. Unable to cope with this 'mass migration', these old communist frontiers were absolute chaos for a long time as the border guards struggled to deal with this new phenomenom, carrying on as they had done previously, checking everything very thoroughly, and virtually taking cars apart in their quest to find 'something'.

Two hours later we cleared the border and headed down to the National Hotel, where, arriving rather later than expected, we had to park out on the access road near the garage. Still we had a bloody good night as Priggy and Cowboy Lillee were there, both on their way back to Germany after delivering tractors to Istanbul.

'Get lost.' Someone was trying to batter their way into my skull.

BANG, BANG, BANG! There it was again. 'Get up you lazy git, it's 10 o'clock.'

'What? Stop doing that, it's making my head hurt.'

'If you're not up in five minutes we're off without you.'

Bugger, I'd overslept and had too many Pivos the night before. I also had a stonking headache.

We had planned on hitting the Harem in Istanbul that night, but now I wasn't so sure.

As I was rolling off my bunk into the driving seat, a bit the worse for wear and half dressed, Steve and Pete were pulling out on to the road. No time for food then. As quickly as I could, I pulled on my shorts and scooted back to my trailer box. I'd got to have something; my mouth was like the bottom of a bats' cave. A bottle of Coke would sort that out as I scrambled back into the cab and fired the old beast up. The bastards weren't waiting for me!

The Coke sorted my headache and refreshed my palate, and by three ciggies I was on top of the world and catching the others up at the top of the climb out of Belgrade, where there'd been an accident not involving a Turk! After we'd managed to squeeze past the gory scene it was down 'gastarbeiter death trap road' to Nis.

This road was in my book most probably the most dangerous on the whole journey. It was the time of year when thousands of Turkish gastarbeiters made their annual trek back to their homeland for their holidays. The problem was that as a money saver they tried to do the 1,600 mile trip in one hit. But as a lifesaver it wasn't always successful. There was usually a car full of people, a family, with sometimes only one driver and the equivalent of the best part of Land's End to John o' Groats and back again. Fatigue usually set in after about 1,000 miles towards the bottom end of Yugoslavia and the proof showed on each trip as there were *always* fresh crucifixes and flowers along the whole 240 kilometres. I'd had numerous close calls myself and little did I know that today was potentially my most serious incident so far, which ended up in a collision of sorts, with the police becoming involved.

The contretemps occurred near Velniko Plana about sixty miles south of Belgrade. I was running third in line and well back from Pete's tail. In Yugoslavia back then the law stated that heavy goods vehicles should travel at least 100 metres apart, to allow easier overtaking for cars and coaches. This was because the road network was 99.9% single carriageway.

Since we left Belgrade there had been a nearly continuous flow of German registered cars overtaking, and on this occasion an old Mercedes was sitting behind me waiting for his opportunity to come past. There was also a flow of vehicles coming in the opposite direction, and for a few minutes he was unable to overtake. In the end, like most of them, he became impatient and even though I could see another truck coming towards us in the distance, the young Turk most probably said '*Inshallah*' and went to overtake me.

There was no way he was going to make it, so I eased right off. When the truck coming towards us saw what was going to happen, there was a blaze of headlights and a full set of air horns. The young Turk was also giving it the big hand on his horn and flashing his lights. I'm not sure what he expected me to do, maybe disappear up my own rectum. Anyway I couldn't and I didn't. The other truck driver and me were as far over to our own sides of the road as humanly possible without slipping off the edge into the field down below.

As our cabs passed each other, the Turkish car was alongside me and the young driver most probably had his eyes closed, because there was a piercing, screeching sound of metal on metal as his car engaged with my truck in a bout of mechanical fisticuffs.

How we never had a more serious accident I'll never know, and as he pulled past me I could see the damage. It was as if I had been a Roman charioteer in *Ben Hur* with twirling blades on my wheels, because there was virtually a circle of metal cut out of his passenger side door where my wheel nuts had engaged with it.

I followed him to the next lay-by where before I could even get down from my cab the whole family started to berate and abuse me for causing the accident, best to stay in my cab and lock the door, I thought. The young driver kept banging on my door and repeating '*polizei*', as if to try and scare me.

Eventually the Yugoslav police turned up and before they had a chance to get out of their car the family had surrounded them, most probably telling them I was a danger on the road and should be hanged from the nearest tree or at the very least banned for life. In their opinion, I had not spotted their overtaking manoeuvre and had turned my wheel to pull out and overtake the fictitious truck in front. As if to emphasise the point the woman kept making steering motions that inferred that I had swung violently to the left which was a blatant lie.

After a while the police thought they'd better have a word with me, and while one of them kept the Turkish family from interfering, the other came up to me and repeated the turning motion with his hands, at which I shook my head vigorously and pointed to my front wheel. With my best hand signals, and drawing in the dirt, I explained that if my wheel *had* been turned to pull out, then surely the tyre would have hit the car, not the wheel nuts. I did my best to show that we were in fact running parallel, and as he had edged closer to me with the truck coming the other way he had got too close and ended up being chewed up by the studs. This he understood and seemed to find it a rational explanation, and what with the number of Turks being killed on a daily basis on this road with their crazy driving was more than willing to give me the benefit of the doubt.

With that he went back to them and explained what he thought had happened, which, judging by their reaction, was roughly what I had told him. They were not happy turkeys, and gave vent to their feelings most vociferously. However the police were having none of it and waved them away. The clincher came when the police looked round the driver's side of the old Merc; the front wing had been battered about by the other truck and was covered in shiny new scratches and tears to the metal. All of a sudden resignation settled in as they all climbed back in their newly ventilated car and shot out of the lay-by nearly causing another accident. I waited ten minutes to give them a chance to get well in front before pulling back on to the road to try and catch up with my two mates, who were oblivious to what had happened.

Twenty miles down the road, there they were in a lay-by, having a brew and totally unconcerned about my welfare.

'Hiya Paul, where you been then, couldn't keep up?'

'Ha ha bloody ha, hilarious, guys.' When I explained what had happened they were even less concerned.

'We'd have given you another couple of hours and then come back to find you,' said Steve with a grin. 'Anyway we'd better make tracks; otherwise we'll never get to Kapic.'

We were off to Nis, and left turn to the Yugo/Bulgarian border at Dimitrovgrad/Kalotina.

What a pain! There was a queue there as well. It was another two and a half hours getting through both sides, so by now we were well behind schedule, and I was very hungry.

'We can have a bite to eat at Dragoman,' said Pete, 'then do a non-stop down to Kapic.'

And that's what we did.

By now it was night time and a very dark one at that. As we were blasting our way through the darkness south of Plovdiv, all headlights and spotlights on full beam, we had the weirdest of experiences when we encountered a 100-yard wide river of frogs; thousands of them.

For the first second or so I thought we'd hit an oil slick as our powerful beams picked out this solid phalanx of shiny backed amphibians slowly making their way across the road. Poor things, it was impossible to miss them, and what a way to go, on your way to the pond in your newly pressed Speedos to meet your girlfriend. Not a very nice sound either, it was like popping bubble wrap. Apparently this was their annual migration, and every year there was this frog massacre.

Over the next couple of years a few culverts were dug under the road to assist the poor creatures, who for some reason didn't understand the Highway Code. Even with the culverts built, many frogs still preferred playing chicken with the trucks. They were most probably the males; it was a macho Bulgarian thing I reckon.

It was midnight by the time we reached Kapitan Andreevo. No Harem tonight my son ...

From there on we had a trouble-free run across Turkey and down into Syria and split at Ramtha three days later, with Steve and Pete heading off into Saudi. I was off to my favourite destination - Amman.

I parked up in the compound mid afternoon and rang Abdul, who came down, collected all my paperwork and invited me up for dinner that night. There were a couple of other Brits parked up as well, Pete, an owner driver, and Jock, from McNeil's. We spent the rest of the afternoon kicking a ball around and generally lazing about. They expected to be here a few days, so we decided to go down to the Dead Sea the following day and check out whether or not it was true that it was impossible to drown due to the volume of salt in the water.

That evening I went to Abdul and his wife Durriyah's house for supper, and had a very pleasant evening with them and their son. In one respect Amman is a bit like Rome in that it sits on seven hills and their house sat up on one of these hills, with a lovely view out over part of the city. Abdul said that if I was still here in a couple of days, he would take me on a sightseeing trip around the town: such kind people, the Jordanians. Later on that night Abdul ran me back to my truck in his beaten-up old Hillman.

The following morning, as usual we were up just after the sun. It doesn't take long for its heat to search out every nook and cranny, of which there were quite a few in my cab. I was living like a slob at the moment and my mobile home desperately needed a good old muck-out - to use the vernacular.

The three of us made ourselves breakfast, a cup of tea followed by a bowl of Weetabix for me, and made ready to visit the Dead Sea. I pushed all my stuff up into a corner so there was enough room for the guys to get into my cab.

There were now four of us: Hercule, a French driver, had turned up and he was keen to go as well.

After dropping the trailer we left the compound and headed out towards Israel, which was only about twenty-five miles away. Now I'd never been out in this direction before, and heading out of Amman the surrounding scenery gave the impression that we were driving through a mountainous region. The rock formations and structures we passed made us think we were 6,000ft up, so it came as a bit of a surprise when after about twenty miles we rounded a bend to a spectacular view of the Dead Sea way down below us. The sign at the side of the road had a line right across the middle that said we were in fact at sea level, with the Dead Sea 1,480ft below the line. So we weren't up in the mountains at all!

As we dropped down round the bends to the lowest open accessible place in the world the heat became more and more intense. Eventually we were down at the bottom and came to a junction at the northern end of the sea where we had no option but to turn left. Straight ahead was an Allenby bridge and across the other side of it was Israel, which would have been a nice idea, but in those days if you entered Israel and got a stamp on your passport then you wouldn't be allowed back into an Arab country.

We drove along the left hand shore of the sea until we came across a sort of shingle strand with, of all things, a shower standing alone at the top of the beach. We couldn't wait to get into the water and see what would happen, and it was true, once you waded in up above your waist, the natural buoyancy in the water took you off your feet and away you floated. The salinity was intense and the water quite brackish. If you took a mouthful it was pretty gross. I was wearing contact lenses and made sure I kept my eyes closed while swimming, but even so managed to splash water into them. Within seconds, my eyes started to burn so I scrambled out back to our towels. Fortunately I was wearing hard lenses and was quickly able to flip them out on to the palm of my hand. Within thirty seconds they were encrusted with salt crystals!

Luckily I had specs with me, because for the next few days my eyes were extremely sensitive. Not only that, but we now realised why the shower was installed at the top of the beach. If you swim in a saline solution and come out and lay in the sun then your skin is going to dry out and wrinkle up like an old leather seat. Best to wash off the salt with fresh water before you look like Yoda.

I really enjoyed the Dead Sea experience, even allowing for the incident with my lenses, and it's a bit of a misnomer to call it a sea because in size it looks more like a lake.

Unbelievably, later when we got back to the compound Abdul told me I was cleared by customs and could tip that evening as the customer was waiting for the goods, so the chance to visit the Gold Souq and the Citadel in Abdul's old chariot would have to wait till next time.

23

A Bit of a Headache

We'd been informed by telex at the Mocamp in Istanbul that Dave Tasker had broken down in central Turkey, somewhere between Zara and Refahiye. Running with me and loving every minute of it was Smudger on his first trip to Iran, a more gregarious and outgoing bloke it would be hard to find and he was behind me when we finally came across Dave parked on a bit of wasteland close by a couple of single- storey buildings.

It was the middle of summer and Dave who was on his way to Islamabad in Pakistan had been broken down here for the best part of a week. This guy was well known for his aversion to the beneficial effects of water, so I'll leave you to imagine the state of his cab and personal hygiene after a week in this intense heat.

We pulled on to the rough ground, our air horns blaring. Our instructions were to tell him that another of our drivers, Pete, was on the way down with the spare parts needed to repair the truck. I parked up nearby, and Smudge pulled up near a standpipe to top up his water container.

Oh no, Dave must be dead! There was zero response to the air horns, *even* in this heat his doors were closed, his curtains drawn, and the windows wound up. I climbed down from my cab, strolled over to his truck and banged on the door, opening it to say hello. I staggered back, as an almost visual odour made good its escape, enveloping me in its foetid smell on the way. This followed by Dave, so there was *no* escape.

At the sight of me staggering back, Smudge cracked up and pleaded a bad leg and double pneumonia as the reason he couldn't get out of his cab to say hello.

There's no doubt about it when you live on your own, sometimes for weeks at a time you become immune to your own smells and, dare I say it, even get to enjoy them. Anyway, other than the odd passing Kurd, and all he wants is a fag or two, who cares? This is obviously a male thing because I couldn't imagine any woman being like that.

It turned out that the standpipe wasn't working anyway which could account for it. That night we stayed with Dave. When I say with, I mean in the same country. Just to keep him company, we did our socialising with a megaphone and the following morning made good our escape!

At Erzincan we pulled into the police checkpoint, only to find no one there. Now what to do? I decided we should carry on to the Erzurum checkpoint and explain what had happened. Were they interested at Erzurum? Not in the slightest. No excuses accepted, go back and get a police stamp. So that's what we had to do, turn round and retrace our steps, 120 miles each way, well over half a day lost, and when we got back to Erzincan, the police were *there*! Driving over any stretch of road in Turkey was bad enough, but to have to drive over the same stretch three times was soul-destroying. We could have been over Tahir and heading to the Iranian border by the time we had returned to Erzurum for the second time.

Halfway back, as we were hot, bothered, and unhappy we stopped near a beautiful clear mountain stream, and fully clothed, went and sat in the icy cold water for the Full Monty, body scrub and clothes wash. Bloody cold and bloody marvellous! Back in the trucks we stopped at the Erzurum police checkpoint for the second time that day and managed to scramble over Tahir at no cost to our health before it got too dark, then dropped down the mountain and parked at the café in Eleskirt. The old maroon Scammell wrecker, Big Bertha, was still there, parked up beside the building. *Who* had managed to drive that old girl all the way from England? A real hero whoever they were.

That old Scammell wrecker parked up in a small Turkish village that struggles to grace even the map of Turkey nearly 3,000 miles from home, spoke volumes about the idiosyncratic British psyche and why the drivers from the rest of Europe viewed some of us as eccentric at the very least.

In the early days of the overland trip to the Middle East, we Brits were driving virtually anything that had four wheels and an engine that started. Absolutely no thought was given to driver comforts until later. Many of the trucks I mentioned in the early part of this book, like AECs, ERFs, and Scammell, mostly non-sleepers, were driven all over the Middle East by tough British men, while Herr Deutschlander and Monsieur Francais looked askance at the mad Englanders ... '*Ah Zo! Mein Gott, zis is how you von ze var*.' Mind you a lot of these old trucks didn't make it in one piece.

The following day Smudge and I reached Bazargan in roasting sunshine, only to find he'd got two shredded tyres on his trailer. Fortunately they couldn't have been flat for too long, otherwise the rims would quickly have been wrecked.

Smudge was hauling a step frame trailer with around seven tons on board. The problem with the much smaller wheels and tyres on a step frame is that they are more enclosed within the trailer than normal sized tyres, and therefore have more trouble dissipating any heat build-up.

Anyway it was out with the tools and jack, off with the shirts and get stuck in. It's a dirty old job at the best of times as you have to crack off[1] ten nuts on each wheel with a brace and an extension bar.

Often the extension bar has to be jumped on to get the necessary leverage to crack one, and sometimes the brace slips off the nut. The resulting flying ironwork can, if you get clumped by it, cause at worst broken teeth or bones and at the very least painful bruising. Two hours later we'd managed to change the tyre on *one* wheel. What a laborious job!

I have total respect for British tyre fitters, out in all weathers trying to keep us on the road. Trouble is, where's a tyre fitter when you *really* need him, 3,000 miles from home?

Finally it's done. You try and stand up, but your back is too stiff. It's broken, the sweat and grime is pouring off you, and the Hilton is 600 miles away. Bring on the Turkish baths in Maku, but first we've got to clear the border which is another two hours minimum.

At last Maku and a bloody good clean-up. Those baths were a godsend, and so refreshing.

When we were done, we decided to pootle down to the Oasis for the night and have an early start for Tehran in the morning.

There's nothing better than feeling clean for a couple of hours and consuming a few beers with like-minded souls. I

[1] Crack off. Truck wheel nuts are tightened to a stage where each small turn of the nut brings forth a cracking sound, hence the term 'cracking off' when undoing them ...

loved the Oasis. I was never quite sure what meat we were eating, but at least it was edible, and they *tried* to cater to our requirements.

In the morning, before the sun had fully made its spectacular entrance, we were up and away - Davis Turner compound here we come. Many hauliers on the Middle East run were driving trucks with Davis Turner loads on, and DT had set up a compound out in the southern suburbs, where trucks would park up for a few days until they were called up for their loads to be cleared by customs. The facilities were good, as next door there was a type of campsite with a pool and a restaurant.

Smudge and I had a clear run down, and by late afternoon we were on the outskirts of Tehran and stuck in a queue not far from customs.

Now very often, when these queues form in the large towns and cities, there is someone wanting to do a 'bit of business' of some sort or another. That day it was money changers. They would walk along the queue looking for foreign trucks and offer to change money. I said no to one guy, so he walked on back to Smudge, who was behind me, and jumped up on to his footstep. It seems that Smudge wanted extra rials, and pulled out his wallet ready to change some currency. Suddenly the queue started to move forward slowly and the bloke saw an opportunity.

While hanging on to the mirror arm with one hand he offered to hold Smudger's wallet while he changed gear. He made no effort to run off with it, but while Smudge was concentrating on driving, managed to substitute a large portion of his European currency for not such a large portion of Iranian rials, then calm as you like gave back the wallet, said his thanks, hopped off the truck and wandered off. By the time Smudge had realised, the guy had disappeared further up the queue. Lesson learned, cost, about £250!

So that night I was parked in the compound with a not very

impressed Mr Leudar-Smith, but hey, you can't keep a good man down, and by the morning it was history as we took a taxi to see our clearing agent, who reckoned on a couple of days at least. Strange how it always took so long, even with two bottles of the hard stuff thrown in. I mean, all we had in our trailers were a pair of doors, and a load of ancillary gear for the preparatory setting up of a cold store. Granted the doors were big, they filled the well in Smudger's trailer, but they were nothing that were important enough to take two days to clear customs, were they? But that was the way it was, the wheels of Middle Eastern bureaucracy only turn very slowly even when oiled by Johnny Walker.

While we were up town I decided to show Smudge a few of the sights like the Golestan Palace, the Azadi Monument, the world famous bazaar and even more importantly have a drink, then it was back to the compound and a couple of hours by the pool.

The following morning we had an almost English-style breakfast in the camp restaurant after which I decided to go to the pool again. Smudge said he was going to clean out his cab as it was a bit untidy. So was mine, I'd do it tomorrow.

Smudge had been gone about five minutes when I heard the sound of tearing metal and shouting coming from the main road which ran alongside the site. With a couple of the other lads I wandered outside to be greeted by a pretty grisly site. A mini-bus had been savagely attacked by the swinging arm of a JCB and the roof had been virtually torn off. There were certainly very seriously injured people in the remains of the little coach but we decided to keep out of the way as there was more than enough help to hand and anyway blood and gore after lunch would have been very unsettling.

It appeared that the truck driver with the JCB on board hadn't secured the arm and bucket of the machine properly and as the bus drove past in the opposite direction the truck had dropped into a pothole. Somehow this had been enough to jog the JCB, releasing the arm which had swung out taking the side of the taxi bus with it. From our vantage point it didn't look a pretty sight, the hubbub was very intense with people milling round all over the place, then the police and ambulances started to arrive. It was time to make ourselves scarce in the sanctity of the camp; you never know we could have got the blame!

At that time I had a favourite piece of jewellery that I wore round my neck virtually all day. Made out of gold, it was a really nice Star of David, quite innocuous I thought, and as I'm Welsh, and St David is the patron saint of Wales, with a bit of lateral thought, I saw no problem with it. But if I went down to any of the Arabian countries I always left it behind.

Anyway there I was sitting by the pool reading an old *Mad Magazine* when a middle-aged couple walked by, stopped in front of me and started chatting in what I thought was Farsi, pointing at my piece of jewellery. They realised I didn't understand, and started talking in broken English, saying they were Jewish, and asking me what part of Israel my parents came from. As soon as I told them I wasn't Israeli, the woman hit the roof, shouting at me, and telling me I had no right to be wearing this sacred piece, that it was a slur on Israel and Zionism when people wore it as a piece of jewellery. That it was hugely important to Jews, and didn't I realise the iconic significance of it? She even tried to reach out for it, but her husband pulled her arm away.

Eventually the ruckus died down and she waved me away with disdain, as only Middle Eastern people can. I was more embarrassed than anything else. To me it was just an attractive piece of jewellery, which I have now passed on to one of my sons, so he can deal with any consequences in the future. It certainly taught me a lesson in how what may seem of little importance to you, can have a much deeper significance to someone else.

Interestingly enough, many of the lads bought gold

artefacts while in the Middle East, as generally speaking it was a cheap buy. I had a gold bracelet made up at Danny's, in the bazaar in Istanbul in 1976 for the princely sum of £136. For his twenty-first birthday I gave my eldest son Lewis the bracelet and he had it valued at £2,000!

A while later Smudger turned up having had enough of cab cleaning and, instead of sunbathing quietly, wanted to mess about in the pool.

'Let's see who can swim furthest underwater,' he said, pushing me with his foot.

'Mess off Leudar, I'm happy doing nothing.'

'Who're you telling to mess off, you little sod?' he said, reaching down to try and pull me into the pool.

'Come on Smudge, don't mess around mate,' I said, scrambling to my feet and trying to get away.

As I started to run off – so Smudger told me later – I slipped on the slabs and hit my head on the ground before slipping into the pool and hitting the bottom head first. Apparently I floated to the top, and Smudge thinking I was messing about, did nothing for a few seconds. Then he realised there was something drastically wrong, at which point he jumped into the pool and fished me out. Luckily he was a big, strong old boy and managed to get me out of the water and on to the side.

Smudge was about to start resuscitation, and *snog* me when I started to come round, belching out water. I reckoned it was the thought of him giving me mouth-to-mouth that brought me to my senses. However there was one important side issue. Blood was running from an open wound on top of my skull, as well as from the side of my head where I had first hit the concrete.

'Bloody hell mate, this leakage ain't gonna stop in a hurry. We're gonna have to find a doctor or a vet.' That was a prescient statement as it turned out.

My head was thumping a bit by now, so Smudge told me

not to move and went off to find the site manager. A couple of minutes later they both came running round the corner, and I thought he was going to faint at the sight of me as he turned a shade of puce and almost went into panic mode.

However he pulled himself together when he realised I wasn't about to croak on him, and together they helped me to his car. Then it was some 'Iranian style' driving to what he called a 'medical centre', somewhere in the suburbs.

That it was a medical centre was not in doubt. There were cubicles all down one side of the room, then halfway along, a full length curtain split the room in two. The other side of the curtain sounded like a vet's surgery. There were certainly animal noises emanating from there. However I didn't care, I had a throbbing headache, and I looked as if I'd been ten rounds with George Foreman and come third.

A man at a desk took down my details, and then directed me to one of the cubicles. Within five minutes two men came into the open cubicle, one was a 'doctor', was he? The other, his assistant. Neither man spoke any English, nor was the 'doctor' that gentle with my head as he started pulling away the congealed hair from around the wound. He then gave instructions to the assistant who picked up a pair of scissors and proceeded to snip the hair away from around the tear, reducing the length, after which I assumed he was going to shave it, but no.

The 'doctor', who had disappeared for about ten minutes to operate on a goat (joke, I hope) came back into the cubicle, inspected my head and then made two injections, one either side of the tear to deaden the pain. Then it was out with the needle and thread and he proceeded to insert four stitches. That *was* painful, as the painkilling injections hadn't taken full effect yet. When he had finished, he said something to his assistant, shook my hand and disappeared, never to be seen again. What he had told the assistant, I later realised, was to cover the wound in iodine to kill any germs. I felt that, even through the numbness of the painkilling injections, and later, as the effect of the painkillers wore off, so the pain from the neat iodine increased.

I don't suppose I was there for more than twenty minutes, and I *still* had dried blood on my face.

Smudger wanted a look, and said: 'Blimey Paul, he's put a top knot in your head.'

'What do you *mean* ... a top knot?'

'Well, they didn't shave all your hair away, and some of it looks like it's been sown into the wound, *and* you've a top knot like some of those young Hindu kids,' he said laughing, as we got back into the car for the ride back to the compound.

The rest of the afternoon was spent in gentle relaxation and recuperation round the pool. After a while Smudge got bored with gentle relaxation and wandered back to the compound.

While I was resting and reading another *Mad Magazine*, a very well-built West Indian guy turned up on the far side of the pool and started to do some yoga-style exercises. He was at it for the best part of half an hour, and very impressive it was too, especially when I found out he was fifty-six! He could have passed for late thirties, no problem. This I learned when he wandered round the pool after he had completed his exercises.

A very interesting bloke, Ron Roberts. He and his wife owned a hotel in Ilfracombe, north Devon. He wasn't a regular on the Middle East run, but over the last couple of years had done a few trips at the end of the English holiday season. He was the most amazing physical specimen of a fifty-six-year-old I have ever seen, and that includes Arnie Schwarzenegger. At that time Ron was on a detox diet, which he told me he completed twice a year, and consisted of seven days of eating *only* boiled rice and water. Delicious or what? He was a genuine guy, and a few years later I booked his hotel for my honeymoon.

Luckily it took three days for the paperwork to be sorted, and by that time my headache had subsided a little. Smudge and I went up to the customs for our loads to be checked, and then it was a couple of hundred miles drive south to Arak to deliver the first load of equipment to the new cold storage complex. A huge amount of tackle was going to be delivered here over the next year, so we expected to be back and forth quite a bit. But, by the time the next load arrived a couple of weeks later, the whole complex had burned down, and they had to rebuild the site all over again.

As for the top knot, I still have the memories and the scar to prove it, and if my hair's cut too short it sprouts out at all angles!

24

Aw Smudger, Don't Do That!

It was summer 1978 and Smudge and I were off on yet another epic trip, this time to Tehran. We'd been doing the job for a while now and felt really settled into it. We always tried to stop at the same places on the way down and back, because at each stopover we knew what to expect. Sounds boring but it made life a lot easier. There were enough complications to deal with anyway so anything that would make the job less stressful was fine by me.

We ran down through the Eastern Bloc as per usual and made good time across Turkey, and within twelve days we were pulling into the Davis Turner compound in Tehran.

There was a good crowd in the compound this trip, and on the second night six of us decided to go into Tehran city for the evening. Most of the guys had done a few trips and knew the ropes, but one of the lads, Gary, was a bit of a pretty boy on his first Middle East adventure.

We took a bus into the city centre, had a wander round some of the shopping malls and bazaars, and bought a few gold trinkets to bring home. Then it was time for a drink. Most truckers aren't hugely enthusiastic about walking, so it doesn't take much persuasion to sniff out a bar and have a sit down.

In the mid-to-late 1970s Tehran was still very much westernised due to the Shah's influence, most of the younger generation wore western-style clothes and played western music. Consumption of alcohol was not frowned upon yet.

It was early evening and we decided to have a look into a few of the hotels just north of what is now Shahr Park and have a beer or two before catching a bus back to the compound later.

Come 10 o'clock we were in our third or fourth or fifth hotel bar. I'd lost track by then, when somehow we were befriended by a guy we assumed to be an Iranian, dressed in the full Arabic thobe and ghutrah, and obviously very wealthy as well, judging by his jewellery and huge diamond-encrusted cufflinks. He just looked the part of a very successful and wealthy Middle Eastern businessman.

It turned out he was from Kuwait and his name was Ahmed. Wealthy? Yes, there were apartments in Tehran, Paris, and a few other places. He seemed like a genuine good bloke and was quite happy to ply us all with drinks for a while, only taking soft drinks himself. What we hadn't realised yet, was that he'd taken a bit of a shine to our young friend Gary, and all this attention he was giving us had an ulterior motive.

By the end of the evening we'd become a bit boisterous and peckish. Trouble is there aren't *too* many Indian takeaways in Tehran, and you know what it's like, lots of beer = must have vindaloo!

So Ahmed says: 'No, no you stay here and we eat in hotel, *after* if is too late, is possible to stay at my apartment.'

Well, we were up for a bit of that all right. We were famished, and Smudge was huge and hugely famished. So we all thanked our kind host profusely, drank a toast to Kuwaiti hospitality and waited to see the outcome.

The guy obviously knew the manager, because in five minutes we were ensconced around a large table in the very plush restaurant perusing the menu in Farsi and pidgin English, which is always good for a laugh.

Our new found Kuwaiti friend had managed to seat himself next to young Gary, not that we were interested or cared. Free drink, free meal, as it turned out, and a free bed for the night. This is why we did the job, for experiences like this. We had a fantastic meal and about midnight we were ready to go. Young Gary had realised he could well be on the menu for afters and spoke to Smudge about his worries.

'Don't worry,' said Smudge, 'someone's got to pay and it might as well be you.' He then broke out into a huge belly laugh at his own joke and a vision of what might happen.

Meanwhile our host had gone off to the bathroom so wasn't aware of the conversation.

Gary was genuinely worried as our wealthy benefactor had made it abundantly clear that he 'liked' him.

'He was touching my leg at the table.'

When we heard this, we all cracked up, as you would. We were half cut and thought it hugely funny.

Ahmed came back and informed us that he had paid for the meal, for which we expressed eternal gratitude and undying devotion to all things Kuwaiti, and asked how we could repay such massive generosity.

'This is not a problem, my friends, I will think of something,' he said.

'Now it is getting late for me and you must rest at my apartment till the morning, this will not be a problem, you have all been very entertaining and this young man here reminds me very much of my young brother.' With that he took Gary by the arm and led us out of the hotel.

'It is only five minutes to walk to my rooms so if you would accompany me we shall go.'

So walk we did, and while we were all laughing and joking in silly mode, poor old Gary was having to put up with the enthusiastic friendship of Ahmed.

The apartment was something else, with a real understated elegance. Not the sort of place us ordinary mortals would normally be frequenting. It was vast with numerous rooms, and one of them had eight or ten mattresses spread around the floor.

'You can sleep here my friends, often I have people sleeping with me.'

We had a quick glance at each other at that remark. He was a kind host and after showing us around his ranch, allowed us to make coffee.

His bedroom was palatial and it was obviously hoping to get some action tonight. Poor young Gary was starting to look a bit peaky, but Smudge told him not to worry as we'd look after him.

About 1 a.m. we all managed to organise ourselves a mattress and were thinking about some shut eye when the bedroom door opened and Ahmed, magnificent in some form of silken bedroom attire, strode across the room and tried to pull Gary to his feet, saying: 'come with me,' with the obvious intention of introducing him to the delights of male to male bonding. With that Smudger lurched to his feet, half cut and swaying like a drunken lamp post. He pointed somewhere in the direction of young Gary and in a slightly slurred baritone voice said: 'Thish ish one very good young man Ahmed, but at the moment he ish not very well, he ish more of a morning man than a night time man, if you know what I mean,' and winked at Ahmed while shaking his hand.

'Ish there anything I can do for you Ahmed?'

This came from a twenty-one stone man of considerable girth and height, who from any perspective would not have been attractive to another man. But hey, what do I know?

Ahmed was clearly extremely miffed.

'No thank you Mr Smudger, I do not require *your* assistance.'

'Shir, you have been more than generous with your hospitality therefore I will personally bring him to you in the morning,' said Smudge still pointing at Gary, whose mouth dropped open with shock. We could hardly contain ourselves.

Clearly still miffed, but slightly reconciled by the offer, he diplomatically decided to withdraw. Mr Terence Leudar-Smith, alias Smudge, was large of body and large of voice, and not someone that Ahmed was going to challenge.

'You are a good and trustworthy man Mr Smudger, I will see him in the morning,' and with that withdrew gracefully from the room.

I was laughing uncontrollably into my rolled-up jacket which I was using as a pillow.

'Thanks Smudge,' said Gary.

'Don't thank me yet,' retorted Smudge, 'just get your Vaseline warmed up ready for the morning.'

'You're kidding me mate, there's no way he's getting anywhere near me.'

'Don't worry Gary, we'll sort it in the morning, now let's get a bit of kip, I'm bloody knackered.'

We let young Gary sleep on a mattress in the middle just in case Ahmed changed his mind and came back. Eventually the room was resounding to extremely loud snoring, most of it Leudar-Smith's, so it was patchy sleep for the rest of us.

About 4 a.m. Smudge stirred. I was on the next mattress, and I heard, 'need the bog'. He was really still in the land of nod, as he staggered to his feet, and *managing* to step over two mattresses, headed across the room to the nearest radiator which was on the far wall.

'Aw Smudger, don't do that, *noooooooooooo*.'

He stood to attention, saluted (ex-army), drew down his zip, extracted his todger and proceeded to urinate all over the radiator. As has been said, Smudge was a big bloke: large bladder, large pee. It sounded like a horse peeing in a trough, like someone had pulled the plug in the swimming pool. It was horrendous, and at that quiet time in the morning, the whole apartment block must have heard.

We were all gobsmacked. Surely Ahmed must have heard *that*. Blithely, Smudger finished urinating, shook his todger and packed it away. He then turned and made his way back to his mattress. The rest of us were wide awake by this time, and as he started to lay himself down to sleep again, I was urgently shaking him and telling him to, '*wake up for God's sake*,' trying hard to whisper.

It was like trying to raise the dead. Eventually he started to wake up, and by that time we were all stood round him still in a state of shock.

'Wassup mate? Put the kettle on there's a good bloke.'

'Sshhh, Smudge, *get up*, you've just peed all over Ahmed's wall, radiator and carpet, and rather a lot of pee at that.'

He was now starting to come round and began to realise the seriousness of the situation.

'It wasn't *me*, was it?'

There was a whispered chorus of: 'Yes.'

'Well then chaps, I think it's time to make a swift and silent exit stage right. What say you?' . . . He was incorrigible.

At 5 a.m. we all crept out of the apartment with shoes or boots in hand and made good our escape. We walked for an hour in a state of high spirits until the early morning sun started to poke its fingers over the horizon, and we were able to flag down a mini-bus to take us back to the compound.

What a night!

25

Human Frailty!

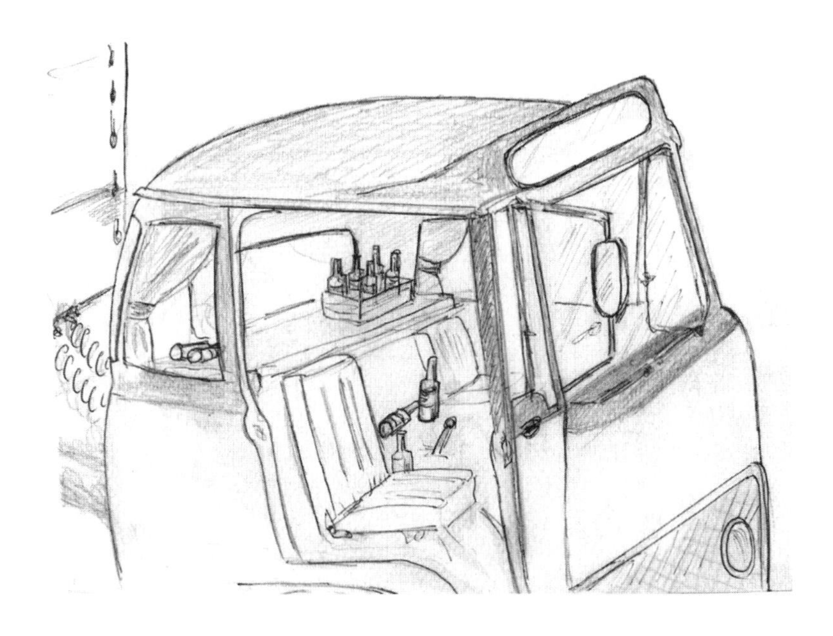

I write this story because I was involved in it and it's a difficult tale to tell as it highlights a case where human frailty can be more than dangerous in a potentially hostile environment.

Early in 1977, Tony Waugh called Freddie Grimble and me into the office. We were both due to be shipping out from Felixstowe on Sunday night for Tehran.

'Look guys we would appreciate you playing mother hen to a couple of subcontractors going to Tehran and Khorramshah. They're both called Jim and have never been on a Middle East trip before, so would benefit from a bit of "coaching" on the way down.'

'Bloody hell Tony, that's all I seem to do these days, is play at being a shepherd. You're sending me and Fred to Tehran. Do you want us to take one of them all the way down to Khorramshah as well?'

We weren't going to say no; we always had this banter. He was a good bloke Tony, and anyway new drivers always added a bit of interest.

'Yeah yeah, very bloody funny, by the time you get to Iran they'll be confident enough to finish the job off themselves thank you, and anyway at least one of them was driving trucks on the continent before you were eating solid food.'

According to Tony, one of the drivers, Jim M, was a bloke who used to be the transport manager at Fridged Freight out at Diss, a well-known continental haulage company, and the other was his very good friend, another Jimmy, who had also been a driver there.

Tony had told us that Jim M had started off as a driver for Fridged Freight back in the late 1950s, running continental trips to Italy in AECs and Scammells, when the only way to ferry a truck over to Europe was for the whole vehicle to be lifted by crane into the cargo hold of a freighter. No roll on, roll off ferries back then!

I wondered what with this guy's history and knowledge of continental work what the hell was I going to be able to teach him with my limited experience.

'However,' said Tony, 'Jim M hasn't driven abroad for a number of years and would appreciate some knowledgeable company and you're all that's left. Scraping the barrel I know, but there you are.'

Jim M came with a fearsome reputation as having been a very hard taskmaster during his time as transport manager, and as I was to find out later, his hard attitude was in part due to his role in the army at the end of the Second World War, when as a soldier in the 3rd Battalion, Parachute Regiment, part of his function was to escort officers of the Third Reich to the gallows! In later life this was something that came to haunt him quite a bit.

So with all this remarkable history, and as one of the pioneers in the world of continental trucking, it was a bit of a surprise to see them roll up at Trans UK driving old Volvo F86s, which, though good trucks in their own right, were not ideal for this type of work. At Trans UK the furthest Bob would send them was Istanbul.

On the Sunday we were introduced to both men and given our documents for the trip. Both were quite a bit older than us but came across as very amenable and more than happy that we would be running together.

The first couple of days were fine. We were running Commie Bloc, into Czechoslovakia at Waidhaus. On the second night we stopped at Hans' restaurant at Bor and spent the evening having a few Pils with him and his wife. I noticed Jim putting away quite a few shorts on top of what we were drinking. Later as we said goodnight to everyone, we agreed on a seven o'clock start the following morning.

At 6 a.m. Fred and I were up and about, having a wash and brush up ready for a brew before we hit the road. Around 6.30 I knocked on both the Jims' doors to offer a cup of tea and tell them we were going to make a move in half an hour. Jimmy emerged from his cab a few minutes later, scrubbed up and joined us for a cuppa.

'Where's your mate then?' I asked.

'He'll be up in a little while,' said Jimmy. 'Had a few last night and didn't get to sleep too early.'

As it was the first time, I let it go and waited till Jim M finally surfaced looking a bit the worse for wear at about 9.30 a.m. We had a few words as I expressed my disappointment, and that he, being an experienced continental driver, surely knew the importance of trying to keep to a schedule, especially on a trip of this length.

'Righto let's get on with it,' said Jim, climbing straight into his cab.

'Great, we should be able to make up for lost time.'

However, within an hour Jim wanted to stop for a brew as he'd missed the one we had earlier. This took two hours. All the time I was building up a head of anger and frustration. I was already beginning to realise he didn't really want to be there and this could be a trip of epic proportions.

That night we reached Brno after a number of unplanned stops. Jim M kept asking if everything was going to be OK. He'd heard lots of stories about the Middle East, not all of them good, so we needed to be careful. I remember trying to ease his worries and said we'd have to have an early start the following morning, about 5 a.m. have a quick cuppa and be away to try and make up for lost time.

No chance! I was up at 4.30 a.m. making a cuppa with Fred, and knocked on Jim's cab door. Zero response.

I woke up the other Jimmy who said: 'Sorry mate, he won't be up for a while yet. Had a few shots last night.'

It was then it dawned on me. We could have a major problem on our hands: only day four and likely to have an 'alky' in our midst.

'What's the score Jimmy,' I said. 'You've done more miles than I've had hot dinners, so you know how difficult this job can be at the best of times, and where we're going isn't Italy, however difficult that might have been back in the 1950s.'

'Sorry mate, Jim likes a drink or two and is obviously worried about this trip.'

At midday Jim M surfaced and very little communication took place. I was finding this difficult. I was twenty-nine, Freddie was twenty-six. These guys were in their mid-fifties and had a wealth of life and driving experience. Were they going to listen to me, a whippersnapper? Bob had said to look after them as it was their first trip, so that's what we were going to try and do.

By the end of that day we had managed to cross the border

into Hungary at Rajka and made it to the service area at the end of the motorway, just before you dropped into Budapest. At that time the Budapest ring road hadn't even been started.

Jim M wasn't prepared to go any further.

'Had a good day today and need a drink.'

When I opened his cab door later that evening I could see a large number of whisky bottles dotted around. I thought this guy isn't going to finish this trip. Fred and I had a chat and decided to telex back home at the first opportunity to let them know of the situation. In total we had already lost a good day and as much as I didn't want to let Bob down I could see this turning into a disaster.

As it happened, the next day we were away by 8 a.m. and things went reasonably well. In fact, we made it to the National in Belgrade. Not a huge day, but better. That night Jim was in his element, chatting to other drivers about his experiences and loving it. He also had a faceful.

The following morning about 11 a.m. we managed to get rolling again. Jim was feeling a bit bullish after the previous night's entertainment, that is until just north of Nis, where he had a close encounter with a Turkish gastarbeiter on his way home to Turkey in an ancient Opel Kapitan. Nothing happened, but it was a very close shave, and we had to pull into the next lay-by to recuperate.

Bela Pelanca was as far as we got that night. We stopped at a roadside restaurant, and then the drinking started. It was horrendous. Until now, Jim had kept his drinking to the privacy of his own cab, but now he didn't seem to care. And as soon as we got back to our cabs after dinner he was offering all and sundry drink after drink. The whole trip was turning into a disaster, and how drunk was he when he was driving? I daren't even contemplate it. I kept thinking: what if he has an accident out here? They'd lock him up and throw away the key. His mate Jimmy was as good as gold and tried to encourage Jim M to ease up on the whisky, but he was having none of it.

It had got to the stage now that Jim M wouldn't drive at night just in case he got involved in a pile- up. He was really shot away, and could easily become a danger to himself as well as everyone else.

I asked Jimmy how a bloke with such a tremendous history of experiences had ended up this way. His response was that it had been a slow process, and that Jim's background since the war, with the Nuremburg trials and all that entailed, had preyed on his mind, slowly eating away at him. Jimmy also reckoned that the very inflexible exterior he presented hid a slightly softer centre, which very rarely showed itself. 'All I can do is be here for him,' said Jimmy.

My feeling was that Jim, for all his years of experience in transport, and before, was actually a little scared and didn't want to be here. He was continually worried that something was going to go wrong.

We managed to get him roused and into the driving position at about 10 a.m the next morning after a very large strong black coffee and decided to make sure that Jim M drove third in our little convoy and that we would overtake other vehicles as little as possible.

That day we managed to transit the Yugo/Bulgarian border at Dimitrovgrad and after a slow drive down to Plovdiv, Jim decided he'd had enough for the day.

To be honest I'd had it up to here, and was all for leaving him to rot. We'd had a number of rows by now and I was almost at the end of my tether.

I remember him saying: 'I used to be a terror to my drivers and they got away with nothing while I was in charge', and thinking it's a pity you don't apply some of that discipline to yourself then mate.

It was another night of whisky and very little food. This guy must have had the constitution of a buffalo, no actually, a herd of buffaloes.

By this time we were almost three days behind schedule

and still hadn't reached Istanbul. Jimmy was still trying to encourage him to keep going. 'It'll be better tomorrow Jim.'

Midday the following day we were on the move again and made it down to Kapitan Andreevo where we joined the queue and waited and waited and eventually got through first thing in the morning. Virtually the whole night, Jimmy had sat with Jim, trying to stop him drinking. Kapicule would not have been a good place to have been found drunk in charge of a truck. By mid-morning we had cleared through Young Turk and Jim, though tired, was sober.

'Look guys, whatever happens we are going to get to the Londra today, OK?'

Five and a half hours later we rolled into the Mocamp and the relief ebbed over me. I felt as if we had won a war.

The plan was that we would have a day off and then move on. Jim M was a new man and looking forward to the next part of the trip.

I telexed back to Trans UK and told Tony of our problems. His response was: 'OK, but if they *don't* leave with you tomorrow, you leave without them. *Is that understood?* They will have to make their own way down, they're subbies and responsible for themselves. We can't afford to lose any more time on this trip.'

So no day off for us then, great!

We told the two Jims what Tony had said, and they appeared to be OK with it, so at 9 a.m. the following day I knocked on Jim's cab and managed to rouse him. Jimmy was already up and wandered over.

'Are you ready Jim, time to go mate?'

'No Paul, we're staying over for a couple of days. You go on and we'll catch you up.'

I knew then that was never going to happen.

And that was that. Jimmy, God bless his soul, true to his friendship, stayed with Jim M. There was nothing more we could do, the whisky was in control, so Freddie and me saddled up and disappeared into the sunset, sadder and wiser so to speak.

Would we ever see them again?

For thirty years I had wondered what had happened to the two Jims, and then recently I had a contact through a website with Jim M's youngest son who was able in some way to bring the story full circle and to a sort of conclusion.

It appears that during the next few days after us leaving the two of them in Istanbul, that they managed to get away and reached Ankara. But that was it. For the next week or so Jim put his liver and kidneys to the sword and was virtually permanently drunk.

Eventually, so it seems, some sanity prevailed or maybe the drink was starting to run out, and Jim M managed to get himself as far as Erzincan, where, according to the man himself, the differential on his truck broke and as the weather was very cold and wintry, he booked himself into a local hotel. While going for a shower, he slipped and cracked his skull on the masonry and ended up in Erzurum hospital for a number of months, recuperating, leaving the not so little problem of what to do with Jim's truck and load.

This predicament only related to Turkey in that once you entered the country your vehicle details were entered on your passport, and once this had happened it was only you who could take the truck across the border. Though not insurmountable, it was a long and convoluted procedure to have the vehicle taken off one passport and entered on to another. It also required a person to be in Turkey to complete the relevant documentation.

Bob's problem was that as both Jims were sub-contractors, in the final analysis Trans UK was responsible for the load. A huge amount of expense was incurred in sorting out the whole mess and the loads were eventually delivered.

Jim's eldest son, also Jimmy, flew out to Istanbul to bring his father back. At the airport while looking for his father,

Jimmy jnr was accosted by a very 'hairy hippy', and not recognising him, Jimmy jnr advised him to mess off, or else. It turned out to be his dad, so covered in facial hair as to be unrecognisable.

Jim M's reputation was at one time huge, but it doesn't matter how big or brave your history is, once the dreaded booze takes hold it's a downward spiral. It is also a lesson in what a sobering experience it is for those who are helplessly caught up in it.

As for Fred and I, we got to Tehran without any more fuss and telexed back to the UK. Tony told us that Jim M was still at the Mocamp, and that we were to carry on as they were dealing with it. Our instructions were that I had to reload in southern Germany, and Fred had to go on to reload out of the Ruhr.

We had a comfortable run back up to Bazargan and a quick passage through into Turkey then as we left the border heading for Agri, Fred's injector pump started playing up. In the end it gave up the ghost completely and I had to tow him on a rigid bar across the rest of Turkey to Istanbul.

This was an exercise fraught with danger especially when the 'kamikaze' bus drivers decided they wanted to overtake, usually at the most inopportune moment and often when another vehicle was approaching from the opposite direction. Of course halfway past, the driver, sorry 'pilot', dressed in the 'uniform', peaked cap, dark sunglasses etc, would realise Fred and I were joined by our umbilical cord, the bar, and you could see panic set in as the assistant driver and stick waver quickly opened the rear door, leaned out frantically waving us to slow down, while futilely bashing our truck with his stick, a la *Fawlty Towers*. Of course we always did slow down otherwise there would have been many an accident to blame on the western trucker.

On our eventual arrival at Istanbul we headed for Aydin's, the 'mechanical magician', who would work night and day to affect a repair on your wagon. And he did - the following day Fred's wagon was once again roadworthy.

Turkish engineering in general was miraculous to behold and they would do anything to keep their beloved Tonkas on the road. There were many tales of prop shafts and half shafts being dropped into a blacksmith's forge and brought back to life. Not always perfectly symmetrical you understand and maybe with a little vibration, but more often than not, after a fashion, they worked.

26

10,000 Miles of Excitement!

We were off again. At the end of November 1978, John was going to Istanbul with a load of second hand tractors and I was heading for Bandar Abbas, right on the Straits of Hormuz, at the bottom end of the Persian Gulf. This was to be my furthest trip, 10,000 miles there and back and 1,000 miles past Tehran. Some of the other lads had been up through Afghanistan to Pakistan, but this was as close as I was getting, about 750 miles as the crow flies from Karachi.

Once again we were into winter, so enthusiasm wasn't as high as it might have been in the spring, but hey, that's the way it was. By now I was a reasonably seasoned traveller and

I would be able to cope with most things the job could throw at me.

This was my second trip that winter. The first was to Tabriz, and the weather, though cold and snowy, was nowhere near as bad as it had been three years previously.

As usual it was out through the Eastern Bloc at Weidhaus where we picked up quite a bit of snow, and even had to fit the snow chains just to get up through the Czech side of the border. By now the customs personnel in the communist part of the world were much less strict in their dealings with western European drivers, and you could usually drift through in around an hour or so. I hadn't run en route with John before. He was a nice guy; our paths had crossed a couple of times at places like the Mocamp and Belgrade, and it made a nice change to have him as a running partner.

Driving down through Czechoslovakia and Hungary into Romania we had a trouble-free passage. It was very cold, down to -15C with occasional light snow, but for those two or three days there was enough traffic to keep the roads clear. And further south there was hardly any snow lying at all.

At Brezoi, about fifty miles north of Pitesti, rounding a bend we noticed a lone British truck parked in a large lay-by. We turned round and pulled in beside him. I thought I had recognised the vehicle, and sure enough it was an old mate.

'Gloopy you old bugger, how's it going?' I said as I jumped out of my cab to shake his hand.

'Hello Paul,' he said rather gloomily. 'Bloody truck's frozen up and won't start; I've been waiting for someone to come by for the last twenty-four hours, I'm bloody freezing.'

Gloopy, proper name Martin, was a really nice guy, so named for his lack of ability in the cooking department. Everything he tried always turned into a gloopy sticky mess. Martin and I had met up and run together a few times in the past. He was an owner driver and his vehicle of choice was a battered old 1924 Mercedes.

'Where are you off to then Gloops?'

'Supposed to be Salonica,' he said. 'I pulled in here yesterday for a bite to eat and when I tried to start my little darling after lunch she didn't want to know. Luckily my gas bottle is, or was full, otherwise I would have frozen last night.'

Martin had been doing this job quite a while now so I was surprised he hadn't tried the usual stuff to get her fired up.

'Where's all your winter stuff then mate?' I said.

'Yes I know, stupid me, I left it in my other trailer and forgot to transfer it over.'

'Well done you silly old fart, we'll see what we've got.'

John and I had our winter gear with us and we were quickly able to heat up his air tanks with our paint stripper guns, and then drain them off through the drain tap, before topping up his alcohol bottle. Meanwhile Martin checked the radiator coolant which seemed OK but when he went to start his truck on the key, no joy, as the engine gave just a couple of half-hearted turns before the dreaded click, click, click of a dying battery.

'Got any jump leads, Paul?' he said.

The one thing we didn't have was jump leads.

'OK, if you could blow my brakes off maybe you could give me a bump start on the bar.'

'Righty oh mate.'

So that's what we did. John hooked up his red air line to Gloopy's trailer and released the brakes.

'Nearly there,' he reckoned. 'Now if one of you guys could hook me up to your tow bar and pull me down the lay-by I'll try and get it into gear and bump start the old bugger.'

John had a decent tow hitch on the back of his trailer so he hooked up and pulled Martin down the lay-by. He managed to find a gear, but as he released the clutch, disaster struck with a loud bang. John immediately stopped to find out the cause of the noise.

We didn't have to look very far to see that a large section of metal plate had been blown out of the side of the gearbox. Very little oil was running out; in fact it reminded me a bit of his cooking. It was congealed and had thickened up so much with the cold that when Gloops released the clutch to engage a gear the pressure inside the box was so great that the side wall blew out.

'Fuck! That's buggered it,' said John.

'Aw, shite, I don't believe it,' said Martin when he saw the mess.

'Fuck it, that's not a repair, that's a new gearbox.'

Poor bloke, he was almost in tears. What could he do? First, it was now impossible to tow him anywhere. Second, he couldn't stay with the wagon in these wintry conditions, and third he'd most probably have to get a replacement gearbox from somewhere - but where?

'Look mate, there's nothing we can do here, *we* can't repair this,' I said, 'and you certainly can't stay here, it's absolutely freezing cold and the middle of winter. Look, you know what I think of Romtrans, they've been very helpful to me in times of trouble so I reckon if we take you down to Pitesti and pop into the Romtrans depot there, they might be able to help.'

'Yeh OK, it's worth a try,' he said resignedly.

With that he drew his curtains round and locked his cab, at least no one was going to steal the old beast.

There was a young girl in the Romtrans office who could understand English pretty well and when Gloops explained his dilemma she called in one of the managers and translated the conversation.

They were brilliant and with much nodding of the head during the discussion, offered to send a fitter back up to Brezoi the following day to assess the situation.

That night we stayed with Martin in a ropey old hotel, which served up a pretty ropey old dinner of potato and cabbage topped with some brown water and washed down by some ropey old local beer. The one bonus was that he felt a little better about the situation now.

In the morning it was only a five-minute drive back to the Romtrans yard. We hung around for an hour or so until things were sorted out and the fitters were ready to take Martin back to his truck. Then we said goodbye and left him in the more than capable hands of *'F troop'* Pitesti.

I met him a couple of years later in Dover and he said they had towed the truck on a wrecker down to Pitesti the following day, and then welded a plate on the side of the gearbox to effect a repair. I never saw the repair so could only believe the story, and why wouldn't I? In countries like Romania and Turkey, running repairs were the norm, and their engineers were renowned for their ingenuity.

It seems that in the intense cold, cast metal can become less consistent and under extreme pressure will shatter relatively easily. I speak not as an expert, but after listening to bar-room 'engineering experts'.

From then on, other than a heavy fall of snow over Stara Zagora in Bulgaria, for which we had no option other than to chain up, John and I had a trouble-free trip down to Istanbul.

For a change, as John was clearing and tipping on the Asian side of the Bosporus, we stayed over at Harem Hotel for the night. It was a good place and many of the 'long in the tooth' Middle East drivers stayed there. This was the place to come if you wanted up to date information on what was happening further down the line.

Once you'd parked up down near the quayside, you'd try and sneak up to the hotel before the young kids started to polish your trainers off your feet. These kids were remarkable. Some were as young as seven or eight, working just to live. They reminded me of street urchins and could have jumped straight out from the pages of a Dickensian novel. As soon as there was any sign of movement, it would be 'shoeshine collega, shoeshine,' as they trotted up with their large wooden boxes hanging off their shoulders, full of polishes, brushes, and dusters. Sometimes the boxes were nearly as big as the kids, and savvy? They'd get you virtually anything you wanted, should you ask, including their sister!

After a pleasant night at the Harem, John and I said cheerio, and I hooked up with Les, an owner driver, going as far as Ankara, before he headed south to Kuwait. An Astran guy on his way back from Iran had said there was quite a bit of snow the other side of Ankara, especially between Erzurum and Horasan.

A couple of days later I was running on my own and ran into heavy snow at Yozgat which continued through virtually non-stop to Sivas and most of the time was spent on snow chains, so progress was slow. Dropping down a steep bank, I spotted a guy waving at me from the edge of the road. There was a snow-covered Saviem truck parked close by so I assumed he was the driver and pulled over to see what the matter was. I could see the number plate now and realised he was French.

'*Bonjour m'sieur*,' he said. 'Hi speak liddle English, *parlez vous Francais*?'

'*Un peu*,' I said. '*Qu'est que c'est?*' (A little - what's the matter?)

Between us, he got me to understand that he had stopped here to brew up a coffee about five hours ago and been unable to restart his truck, and now the battery was flat. He was freezing cold and could I give him a jump start with his leads. I felt a bit of déjà vu at this point!

'*Pas problem m'sieur*.'

I pulled up alongside his unit, so we were battery to battery so to speak and attached the cables. With that he tried to start his truck - nothing, not a murmur, so we checked the terminals, and the connections seemed good. We messed around for a while, changed the leads around, anything to see why it wouldn't turn over, but still nothing, not a peep.

While we were trying to get him started a Friedrich's truck from Switzerland pulled alongside and offered to try, so I pulled out of the way, and wouldn't you know it, as soon as the cables were connected to him the engine swung over and kicked into life. That was good news anyway, so I left them to it as they were running back empty, and climbed back into my truck.

I'd only driven a couple of miles when I noticed my ignition warning light on. What was this all about? Don't tell me that my trying to help the French guy had knocked out my electrics? If so the batteries would be drained by the end of the day, which would mean no electrics at all and *no heater* - bugger.

Back in the days before all the newfangled electronic devices fitted to modern vehicles, if your diesel engine was running, no electrical input was required to keep it running, so it was now the time to remember the old adage, whatever else - *Do not switch your engine off.*

It was after the climb over Refahiye that I began to notice the heater dying and the cab getting colder. Checking the indicators, they were only giving off a weak signal. I needed to think. Luckily, I was through this range of hills and on the reasonably gentle drop down into Erzincan. As soon as I could I stopped to take the chains off and hung them out to 'dry' under the side of the trailer. I'd have to plan for an early stop tonight before the light got too bad.

Managing to find a reasonable place to park at Tercan, I quickly got the gas bottle alight. This would give me respite from the cold for a few hours until I went to bed. After a cordon bleu meal of chicken soup with beans, and topped up with the ubiquitous instant mash, I felt a lot better. The cab was a lot warmer, and the engine was ticking over nicely even though not giving me heat.

Tomorrow, all things being equal, I'd get to a garage in Erzurum that I'd used once before on a previous trip when my gear selectors jammed and see if they could help me.

That night I kept all my clothes on and put one sleeping bag inside the other. My main bag was supposed to be good for -20C. I'd find out tonight! I took out my contact lenses, switched off the gas bottle, pulled the hood tight round my head and tried to sleep. The temperature outside was certainly -20C, hopefully the engine wouldn't die on me before morning.

It was a very fitful night's sleep, I'm not sure I had any, maybe a catnap or two, and even in my super duper sleeping bag I felt the chill. I must have dozed off in the early hours of the morning, because when I awoke it was daylight. The problem was I couldn't see out. All the windows of the cab were covered in ice, on the inside as well as out! Not only that, my contact lenses were frozen in their solution. What now? Even if I could light the gas bottle, it would struggle to clear all this ice away.

Still wrapped in my sleeping bag, it was an effort to get into the driver's seat, but I wasn't getting out of it until I knew the gas bottle would light. It was mind-numbingly cold, but at least the engine was still running. Eventually I managed to squeeze myself into the driver's seat making sure I kept my feet away from the exhaust brake. If I stepped on that it would be disaster as the engine would immediately cut out.

Finding my lighter, I turned on the Calor gas bottle. Bollocks, there was very little gas coming out, so I flicked the lighter switch and the small flame was picked up by the gas bottle, but the flame was so low as to be almost indistinguishable. What now? I could be in the poo here.

Then for some reason or other, and I don't know to this day why, I leaned over and turned off the ignition key and then turned it back on again.

Hallelujah! The Great Electrician in the Sky had come to save me. As I took my hand off the key, hot air roared out of the vents. I switched on the eight-track, and it worked! Within ten minutes water was running down the inside of the windows as the heater did its job and defrosted the cab. I was ecstatic and felt a huge weight lifted off my shoulders. The thought had crossed my mind that this was going to be 1976 all over again. Luckily not!

Later, when I had a chance to ask an electrician what had gone wrong, he said there was a good chance that the Frenchman's truck batteries were positive earth, while mine were negative or vice versa and if that was the case it most probably knocked out a regulator which, when I turned the key on and off, reset itself. Who knows? I just thanked God for his intervention.

This was fast becoming an 'interesting' trip!

Eventually I sorted myself out, had the magic brew and was ready to roll at 10 a.m.

Around 1 p.m. and climbing the hill out of Erzurum, I watched as a German wagon and drag dropped down the hill from the other direction. The road was covered in slushy snow and I could see he was going much too fast to negotiate the roundabout at the bottom. It was one of those situations when you knew before it happened that here was an accident in the making.

The driver must have forgotten the roundabout existed. At the last second realisation must have hit home and he obviously applied his brakes, because as I watched open mouthed, the whole outfit crumpled up as the trailer jack-knifed round, and pulling the truck with it, truck and trailer mounted the roundabout virtually sideways, bumping and bouncing across the raised grass centre then as if in slow motion the trailer toppled over and both halves of the outfit came to rest facing back the way they had just come, but with the trailer on its side.

I stopped my truck and as quickly as I could made my way across to the stricken vehicle, just as two more outfits from the same company came into view and in low gear crept slowly down the hill. I checked that the driver was OK and asked what had happened. For a moment or two he was too stunned to say anything, then slowly he focused on me and shook his head.

Apparently it was as I'd thought. He had forgotten the roundabout was there and by the time it had registered in his brain, it was too late. His mates had pulled up by then, so I left them to sort out a tricky situation.

Back in my truck I moved on from Erzurum heading for Horasan and the infamous climb over Tahir. For the next sixty miles the road ran across a flat plateau at about 4,000 feet. The snow between Pasinler and Horasan lay up to two feet deep at the side of the road and there was enough snow and ice so that the road surface wasn't visible, but there was no traffic at all and visibility was good, so I plodded on at a steady 30mph not wanting to stop and fit the snow chains unless I had to.

This was a big country and as far as the eye could see in any direction there was, snow, snow and more snow. It was one of those times when everything felt good, when you felt at one with the world. For me these moments often happened in times of solitude, when you could be the only person for hundreds of miles around.

Little did I know that this last twenty-four hours of excitement hadn't yet come to an end.

Half an hour later, in the distance behind me, I spotted another vehicle slowly closing with me and within ten minutes it had caught up. I could see it was an Astran wagon and drag so I eased over and slowed down to let him pass.

Now the problem with these snow-covered roads was that with a two-foot snow bank either side, it was impossible to judge the actual width of the road surface. As I felt for the edge with my right front wheel the Astran truck came by me with a thank you blast on his air horns. At that same moment I knew I had gone past the point of no return and my unit was starting to slip down into the snow bank. Panic!

As luck would have it by now I was only doing 15mph, and with the snow acting as a buffer I came to a stop very quickly with the cab at a 45 degree angle down the bank and embedded in a drift. The Astran driver, Pete, had spotted what had happened and stopped about forty yards ahead. He quickly reversed to see if he could help. There was no way I was getting out of this on my own. I certainly couldn't drive forward as I was stuck in the deep snow, and I wouldn't be able to reverse out even with chains on. So precarious was the position of the unit that all I would do was slide further down the bank.

We had a conflab and decided he would reverse behind me and attach a tow rope to the towing eye on the back of my trailer and try to pull me out the way I had gone in. This is the perceived wisdom in situations like this. Pete had already got his snow chains on so traction wouldn't be a problem. Slowly but surely he reversed up the road dragging me out backwards and with the sweat of tension pouring off me, even in this cold, five minutes later I was back on terra firma. Lucky old me, very lucky old me! For a while there I could have been just another accident statistic on the Middle East run.

The whole time we had been there, about half an hour, not one other vehicle had come past, very easy to feel isolated out there. Solitude was fine, but isolation?

I thanked him and offered to buy dinner at the café in Eleskirt that night should we get there. He was up for that and gave me a hand to put my chains on for the crossing of Tahir Mountain.

The climb over was uneventful at least, with no sign of the kids. Mostly, they kept away from the roadside in winter, though on a sunny winter's day they had been known to make their presence felt with the odd boulder or two – lovely kids! Then it was down the other side to Eleskirt, and a stop for the night at the restaurant. There were a couple of Tonkas there already. Anyway true to my word, I paid for the grub as we watched the snow start to fall again through the misted-up windows.

With my heater restored and on its very best behaviour, I had a very comfortable night's sleep and woke up to a cold, bright and sunny morning. The snow had stopped, and after checking round the truck and making sure the chains were still in one piece we pulled out for Bazargan, about ninety miles away. Considering the conditions we made reasonable time, and four hours later arrived at the border.

Looking down into Iran from the top of the Turkish escarpment the roads looked clear and Pete hoped to be in Tabriz today. I thanked him once again for his help and we said our goodbyes. He was a nice guy and I never saw him again, which was the way more often than not. Occasionally you'd catch up with someone on a regular basis, usually at one of the popular stopovers, but such was the diversity of destination, and so huge were the distances involved that the chances of being somewhere on the same day at the same time as a buddy were pretty remote.

Eventually I was through into Iran and heading to Bandar Abbas still another 1,600 miles to the south east. At Marand I pulled into the police checkpoint and over the weighbridge, only to find that they thought there was a discrepancy with my load weight. After calling the Chef and a further discussion they accepted that my full belly tank was most probably the cause, 300 gallons weighed 3,000lb, which was about the difference. Strange, because I'd never had that query before or after, and I'd never known them to check that thoroughly either.

My aim was to try and get to Takestan that night. It would be late, past midnight, but that would allow me two more days to hit Bandar and get my paperwork in. The weather conditions had improved and the roads were clear even though there was plenty of snow about.

I got held up for two hours at Miyaneh: the scene of a horrific accident, with one truck ploughing into the back of another. The truck that had done the ploughing was an ancient, long-bonneted International which was carrying a load of steel, some lengths of which were in excess of eighty feet! There was no sign of a headboard at the front of his trailer to protect the cab, so when he had hit the rear of the other truck the load of steel had shot forward with huge force and gone straight through the cab and was in fact embedded in the rear of the vehicle in front. No part of the cab was recognisable and I would think the driver would have had at the very least a severe headache! In fact he would have been very dead! Health and safety wasn't an issue in this part of the world as it didn't actually exist. All was in God's hands, and it was a good job he had big ones the way they loaded their trucks and drove them.

I had to stop south of Miyaneh. I couldn't go any further. It was 11 p.m. and I was absolutely knackered.

Driving at night in this part of the world could be a very hit and miss affair. The Iranians, Saudis, Jordanians, Pakistanis, Koreans, Uncle Tom Cobley, in fact every trucker in the Middle East loved their lights, and the more colours the better. Much to our consternation there never seemed to be any rhyme, reason or pattern in the way they were used.

Overtaking at night could be a very precarious operation.

For example you might be driving behind another vehicle looking for an opportunity to overtake, and looking up ahead you see in the distance a set of red lights, often interspersed with other colours, so you would pull out thinking that the lights you could see were the rear lights of another truck going in the same direction. Suddenly, halfway past the vehicle you were overtaking there would be a blinding flash of headlights as the truck you thought was going in the same direction as you was actually a truck rapidly bearing down on you from the opposite direction, with his headlights now on full beam! It was, either slam on the anchors and hope to get back in behind the truck you were passing, or swerve out on to the scrubland and hope there were no rocks or potholes in the way. Either way it was a real 'make sure you'd got the right coloured shorts on' sort of situation. Most unnerving, and bloody suicidal! I got caught out like this a number of times.

Even though it was midnight before I got to sleep, I was up at 5 a.m. and after a quick cup of tea and a few stale biscuits, was on the road. It was still about a thousand miles to Bandar, and I wanted to be there the following night, if at all possible. There was very little snow now, though it was still very cold. Down on the Gulf it would be at least 25C I reckoned. A bit of sunshine would do me a power of good.

By 10 a.m. I was around Tehran, and heading down towards Iran's most holy city, Qom, where I stopped for bite to eat and a bottle of Coke from a roadside stall. The sun was shining and there was a spring-like feel to the air. Maybe it just wasn't that cold. About midday I was back on the road and hooked up behind a convoy of seven French trucks for around three and a half hours before they pulled off into Esfahan. With a blast from my air horns, I went past them only to be nearly blown off the road by the volume of the response.

Even though I was still travelling through the hills and valleys of the southern mountains, it was getting noticeably warmer. I'd had a brilliant day's driving and covered 630 miles, stopping outside Abadeh, a small town between Esfahan and Shiraz.

I'd only seen two other Brits all day, and they were going the other way. The following morning I had another early start and leaving Shiraz behind I had only about 320 miles to go (London–Carlisle). I should knock that off pretty quickly. With about fifty miles to go and the weather improving by the mile, I dropped off the plateau, out of the hills and on to the arid semi-desert scrubland leading to Bandar Abbas. Here the temperature was up into the high twenties and I soon had my window wound down.

I was loaded with machine parts for a textile company down near the docks, and as I approached Bandar, I stopped at a filling station to top up and get directions. When I finally got someone to understand, a passenger in another truck on the forecourt offered to jump in with me and direct me. What nice people, these Bandaris! It was a good job I did have company because as we entered Bandar a heavy fog drifted in over the town, and without his assistance I would have struggled. As it was he guided me straight to the factory and when he jumped out I realised his mate had followed us down in his truck. That *was* a genuine kindness; I passed round some packets of ciggies and said my thanks as a couple of guys came out from the reception, introduced themselves and took all my documentation.

'Tomorrow will be underloaded,' said one of the gentlemen. Now that was good news.

I asked if there was a shower. 'No,' but there was a washroom, with vast tin sinks, so I made the best of that and felt pretty refreshed by the time I had finished my ablutions. I couldn't park outside the factory and as far as I could tell it was only about a quarter of a mile to the quayside. So I drove down towards the southern end of the dock, where I found a piece of rough ground out of harm's way.

Here I was, 5,103 miles from home looking out over the Straits of Hormuz, the gateway to the Gulf. The mist had cleared and as far as the eye could see in either direction were hundreds of fishing boats bobbing up and down on their moorings. It was a most unexpected and remarkable sight.

True to his word, the following afternoon I was 'underloaded', and ready for the return leg of this odyssey.

My instructions were to get back to Yugoslavia, pick up a load of bicycles from Sarajevo, and try to get home for Christmas, so it was up sticks and try to get a couple of hundred miles under my belt that night.

Before long the 25C temperature was a distant memory, and four days later I was back in the cold and snow of central north Turkey about to get myself into another fix.

The roads were pretty clear and had been recently scraped by a grader, and other than putting the chains on for Tahir, I had managed with little trouble to reach the bottom of the climb up Refahiye. As I was empty I thought the climb wouldn't be that difficult as it was pretty straightforward, about 6,500 feet with no real hairpins.

Then, close to the top, on a particularly icy stretch, I started to lose traction. It was cold, getting dark and not a good time to be messing around with snow chains. I came to a halt close by a six foot high snow wall and put on the handbrake. Well wrapped up, I climbed out of the cab and got to work. With the reversing light from the back of the cab shining I had plenty of light and soon had both chains laid over the drive wheels. I was on the nearside of the trailer and there were only a couple of feet between the truck and the snow wall. As I got on my hands and knees to reach round the back of the wheel to attach the hook and locking loop the truck juddered and infinitesimally slowly started to slide sideways towards the snow wall, with me sandwiched in between.

I have never been as scared as I was in those few seconds. I managed to stand and was actually trying to push against the trailer, obviously to no avail! What was I expecting? Then, as suddenly as she had started to slip, she stopped, with less than a foot between the trailer and the snow bank. I didn't move for at least ten seconds, uncertain what to do, my heart pounding like machine gunfire in my chest. Somehow I'd got to do up this chain. Creeping out from the inside I went round to the outer wheel and finished that first then waited five minutes before I built up enough courage to crawl back under the nearside and somehow, in that confined space, completed the task.

Experience taught me very little, I knew best. How stupid! I always tried to do that extra five miles without chaining up. Why, I don't know, as snow chains could often be a lifesaver. There was most probably some inherent failing in my character.

After pushing hard and completing long driving days I got back to Sarajevo in time, but as it transpired it was a wasted effort as not all the bikes had been built, so there was a delay in loading.

Waiting for the load would not have given me enough time to get back for Christmas, not too popular an idea on the home front, so it was decided that I should wait for the load, then drive back to Belgrade and park at the National. All things being equal I would have enough time to fly by JugoTrans from Belgrade International Airport back to Heathrow, getting back indoors late Christmas Eve.

I finally got loaded on the 23rd and hammered it back to Belgrade, only to find the car park at the National Hotel was full of trucks parked up for Christmas. One or two of the lads stayed over, nothing to go home for. Very sad, but not for me! I would get a taxi to the airport.

My only option was to park on the bridge over the motorway that accessed the hotel and hope for the best.

But when I got back from my winter's break a week later and checked the trailer I spotted the seals had been broken off and forty-four boxed up bikes had been 'borrowed', never to be returned.

My next problem was, how was I going to get out of the country having had my TIR cord tampered with and forty-four bikes missing?

Not a problem as it turned out. Once I'd explained as best I could in 'Serbo Croat', in which I'm fluent,[1] what had happened, the customs officials at Subotica were very helpful, and after noting the info on the carnet and re-sealing the tilt, I was allowed through into Hungary.

It was quite strange how trips turned out. Most of the time they were so well organised there was little to write home about, and as with most jobs, it became mundane and settled into a routine. We stopped at the same places each time, and generally tried to keep out of trouble, but just occasionally things happened that brought a whole new meaning to the word danger! This had been one such trip and I was more than happy to get back in one piece.

[1] This is of course a lie; I am totally 'unfluent' in any Yugoslavian dialect.

27

A Different Tack

By 1979 it was time for a job change, because by now I'd acquired a wife who preferred me to be home occasionally. So I applied for a post at Tolemans Transporters in Ipswich as transport allocator on the Volvo contract, and fortunately for me, as third choice, I got it. Third choice!!

Over the next few years I was successfully taught how to run a fleet of vehicles and how to become a normal member of society again as I settled into married life and a seven-five job.

Eventually fatherhood arrived, with my two sons Lewis and Leigh being born in the early 1980s. Their arrival put different pressures on the family income and more money was required, so as soon as a vacancy on Tolemans driving staff became available I applied for it. At this time car transporter drivers were the highest earners in the haulage industry, almost double that of the allocator. After a week's driver training, which was very much needed as loading and driving a car transporter required a different level of skill to mere mortals, I was back in the saddle again, delivering Volvo cars to dealerships in various outposts of civilisation in the UK, from Ipswich to Falmouth to Thurso to Ullapool and even to Llanfairpwllgwyngyllgogerychwyrndrobwllllantysiliogogogoch.

It was good to be back on the road again, where I felt comfortable and in my element. Even though it wasn't the Middle East, it had its moments.

There were a good number of Volvo dealerships in Scotland which meant each week ten or more transporters made the trip up north, often twice. The normal stopping place on the Scottish runs was Penrith Truck Stop in Cumbria, and if you were doing two trips a week, it would be normal to stop over there four nights a week. It was a very sociable place where Tolemans drivers from many depots met and had a drink or two together while resolving the world's problems.

If you stopped there on a Friday night, the usual practice was to get up about 2 a.m. on the Saturday morning, still dressed in your previous night's going out gear and hoss it back to Ipswich, load up ready for Monday and be home in bed by 10 a.m.

One particular Saturday morning in the summer of 1985, six or seven of us left Penrith early to cross the A66 and hammer it home to Ipswich. That particular morning it was raining heavily as the usual culprits, Herbie, Eddie, Wilf, Henry and three or four others left Penrith. Henry was the last to leave, still dressed in his smart casuals from the night before.

Once on to the A66 it was pedal to the metal as there was little traffic about that time in the morning, although we were a little more circumspect on the single carriageway due to the monsoon-like rain, but once on the dual carriageway over Stainmore it was plain sailing.

Flat out at the rear and doing about 65mph Henry noticed a pair of headlights in the distance in his rear view mirrors. Ever so slowly the lights caught up and pulled out to overtake. As they drew alongside Henry looked down and saw the telltale red stripe of a 'jam sandwich' as it pulled in front of him, put on the blue flashing lights and directed him into the next lay-by about half a mile ahead.

'Oh bollocks,' said H on the CB radio, 'just been clocked by the law.'

Oh good, that meant we were safe and we all kept going, silently thanking him for taking the rap.

Having stopped Henry, one of the policemen got out of the car in the driving rain, put his waterproof jacket on and made his way to Henry's driver side door. He, not wanting to get even the slightest bit wet wound his window down about two inches.

'Open the other side please driver, I want a quick word,' shouted the copper.

Henry reached over and unlocked the passenger door of his F86 as the officer walked round and climbed in, rain dripping off his peaked cap and on to his nose.

'Thank you driver, do you know why we stopped you?'

Henry not admitting to speeding said: 'No sir.'

'Well there are a couple of things,' he said, checking Henry's licence. 'Firstly the speed, do you happen to know what the limit is on this road?'

'Fifty,' said Henry.

'Correct Henry,' said the copper, 'and what speed were you doing would you say?'

'About fifty-five or so.'

'I prefer the 'or so', it was nearer sixty-five driver, and in these conditions a little too fast.'

'Sorry officer,' said Henry, 'I was following my mates who appear to have left me in the lurch.'

'Just so. The other reason we stopped you is that something seems to be hanging down under your unit, and we'd like to know what it is.'

'I've no idea mate.'

'Shall we have a look driver?'

The rain was thrumming incessantly on the cab roof.

'Can't be anything serious,' said Henry, nice and warm and dry in his seat.

'Won't know till we have a look, will we Henry?'

So H, with the policeman, had to get out of the cab in the pouring rain in his best clobber.

'It's under there,' pointing under the front of the cab.

Henry sort of bent his neck to have a look. 'Can't see anything officer.' Already the rain was running down his back and he was getting very wet.

'It's definitely there driver, we saw it as we came past, better get down and have a proper look.'

With that Henry had to get on his hands and knees and look under the cab. He got up, his hair plastered to his head, and looking like a drowned rat.

'Sorry officer can't see anything.' The water was dripping off his top lip.

The policeman bent down to have another look and said: 'Sorry driver you're right, it's gone. Oh no, there it is,' he said pointing, 'it's that thing on the end of your leg, your right boot!! Try putting it on the brake pedal.'

With that he made his way back to the police car, took his waterproof off, got in and they drove off without a backward glance. Just a lesson taught in a very succinct way. Poor Henry had to dry himself off as best as he could and change his clothes before continuing on his journey home. He caught up with us on the A1, at the Boot and Shoe filling station and gave us the story verbatim. I'm just glad I wasn't at the back of the convoy.

28

Monte Carlo or Bust!

'Paul, how do you fancy a trip down to Monte Carlo?'

'You what Robbie?' I replied, mildly shocked.

'Yep mate, I've put your name forward as one of a team of four drivers taking two transporter loads of vintage Bugattis and Ferraris to Monaco for an auction being held by Christie's at some famous hotel.'

'Cheers Robbie, but why me, there must be loads of blokes would love that number?'

'Well there's Phil Parsons from Harwich, Del Thompson from Dagenham, Hughie High from Milton and it should have been Les Taylor from our depot, but he'll be away on holiday so I suggested you as you've had loads of continental experience and you speak a bit of French.'

'I don't know what to say Rob. Well I do, thanks a bunch and when do we go?'

Robbie Blackwell was our shop steward at the Ipswich depot and could have proposed anyone so I was really grateful for his support.

Two weeks later I was down in Toleman's head office in Brentwood for a preliminary meeting on the logistics of the trip.

It appeared that this was the first time a specialist two marque auction of very important vintage and classic Bugattis and Ferraris had been held and it was expected to be the most prestigious event of its kind, ever.

The auction was to be organised by Christie's at the famous Loews Hotel in Monte Carlo two or three days before the Monaco Grand Prix.

Normally these 'works of art' would be transported down in ones or twos in the back of small covered trailers. Tolemans management and advertising team tendered for the contract and came up with the best package in terms of price and service, so during the next few weeks numerous days were spent at our Griff engineering depot in the Midlands completing load trials with various mechanical loading devices and extra ramps. We were told that the ground clearances on some of the cars could be measured in centimetres and great care would be needed during loading as individual car values could be in the hundreds of thousands of pounds. Eventually it was decided to use a manual winch to load them as you could instantly respond to any potential crisis whereas an electrical winch would not have been as sensitive to the minute adjustments that needed to be made.

A week before the off we were all invited down to our head office in Brentwood where interviews were being conducted by various media companies, such as the BBC World Service.

On 23 May 1987, we four drivers found ourselves at a warehouse in Middlesex carefully loading thirteen very rare and precious classic cars, while waiting for the fourteenth car to arrive from Cornwall.

Apparently the owner, a doctor who lived in the West Indies, wanted one last drive of his beloved Ferrari, a 275GTB2 and had flown over with his girlfriend to collect the car from Cornwall and drive it up to Middlesex.

Now, we were loading *outside* the warehouse with our trucks facing forward looking out over a foot-high concrete drop on to the estate road below. We were about halfway through when we heard the Ferrari roar into the estate and up the ramp. What an evocative noise a V12 Ferrari makes!

We stood watching in awe as the owner swung alongside the trucks, we presumed to park the car ready for us to load, but no!

There was a deafening, screeching, metallic noise as the good doctor drove his pride and joy over the lip and came to a grinding halt 'a la Italian Job' virtually balanced on the edge of the concrete, badly damaging the underside of his car and instantly knocking thousands of pounds off its value. Red faced and extremely embarrassed, the driver and his attractive colleague made a none-too-graceful exit from the car and with mumbled apologies disappeared into the manager's office.

After the loading was completed we drove to a nearby stately home, unloaded some of the cars and set them up for the motoring journalists to do all the necessary photo shoots, these usually with an attractive young lady draped languorously over the car. Poor old Del was roped in to sit in a Bugatti-type 35 and pose as a 1920s racing driver. Mind you, he looked the part, with his balding pate and gaunt features.

Eventually after all the posing had been done and the photographers were satisfied, food and wine was provided in the manor house for the media guys while we loaded the cars back on to the transporters and made our way back to the industrial estate, parking up in the warehouse for the night.

The following morning the 'classic car experts' arrived to cover the valuable cargo with protective packaging for the trip down to Monaco. I say experts advisedly. As supposed 'experts' ourselves we could see that the flimsy coverings of cardboard, polythene and tape being used to cover the cars wouldn't last as far as Portsmouth, but no, these guys knew best. All I will say is that as we drove down the M3 that afternoon bits of packaging and sheeting were slowly being torn from the cars and deposited in nearby fields and by the time we reached Portsmouth docks not a shred of covering was left. Hopefully the weather would hold for the next couple of days!

One or two of the national newspapers such as the *Daily Telegraph* gave good coverage to this 'momentous' trip with pictures of us drivers standing with our loaded car transporters and interestingly once we were on the ferry to Dieppe a number of passengers asked us to sign their newspapers with our pictures in. How self-conscious did we 'celebrities' feel doing that.

The plan was for us to double-drive all the way to Monaco in sixteen hours, only stopping for diesel. Low profile security was to be provided by the gendarmes who would keep a watchful eye on our valuable load all the way. We never saw them once! Now that's what I call low profile.

It was a superb drive down, even though we took a wrong turning off the Perepherique in Paris and got lost for a little while. Luckily the weather was magnificent and the sun shone all day. With Gary and Michael Toleman flitting back and forth between us in their Range Rover, keeping an eye on us all the way down to Monte Carlo, it was a perfect trip, and the temperature when we arrived in Monaco was 84F. Perfect!

Normally large vehicles aren't allowed into Monte Carlo,

but on our arrival at Nice we met the relevant police authority from Monaco who wanted a structured arrival so that there would be no hitches. They had to give us written dispensation to deliver the cars directly to the Loews Hotel.

In the afternoon we had a police escort into the city and followed the route of the Formula One track to the Loews Hairpin where police stopped all traffic while we reversed up the hill on to the hotel forecourt and there, in front of various dignitaries and VIPs began the laborious process of unloading. Everyone wanted to give their two penny worth as to the best way of unloading these fabulous beasts. Even Christie's senior auctioneer Robert Brooks was there clucking round like mother hen. Mind you, with the potential value of these cars, so would I. Eventually all the cars were safely unloaded and ensconced in the Loews auction room ready for the big day.

The plan once the cars were unloaded was for us to drive back to Nice and have a relaxing evening in a pleasant hotel, then make our way back home the following day. However, as a thank you and because the trip had been so successful, Gary and Michael, the Toleman twins, booked us into Loews Hotel, for two nights.

First, the trucks had to be driven back to Nice and parked up, then the boys picked us up in the Range Rover and ferried us back to the hotel. We were treated like visiting dignitaries by the staff, and made to feel really welcome. This was a different world, inhabited by the super rich and people from other planets, certainly not for the hoi polloi. I know that the bill for our small room per night was £360, and that was in 1987.

And that wasn't all: one of the many restaurants in this magnificent hotel had its own show, similar to the Folies Bergeres in Paris and that night we were invited to attend. On our arrival at the restaurant the Maitre D, very apologetically, said that suits or blazers, shirt and tie were de rigueur, and he couldn't allow Del and me in as we were wearing leather jackets. I'd got a tie on, but had no blazer; Del had neither tie nor blazer.

'*Pas problem, messieurs*,' said the Maitre, opening a small door in the wall and pulling out a twenty-foot long rail of casual jackets for us to try.

What class! I tried on numerous jackets before selecting a maroon one to clash with my green shirt, tie and slacks. It was a fabulous evening finished off by a visit to the casino, which thronged with Chinese businessmen from Hong Kong. We even saw one customer place a 50,000 franc bet on the roulette wheel. How the other half live. Maybe that should read how the other 0.000025% live!

In the morning it was coffee and croissants in one of the many casual seating areas on the ground floor, then after breakfast, a lift up to the swimming pool on the top deck. On our arrival we were each provided with a towelling robe by the pool manager, who then guided us to available sun loungers, where we made ourselves comfortable among the glitterati who had arrived for the auction and Grand Prix.

For lunch, Mike and Gary suggested we pop across the border into Italy. No argument from us, so we all piled into the Range Rover and drove out through Menton on to the Italian Riviera and headed for San Remo, where sitting by the edge of the beach overlooking the Med we were treated to a fine lobster lunch. Mind you though, having to select your own live one was a bit of a trauma

Then it was back to Monte for a bit of sightseeing in the evening. By now the place was a hive of activity as work was in progress setting up all the paraphernalia associated with the most famous Grand Prix in the world. Tomorrow morning we would be off and back to the real world, but just for a short time it was a wonderful experience to feel part of such an important social and sporting occasion.

The following morning we checked out, and in a more

sober mood the twins drove us back to collect our trucks from Nice ready for the non-stop haul back home again.

We later found out that the auction had been an overwhelming success and the cars that we had carried down to Monte Carlo had fetched over £4 million. I believe the total value of all the cars offered came to over £8 million, by far and away the most expensive ever sale of vintage and classic cars. The car that fetched the highest price was one that we had transported down, a 1958 Ferrari Testarossa that went for just over £1 million, and as to the Ferrari that had been damaged by its owner, it realised only half its expected value. This period was a boom time for the sale of rare and exotic cars and within a couple of years these spectacular auctions were springing up all over the world. I was glad to have been involved in one of the first and most successful of the era. Robert Brooks, the Christie's auctioneer, made a great success of the sale and within a very few years went on to set up his own hugely successful classic auction house.

For a few days it had been a wonderful piece of escapism. Les didn't know what he had missed; still his misfortune was my gain. Thank you very much Les, and thank you very much Robbie!

29

Make Do and Mend

In 1993 after having been away from continental work for a number of years, I was at a loose end, as my job with Tolemans had come to an end.

I responded to an advert in the local paper, and realised I was speaking to Fred Archer, a guy I had met a number of times during our Middle East days, when he was an owner driver pushing a 1924 Mercedes overland to Iran.

Working with Fred was a challenge to say the least. Personally I found him a decent kind of bloke, though he wasn't to everyone's taste. The problem was he was a bit slapdash and a make-do-and-mend type of guy. I should have realised from our time abroad that a leopard doesn't easily change his spots!

He was running a company called Ultrahaul European. Anyway he and his wife Shirley offered me a job for as long as I needed one. I went to work for him doing mostly Italy and the old Eastern Bloc and really enjoyed it, and even took my good lady on a trip or two to Italy. Then one day having just returned from Verona he called me into the office.

'Got a change of truck for you Paul, a nice old DAF 95 left hooker and ideal for you! Anyway you're shipping out of Dover on Thursday to Resita in Romania.'

Oh great, I thought, haven't driven a left hooker for more than twenty years, I've got two days to get unrusty. I mean, it would be nice to have a decent wagon, as the best that could be said about the MAN 320 I had been driving was that it resembled a colander, and was a bit of an old dog.

'OK Fred, cheers for that, I'd better have a couple of days shunting it around the dock before I go,' and I did.

Left hookers aren't a problem. It's just that when you go from right hand drive to left hand drive, and you haven't done that for a while then add in driving on the right in Europe, if you don't give yourself a chance to acclimatise, the truck feels twice as wide!

Anyway things went fine. I felt a bit edgy for a while, but got to Resita in Romania without a hitch and delivered my load of train axles and wheels to a large foundry on the outskirts of the town. Apparently the Romanians had a contract with British Rail to service and recondition bogies and wheels. It was cheaper to haul them down to Romania and back than find a blacksmith back home, it seemed.

My reload instructions were to collect barrels of strawberry jam from a farm in northern Romania.

I headed to Baia Mare and parked on the outskirts of the town. This was really rural countryside and nearly everyone seemed to be driving or riding on the ubiquitous east European style horse and cart. Nothing much had changed since I was last there in the 70s.

The agent's address was scribbled down on a piece of paper, but obviously I had no idea how to find him, and street maps of Baia Mare didn't seem to be readily available. I showed the address to a number of locals, none of whom showed any interest.

Finally I approached a bloke standing next to an ancient tractor. Hey presto! He knew the address, and even better, I was invited to scramble onto his belching old tractor. Sitting sideways on the mudguard and inhaling a fog of smoke from his exhaust, he bounced me through the centre of Baia and delivered me to the agent. The old boy even waited for me, and returned me safely with a bruised and battered backside, to my truck. Such natural generosity is hard to beat and uplifts the soul, and he was very happy to accept a bottle of Bells as a token of my gratitude.

Apparently the farm was outside a village thirty miles north, and adjacent to the Ukrainian border.

When I arrived in the village I found the address pretty easily, and sure enough the border watchtowers were in clear view. It was a hell of a squeeze trying to jackknife the trailer into the farm entrance. Those two stone walls guarding the entrance were more designed to accept a horse and cart rather than lorries, and it was obviously the first time any foreigner had been there because the whole village turned out to see this huge truck from 'Anglia' arrive.

Anyway the farmer and his family were very friendly and invited me into their farmhouse. Very strange, I almost had a sense of déjà vu, in that the inside of the house reminded me of the inside of a North American Indian's tepee, the walls and floor were covered with the most colourful rugs, animal skins, icons and old farming implements.

I was well fed and watered, while the workforce, who consisted of half the village, loaded up my trailer. The jam was in blue forty-five gallon plastic drums, the sort that many people use as water butts, and as there was no mechanical device for loading, everything was manhandled on the trailer, *and* double stacked, by force of numbers.

Finally I was loaded and had to drive back to Baia to get the documents from my agent. Pulling out of the very tight gateway and turning right there was an explosion as one of my trailer tyres blew out. And when I walked back to check there was a huge split in the sidewall. Now being one of Freddie's 'best' trailers, there was a distinct lack of anything resembling a spare wheel. In fact there wasn't one, and looking at the place where it should have been, and judging by the rusting mechanism, there probably hadn't been one there for years. What to do now? It was impossible to phone from this outpost of civilisation, there was no GSM in Romania at that time, and there certainly weren't any ATS tyre fitters within shouting distance.

On hearing the explosion the farmer had come trotting down and realised that I would need a replacement. So he had a word with one of the guys standing around who quickly disappeared on a vintage tractor.

An hour later this guy reappeared towing a trailer with four truck-sized tyres on. When I saw them my heart sank, they were all the right size, but all were past their sell-by-date and totally illegal in western Europe.

Here in Romania there still weren't laws concerning depth of tread and general condition of tyres, so basically people drove on them till they went pop. These tyres had obviously come off some other foreign trucker who had decided they were too dangerous to drive on and replaced them leaving these discarded at the side of the road. As nothing gets thrown away in Romania, some enterprising individual had picked them up and now here they were assembled for my perusal.

All I can say is that even the best of the four tyres displayed in front of me was beyond safe usage. However I had very little choice. Loaded to thirty eight tons I needed all my wheels to have tyres on. Sometimes, if you were lightly laden it was possible to tie an axle up out of the way, but not this time. I selected the 'best' of the four tyres, which was almost totally bald *and* had large areas of the steel wire core showing through. Then it was all hands to the wheel brace as everyone mucked in to help me change it; in fact they moved me out of the way and took over.

Finally it was on and about 80lb pressure was blown in through the truck compressor. I said my last goodbyes and very gingerly drove off. Would this scrap tyre get me through to Austria?

Well, it did - all the way across Hungary at 40mph trying to preserve it, until finally I pulled through from Hegyeshalom to Nickelsdorf on the Austrian side of the border.

'Oh no, I don't believe it.'

The Austrian police and their version of the transport ministry were doing vehicle checks, and even though I hadn't yet driven on Austrian roads in anger, as far as they were concerned this was Austria and my tyre was - can you believe it? - illegal. How could they say such a thing?

But worse was to come, not only did I have to buy a new tyre, which I was going to do anyway, but I also had to pay a 2,500 schilling (£178) fine for having an illegal one. Now *that* I did rail about, and thought it was very unfair. The police even took me to a cash point to withdraw the money!

Needless to say, Fred was less than pleased. 'Huh, all the profit gone from that trip then.'

'Well Fred, if there had been a spare on the trailer we might have been OK.'

30

Too Much Potential For Grief?

'Fancy a trip to Belgrade Paul?'

'Not sure if I do Fred, there's a war going on down in Serbia, isn't there?'

'Can't see too much trouble mate, it's a load of medication through the United Nations High Commission for Refugees (UNHCR), most probably it'll be convoyed from the border.'

I should have stopped then when I heard those words slide out of Fred's mouth ... *most probably*, but I didn't. I said yes.

Anything for a new experience, and it might rekindle old memories, as Fred said: 'UN job ... no problem, safe as houses.'

But this job turned out to be one of the scariest I had ever done.

Off I went to Manchester to load up with medical supplies, and to get tipping instructions. Apparently I was to try to phone this guy in Belgrade from Szeged, in Southern Hungary, and transit into Serbia through the Tompa/Kelebija border. Once across into Serbia I was to wait at the border for some 'support' to accompany me from the border to Belgrade. Apparently conditions in Serbia weren't that good as UN sanctions were having some effect.

On top of that, once I had cleared and unloaded, I had to drive 50 miles west of Belgrade to collect date expired medication from a UN compound near a town called Sabac, and return them to England.

I had a problem-free trip down to Szeged and tried to phone my contact in Belgrade. Of course, there was no response, just a dead line. The only thing to do was go through the border and try him from there.

The border at Tompa was absolutely chaotic, with a couple-of-mile-long queue of cars waiting to cross into Serbia. It was around 7 p.m. It was dark and raining lightly. The cars were parked very haphazardly on both sides of the road, making it difficult to manoeuvre through and a few angry words were spoken trying to get cars moved so I could get down to the frontier crossing.

I already had a gut feeling about the trip, which wasn't good.

Back in the 1970s we had crossed the Tompa and the Subotica border tens of times with no fuss and no traffic. Then, there wasn't a huge amount of private vehicle movement between Eastern Bloc countries.

I got to the front of the queue and found myself behind a couple of Csad[1] trucks from Czechoslovakia. I walked into

[1] Csad was the government controlled national haulage company from Czechoslovakia.

the customs office to get my paperwork done and stood behind one of the drivers. We managed to say hello and converse a bit in very rough German. When I told him I was going to Belgrade, his response was not positive.

'*Beograd problema college. Beograd grosse problema.*' Which was pretty much a self-explanatory comment.

The carnets were quickly stamped, passport control done, the barrier lifted and I was out of Hungary. Having cleared that border crossing, it used to be no more than 200 yards to the Yugo side which you could normally see.

But now all I could see through the beam of my headlights was rain and pitch blackness all around.

I was in no-man's-land, and it was a very eerie experience. Where was the Serbian frontier? I drove on very slowly, unsure what to expect. I'd driven for about three kilometres when rounding a bend I could see some lights in the distance. As I approached I could see they were very powerful arc lights shining down on what was the biggest, heaviest, and ugliest looking barrier I had ever seen. It must have weighed tons. Nobody was going to break out of here in a hurry!

There were a number of people at the barrier which was swung open horizontally while a couple of guys in combats, flagged me down with their Kalashnikovs.

'*Kabin Control,*' barked one of the guys. They had a thorough search of my cab, found my camera and without a by your leave confiscated it, just like that!

'*Nema fotograf, nema fotograf,*' shouted one of the guards.

Bugger, am I ever likely to see that again?

A couple of the 'soldiers' jumped up, one either side of the truck, waved me forward and pointed at where I was to park. Then, putting their hands up, instructed me to wait in the cab.

The parking area was a small open compound next to a block of offices and the whole area was lit by massive stadium lights. There were people busy everywhere, some dressed in different coloured combat fatigues, some just in ordinary clothing, but all carrying guns. There was an air of menace about the place, and though I wasn't frightened, I felt very uncomfortable and ill at ease.

It was midnight and the rain was still arcing down through the lights. My truck certainly looked out of place, a virtually new, bright red Scania 113, parked next to some dreary looking Serbian TAM trucks.

Ten minutes later a couple of soldiers came to fetch me and took me into the office block to a desk where I was told to sit and wait. Another five minutes passed before an officer came across and sat down at the table opposite me. He spoke reasonable English with a Slavic accent.

'Your papers collega, what is it?'

'Medical supplies for United Nations,' I replied.

'Pfffh, United Nation no good, is big problem Serbia.'

He spent ten minutes leafing through the paperwork.

'Have you for drugs collega, is big problem Serbia?'

I shook my head.

'OK, have you special visa? OK, have you permit for Serbia. OK, you must change money for dinars, OK yes?'

Great! Fred had given me £300 running money. How much was *this* going to cost?

'I must speak to this man please,' I said, indicating the name of the contact I should call.

'Yes, yes is not problem collega, first you must have visa and permit. Is new law in Serbia?'

'How much?' I said resignedly.

'Is no much dinar, now you must sleep. In morning speak Chef (chief) and pay dollars.'

A soldier escorted me back to the cab. I had very little sleep, and even with the curtains closed the lights were too powerful, and the best I could manage was a disturbed nap.

I suppose I must have slept a bit because I was woken with a bang on the door at 8 a.m. and told to get ready to see Chef. During the night the Csad wagons had come through as well and were parked next to me.

I was escorted back to the office by two more guys, this time not in combats, but still carrying the ubiquitous Kalashnikovs. The Chef was in the office and waved me to sit while talking on the phone. As I was waiting the officer from the night before came in. He was going to be the translator, it seemed.

'Good *Morgen collega*, your passport please.' I handed it over.

'How you say this name?'

'Rowlands,' I replied.

'OK Mr Rawlans, you must pay for visa for Serbia $300, and for permit $250, and for to change dinars, $200.'

'What is permit for?' I asked.

'Permit is for allow you drive on road Mr Rawlans.'

The Chef, who hadn't made any comment up to now, spoke to the officer, who nodded.

'The Chef asks if first time is in Serbia?'

'No,' I said. 'I used to drive here eighteen years ago when it was all Yugoslavia and Marshall Tito was president.'

The officer translated and the chef seemed impressed and was obviously a Tito man, as he nodded when the name was mentioned.

'Have you dollaarrs,' said the officer.

'Not enough, only £200.' I lied. If I gave them everything I would be really stuck. The officer tallied up on his calculator.

'Collega is only $300, you must pay $750.'

'Do you have bank machine?' I asked, knowing full well they wouldn't.

'Mr Rawlans, this is not possible, you cannot come in Serbia without pay.'

'Can I phone this number?' I said, pointing to the contact name.

A conversation with some joint nodding took place between them both.

'OK, we phone and speak for you.'

Ten minutes later I was talking to my agent Milos in Belgrade and explaining my financial dilemma to him. He said he would bring some cash to the border and we would sort out any further problems when he arrived in about three hours.

Good to his word, Milos arrived at 1 p.m. I'm not sure that $750 dollars exchanged hands, but within half an hour I had my visa and permit and was ready to roll.

'I understood there would be a convoy,' I said to Milos.

'Who told you that?' said Milos. 'You only have convoys in war zone areas.' Good old Fred! Say anything to keep you quiet.

'What you must do is stay very close to me though because the people are not happy about UN sanctions. There is very little fuel in the country.'

I followed Milos down to Novi Sad without too many problems; the road was in a state of disrepair and looked as if nothing had been spent on its upkeep since I last drove down it in the 1970s. From Novi Sad on it got more hairy, as the closer we got to Belgrade the more people were stood at the side of the road with bottles and containers trying to wave anyone down to scrounge some fuel.

I followed Milos to ... guess where? The National Hotel! But this was a different National Hotel to the one I fondly remembered; sadly the place was packed with wrecked trucks and looked more like a scrapyard than a hotel car park, and all the Georges were gone!

'You must wait here for two hours,' said Milos. 'I will leave my friend to look after you.'

'What for?'

'I must make arrangements for customs clearance.'

It was a long two hours before he returned.

'Now we must go to the customs at the airport where you

must wait for maybe, one day, then I will collect you and we will unload.'

I followed him to the compound at Belgrade Airport and found somewhere to park.

If I said it looked like a scene from *Mad Max* I wouldn't be exaggerating. Even though there was security on the gate, people were driving, and strolling in and out as if it was market day. The place was like a huge rubbish dump, broken down and burnt out vehicles lay everywhere. There were hawkers trying to sell all sorts of rubbish. Most of the trucks in the compound were driverless and their diesel tanks had been ransacked. It would seem that even if locks had been fitted to the tanks that thieves just drilled in from the top and siphoned out the fuel. There were tens of trucks with holes in the top of their tanks. Those drivers who had trucks were sticking to them like glue.

Sanctions appeared to have had some effect, it seemed.

'This is not a good place' said Milos. Can't argue with that, I thought.

'I will get guard for you tonight,' and he sent off his colleague to sort it out. Ten minutes later he returned with a 'tramp' is the best way I could describe him, but he had a gun. It turned out he had three guns; a veritable one-man army.

Milos said he would see me tomorrow about midday, and not to worry as this was a good man who had been in the army, and he would look after me. The guy spoke not one word to me the whole time he was there and in fact I had a decent night's sleep knowing he was there.

At noon the following day Milos came to collect me and I followed him to a small compound somewhere in Belgrade to unload the medicines. Obviously with the situation in Serbia many people were out of work and when we arrived there must have been thirty men and women waiting to help unload. By 2.30 p.m. I was empty and ready to roll.

'No you don't go tonight, you stay, and we have good food, drink in friend's restaurant, and go to Sabac in morning.'

'Is it OK in Sabac, Milos?' I said, explaining my concern at how close it was to the war zone.

'Not problem Paul, is fifty kilometres from trouble area.'

I was able to leave the truck in the compound with our strong, silent guard still keeping an eye on it while Milos took me back to his for a shower and a change of clothing. Then at 7.30 p.m. Milos, his wife, two daughters, his best friend and I walked about half a mile to his mate's restaurant. It was a really entertaining night out and after an unusual potato-based meal and numerous Pivos I felt very confident about tomorrow . . .

Making my way out of Belgrade the following morning my confidence seemed to have ebbed a bit, actually a lot. It was a miserable old morning with not too many people standing beside the road with their fuel containers. They wouldn't have got much anyway as I only passed two vehicles on the entire fifty km run to Sabac.

I found the walled compound quite easily, and as I arrived, had to wait outside as a convoy of white UN trucks pulled out to go somewhere near the war zone I presumed. There were a few air horns blown and I responded. Maybe a few English guys were driving for the UN, I don't know.

I reported to the main office and spoke to a Belgian UN representative. The medication was ready, and within an hour I was fully freighted and with paperwork in hand left the compound heading back to Belgrade. Before dark I was back in Tompa. Luckily it rained all day which kept people away from the road. Having been through the border process on the way in, it wasn't nearly as scary on the way out. It never is.

Amazing really, to think that even in times of war that the expiry date of medicines was still of critical importance. Four days later I was back where I started, in Manchester unloading the old medicines and reloading the trailer for someone else.

When a few weeks later Fred asked me to do another trip to Belgrade, I declined. There was too much potential for grief. Could be the title of a book, and certainly over the years I was very lucky to get away with so little personal 'grief'. In that time I have completed most probably in excess of two million miles and I've only been involved in a couple of minor scrapes. Maybe I ought to throw away my licence now because by the law of averages ...

I have had some wonderful times and visited some wonderful places. I would just like to thank the many hundreds of people whom I met over the years for helping me to enjoy it so much.

Bye for now,

Best regards,

Paul Rowlands aged 63 years and 77 days ...